Speak Freely

CONVERSATIONAL AMERICAN ENGLISH

Elliot Glass
Queensborough Community College
of The City University of New York

Paul Arcario
Queensborough Community College
of The City University of New York

HARCOURT BRACE JOVANOVICH, PUBLISHERS
San Diego   New York   Chicago   Atlanta   Washington, D.C.
London   Sydney   Toronto

This book is dedicated to
Barbara and Don

Cover and chapter opening illustrations by Russel Redmond.

PREFACE

Although intermediate level students of English as a Second Language are familiar with many key structures and grammatical concepts, they often are able to communicate effectively only in a classroom setting. Such students may be lost when they step outside the class into a world where fluency in common grammatical structures and knowledge of colloquial English are necessities. This is especially true for those who have studied English in their native countries. *Speak Freely* integrates the colloquial language found in conversation and idiom texts with the structural patterns found in grammar books and provides intermediate students with a ready means for mastering structures and achieving a solid working knowledge of the spoken language.

Speak Freely contains twelve text chapters and three review chapters. Each chapter has a theme that focuses on an area relevant to students' daily lives, such as transportation, university life, emergency situations and social situations. Although the chapters progress to more complicated structures, instructors may use whole chapters or sections of chapters in different sequences to suit students' needs. Teaching the chapters in sequence, however, will preserve the continuity of the narrative. The review chapters present exercises that reinforce the more important grammatical items (tenses, comparative and superlative, passive voice, and conditional) and allow students to work in a less structured way with the idiomatic expressions they have learned. Dialogues, narratives, and exercises include a large number of colloquial expressions, idioms, and clichés that are defined either in context or in footnotes. A "Glossary of Colloquial Terms" appears at the end of the book. Consistent with the text's emphasis on spoken American English, "who" has largely replaced "whom" in dialogues and other conversational settings.

NARRATIVES—Each chapter opens with a third-person narrative that presents the grammatical structures and idioms of the chapter in the context of the experiences and problems of a Chinese student, Lin Le-Tian, as he begins to adjust to life in the United States. By following Mr. Lin as he meets various people, students encounter numerous real-life situations that they too are likely to experience. In this manner, they learn vocabulary, expressions, and conversational patterns necessary to communicate in these situations. Questions following the narrative require students to use the target structures or expressions in their answers.

DIALOGUES — Events in the opening narrative appear as brief conversations introducing additional vocabulary and idioms. Comprehension questions follow each dialogue and encourage students to use new vocabulary words and expressions.

GRAMMAR — Examples taken from the narrative are followed by concise grammatical explanations and extensive exercises using the structural item. Exercises take the form of brief conversational exchanges such as two-to-eight-line "mini-dialogues." Students take part in these conversations by supplying the target structures or phrases; consequently, they learn by doing.

Intermediate students often have difficulty *using* verb tenses correctly. Consequently, special exercises in the grammar sections in the earlier chapters have been designed to help students master the tenses by contrasting one tense with another. For example, in Chapter 3, which introduces the present perfect tense, students work on dialogues contrasting the present perfect with the past tense.

EXPRESSIONS AND IDIOMS — This section defines commonly used idioms introduced (in bold type) in the opening narrative of the chapter. Mini-dialogue exercises provide opportunities to use these idioms in a conversational context.

SITUATIONAL DIALOGUES — These dialogues introduce situations that are related to the theme of each chapter but not included in the Narrative and Dialogue sections. These situational dialogues further demonstrate the use of colloquial English as the characters converse with friends, doctors, salespeople, teachers, and others.

VOCABULARY BUILDER — The vocabulary builder extends students' vocabulary while showing them how some words combine to form new words and phrases.

ROLE PLAY SUGGESTIONS — These suggestions for role playing are based on the situations already covered in the chapter.

PREPOSITION PRACTICE — This section is divided into two parts: *Prepositions* covers the definition and usage of prepositions; *Verb + Preposition Combinations* introduces verb + preposition idioms. The exercises in both parts of this section consist of mini-dialogues that are thematically related to the rest of the chapter.

SUGGESTIONS FOR USE

Speak Freely accommodates different teaching approaches. Here are some suggestions you may find useful:

NARRATIVE — Students can read the narrative silently before class as a preparation for the chapter or aloud in class for pronunciation practice. It can also be used for listening comprehension practice, dictation, or as a springboard for discussion of students' similar experiences or of American cultural practices they have noticed.

DIALOGUES — The authors have deliberately avoided lengthy dialogues that often become mere reading exercises. The conciseness of the dialogues enables the instructor to use a "coaching" system that creates maximum student participation. The coaching system works as follows:

    1. *Presenting the Dialogue* — The instructor presents the dialogue by assigning students to read aloud from the text. The other students follow along with books open or closed. The instructor explains vocabulary and structural items if necessary, and students ask each other the questions at the end of the dialogue to ensure their complete comprehension.

    2. *Performing the Dialogue* — A dialogue with two characters in it may be practiced by four students: two perform the dialogue without the text; two others act as coaches and may look at the text. The performing students need not worry about having to recall the dialogue word for word because the coaches will give them cues—key words from each line of the dialogue. Of course, the instructor can also serve as coach and prompt the performing students. Although the students need not recite the lines exactly, they should produce grammatically correct sentences. Because the "coaching" system leaves room for improvisation, students retain a degree of freedom within a guided structure.

    The students can also pair off to practice the dialogues. This approach works especially well with the mini-dialogue exercises, which for the most part consist of only two characters (A and B). Having the students work on their own in pairs maximizes the amount of speaking time for each student, because all the student pairs can speak simultaneously. Students can discuss the choices and work out the answers for each exercise with each other. It also eliminates the "audience effect" that often inhibits students' performance in front of a class. Students should be clear about what they need to do on each exercise before working on their own. Pre-teaching vocabulary and practicing the example at the beginning of each section will facilitate this.

SUPPLEMENTARY VIDEO TAPES

Speak Freely has a companion series of video tapes that parallel in theme the chapters in the text. The series, which is in color and in all formats, is available through Crossroads Video, 15 Buckminster Lane, Manhasset, New York 11030.

ACKNOWLEDGMENTS

We would like to express our appreciation to Al Richards, our acquisitions editor, for his encouragement and thoughtful guidance. Thanks also to Gene Lettau, Jamie Fidler, Avery Hallowell, Lynn Edwards, Julie Etow, and Cate Safranek of the HBJ staff. Special thanks to Sue Nahmias and Joan Winant of Queensborough Community College, CUNY, for their patience and support. We thank Professor Teresa Dalle, Professor Barbara Auerbach, the late

Roseanne T. Harrison, and Professor Beth E. Snyder, Brooklyn College, CUNY, for their careful reviews of the manuscript. We are also grateful to Professor Carolyn Raphael of Queensborough Community College, CUNY, for her suggestions. Finally, we would like to acknowledge our debt to the students at Queensborough, particularly those in the Port of Entry Language Development and Cultural Orientation Program, with whom we class tested this book.

CONTENTS

1 THE BAGGAGE CLAIM CHECK INCIDENT

I. NARRATIVE

Kennedy International Airport in New York is usually a madhouse[1] on weekends, and the weekend of Lin Le-Tian's arrival in America was no exception. Because of heavy air traffic, Mr. Lin's plane had to circle the airport for about an hour. Several passengers became impatient. "I can't believe this is happening," complained one. As the plane touched down,[2] another passenger sighed, "This happens to me every time I fly into JFK."

After he left the plane, Mr. Lin discovered that his baggage claim ticket was not in his wallet. He quickly checked his pockets and carry-on bags, but with no luck.[3] Suddenly, he spotted[4] a flight attendant. He ran over to her and asked her what to do. "Oh," she said, "people are always losing their claim tickets. Don't worry. But **you'd better** go over to the baggage claim area right away and speak to the supervisor." Unfortunately for Mr. Lin, the supervisor spoke very quickly and had a strong foreign accent. Mr. Lin couldn't understand what she was saying. When he asked her to explain it to him again, she gave him a dirty look[5] and snapped back,[6] "Can't you see we're shorthanded[7] today? Here, just fill these out." She then handed him several forms. Mr. Lin **had a hard time** understanding them and was almost ready to **give up** when a student came over and said, "Hi, my name is Mary Cunningham. It looks like you can use a hand[8] with those forms."

"Yes," Mr. Lin replied, "I always have trouble filling out forms, especially when they are in English. Can you tell me what I have to write on these?"

---

[1]madhouse: a very crowded, noisy place.
[2]touch down: to land.
[3]no luck: (1) to be unlucky; (2) not to succeed in doing something.
[4]spot: to suddenly see something or someone.
[5]dirty look: a look showing anger or dislike.
[6]snap back: to reply in an impolite way.
[7]shorthanded: not enough people to do a job.
[8]a hand: help.

"Sure," Mary said, "I can help you with them."

Together they spent about fifteen minutes filling everything out. Mr. Lin then handed in the forms. After a half hour wait, the supervisor called him over[9] and said, "Unclaimed luggage usually comes in on the conveyor belt on your right, but since it's broken today, all luggage is coming in downstairs at gate 5. You can go down now; your bags are there." Mr. Lin thanked the supervisor, went downstairs, and finally got his luggage. As he headed for[10] the customs area, he thought to himself, "What other adventures are in store for[11] me?"

QUESTIONS

1. What is New York's JFK Airport like on the weekends?
2. Why was Mr. Lin's plane delayed?
3. What always happens to the second passenger when he flies into JFK?
4. What did Mr. Lin discover after he left the plane?
5. Where did he look for his baggage claim ticket?
6. What did the supervisor do when Mr. Lin asked her for the same information again?
7. Who offered to give Mr. Lin a hand?
8. Where does the unclaimed luggage usually come in?
9. Where is the unclaimed luggage coming in today?

II. DIALOGUES

1. Mr. Lin realizes his baggage claim ticket is missing.

    MR. LIN: Excuse me. My baggage claim ticket is missing. What should I do?

    FLIGHT ATTENDANT: Well, let's see. You can't go back on the plane now. You'd better go to the baggage claim area right away and see the supervisor.

    MR. LIN: How do I get there?

    FLIGHT ATTENDANT: Go straight ahead. Then turn left at the duty free shop.[12] The baggage area is on your right, just past the rest rooms.

    MR. LIN: Thanks a lot.

QUESTIONS

1. What is Mr. Lin's problem?
2. What does the flight attendant tell him to do?
3. How can he get to the baggage claim area?

---

[9]call (someone) over: to ask someone to come to you.
[10]head for: to go towards.
[11]in store for: likely to happen.
[12]duty free shop: an airport store where you can buy things without paying tax.

2. A student comes over to help Mr. Lin.

STUDENT: Excuse me, my name is Mary Cunningham. It looks like you can use a hand with those forms.

MR. LIN: Yes, I can. I always have trouble filling out forms, especially when they are in English.

STUDENT: Well, let's see now. How many pieces of luggage do you have?

MR. LIN: Two suitcases and a shoulder bag.

STUDENT: What color are they?

MR. LIN: They're all red.

STUDENT: Do they have ID tags on them?

MR. LIN: Yes, but everything is in Chinese.

STUDENT: What's in the bags?

MR. LIN: Just clothes and personal items.

STUDENT: Okay. That's it.[13] We're done. Just hand these to the supervisor.

QUESTIONS

1. How does the student help Mr. Lin?
2. Why can't Mr. Lin fill out the forms by himself?
3. What do Mr. Lin's bags contain?

III. GRAMMAR

A. Present Tense

Use the Present Tense to talk about (a) an action that happens regularly, usually, or every day, and (b) an action that is a general truth.

FORM: | Subject + Verb (base form)

Affirmative: I *fly* to Phoenix once a month.

Negative: I *don't fly* to Phoenix once a month.

Question: Do you *fly* to Phoenix once a month?

Wh– Questions: How often *do* you *fly* to Phoenix?

Who/What/Which as Subject: Who *flies* to Phoenix once a month?

Note: Form for *he, she, it*: | Subject + Verb-s/-es

---

[13]that's it: it's finished.

Affirmative: He usually *orders* a special in-flight meal.

Negative: He *doesn't* usually *order* a special in-flight meal.

Question: *Does* he usually *order* a special in-flight meal?

Wh– Questions: What *does* he usually *order*?

Who/What/Which as Subject: *Who* usually orders a special in-flight meal?

TIME EXPRESSIONS

We often use these time expressions with the Present Tense to show frequency (how often we do something). They may also be used with other tenses. Place these after the verb *be* and before other verbs:

always	seldom	occasionally*
almost always	rarely	sometimes*
often	hardly ever	frequently
usually	never	

Place these at the end of the sentence:

all the time	once a month	from time to time*
every day	three times a day	now and then*
every other week		

*These can also be placed at the beginning of the sentence.

B. Present Continuous Tense

Use the Present Continuous Tense to talk about what is happening now.

FORM: | Subject + be + Verb-ing |

Affirmative: The airport bus *is leaving* now.

Negative: The airport bus *is not leaving* now.
                                          isn't

Question: *Is* the airport bus *leaving* now?

Wh– Questions: Where *is* the airport bus *leaving* from?

Who/What/Which as Subject: Which airport bus *is leaving* now?

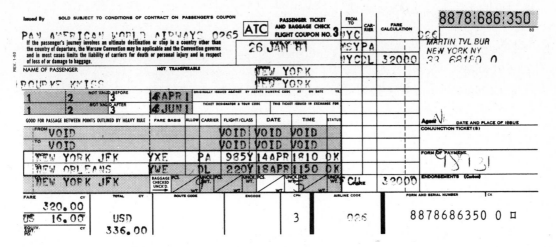

Airline ticket

Baggage claim ticket

Use the Present Continuous Tense to talk about what is happening nowadays or these days, especially when you want to show change.

Example: Credit cards *are becoming* very popular nowadays.

Use the Present Continuous Tense to emphasize that an action occurs frequently or habitually, often with the idea of showing dislike or disapproval.

Example: Sam *is* always *misplacing* his tickets. [The speaker doesn't like the fact that Sam frequently misplaces his tickets.]

Note: We rarely use the Present Continuous Tense with certain verbs. These verbs include:

appear	hate	love	see	understand
believe	have	need	seem	want
belong	hear	own	smell	wish
exist	know	prefer	sound	
forget	like	remember	taste	

Use the Present Tense with these verbs to talk about now:

Correct: I want to leave now.

Incorrect: I am wanting to leave now.

Dialogues

Complete the following dialogues using either the *Present Tense* to show what usually happens or *Present Continuous Tense* to show what is happening now.

1.   Carolyn and John are in the office. Carolyn is making a phone call.

JOHN: Who _____ you _____ ?

(call)

CAROLYN: I _____ a cab to go to the airport.

(call)

JOHN: Oh? _____ you usually _____ the air-

(take; negative question)

port bus?

CAROLYN: Yes, I usually _____ , but I _____ late[14]

(run)

today.

---

[14]run late: to be behind schedule.

QUESTIONS

1. How does Carolyn usually get to the airport?
2. Why is she taking a taxi this time?

2. Andy and Ralph are boarding United's 9 A.M. flight to San Diego when they suddenly spot each other.

ANDY: Hey, Ralph! I'm surprised to see you here. _____ you

always _____ TWA?

(fly; negative question)

RALPH: Most of the time I _____ .

ANDY: So why _____ you _____ United today?

(fly)

RALPH: I _____ this flight because I need to be in San Diego by

(take)

noon.

ANDY: TWA also _____ a 9 A.M. flight, _____

(have)

they?

RALPH: Sure they _____ , but it's full.

QUESTIONS

1. What airline does Ralph usually fly?
2. What airline is he flying this time?
3. Why isn't he taking TWA's 9 A.M. flight?

3. Mr. Lee flies from Chicago to Boston on business every week. His colleague, Mr. Cobb, asks him why he is leaving so early this time.

MR. COBB: _____ you usually _____

(leave; negative question)

for[15] the airport at four o'clock?

MR. LEE: Yes, I usually _____ .

MR. COBB: Well, why _____ you _____ so early?

(leave)

It's only two-thirty.

---

[15]leave for: to depart (to a specific place).

MR. LEE: I _____ now because it _____ .
                 (leave)   (snow)

MR. COBB: You're right. The traffic _____ bad every time it
                                                  (be)

_____ .
    (snow)

QUESTIONS

1. When does Mr. Lee usually leave for the airport?
2. How come[16] he's leaving so early this time?
3. Why does he expect the traffic to be heavy?

4. Mr. Lorca is on the telephone. Ms. Kim tells Mr. Lorca's secretary, Mr. Como, that she would like to see him.

MS. KIM: I'd like to see Mr. Lorca, please.

MR. COMO: He _____ on the phone now. He _____
                             (be)   (make)

plane reservations to Los Angeles.

MS. KIM: Oh? _____ he always _____ his own
                                               (make)

reservations?

MR. COMO: No. I usually _____ it for him, but I _____
                                  (do)   (be)

too busy. I _____ to cancel his reservations to Detroit!
                    (try)

QUESTIONS

1. How come Mr. Lorca can't see Ms. Kim now?
2. Who usually makes Mr. Lorca's reservations?
3. Why is Mr. Lorca making his own reservations this time?

Complete the following dialogues using *Present Tense* or *Present Continuous Tense*. Note the use of *Present Continuous Tense* with *always*.

5. Georgia and Tina are flight attendants. They are on board a flight.

TINA: Georgia, the passenger in seat 8B _____ about the food.
                                                   (complain)

---

[16]how come: why. Note the question forms for *how come* and *why*. How come he *is leaving* early this time? Why *is he leaving* early this time?

GEORGIA: Oh, 8B? That's Mr. Picayune. He _____ with us a couple
(fly)

of times a week. He never _____ the food.
(like)

TINA: Well, _____ he _____ often?
(complain)

GEORGIA: Are you kidding? He _____ always _____
(complain)

about something!

QUESTIONS

1.   How often does Mr. Picayune fly with this airline?
2.   What is he complaining about this time?
3.   Does he complain a lot?

6.   John and Lawrence are in their store. Their colleague, Bob, is on the phone.

LAWRENCE: _____ Bob _____ the phone again?
(use)

JOHN: Yes, he _____ .

LAWRENCE: I don't know why he _____ always _____
(use)

that phone for personal calls.

JOHN: Don't be angry. I know he _____ a lot of personal calls, but
(make)

he _____ this time. He _____ plane
(be; negative)   (make)

reservations to Salt Lake City. He has to attend a sales meeting there next week.

QUESTIONS

1.   Why is Lawrence angry?
2.   Why is Bob using the phone this time?

Complete the following dialogue using *Present Continuous Tense* or *Present Tense* to show
what is happening *nowadays.*

7.   Mr. Pan is buying a ticket on Southwest Airlines. He is talking with the clerk.

MR. PAN: I'd like a one-way ticket to Flagstaff on the seven o'clock flight tonight.

CLERK: Okay. Let me check the computer for availabilities.

MR. PAN: Southwest Airlines has a computer? I'm surprised. You're such a small outfit.[17]

CLERK: Oh, nowadays all the airlines _____ computers. We're no
(use)

exception. Okay. We do have a seat. How would you like to pay?

MR. PAN: Cash. I suppose most people _____ by credit card
(pay)

nowadays.

CLERK: Yes, they _____ .
(do)

MR. PAN: Well, plastic money[18] _____ popular all over[19] these days.
(become)

CLERK: It sure is. After all,[20] credit cards are convenient.

QUESTIONS

1.   How are all the airlines handling their ticket sales nowadays?
2.   How do most people pay for their tickets?
3.   Why are credit cards becoming popular all over these days?

C. Sentence Patterns

Recall this sentence from the narrative:
He ran over to her and asked her *what to do.*

PATTERNS

Subject + Verb + Question Word + to + Verb

Nobody knows what to do.

Verb + Subject + Question Word + to + Verb

Can you tell me how to get there?

---

[17]outfit: company, organization.
[18]plastic money: credit cards.
[19]all over: everywhere.
[20]after all: for a good reason which you should know.

Complete the following exchanges with a *Question Word + to + Verb* pattern.

> ***Example:*** A: Should I leave now or wait a while?
> B: I don't know. You'd better ask the customs officer *when to leave.*

1. A: I don't know where my passport and plane ticket are. What should I do?

   B: I don't know. You'd better ask the flight attendant _____ .

2. A: It's time to leave for the airport.

   B: I'm not sure of the way. We'd better ask someone _____ .

3. A: I'm really in a dilemma.

   B: I can't tell you _____ . You have to decide for yourself.

4. A: Where do you plan to go on your vacation this year?

   B: I don't know yet. I always have a hard time deciding _____ .

5. A: Can we start boarding the plane now?

   B: Don't ask me. You'd better ask the flight attendant _____ .

Recall this sentence from the narrative:
Can you tell me *what I have to write on these?*

Indirect Questions (Wh- Questions)

Subject + Verb + Question Word + Subject of clause + Verb of clause

She's not sure what time the plane departs.
I wonder why he's not here.

Verb + Subject + Question Word + Subject of clause + Verb of clause

Do you know where gate 12 is?

Indirect Questions (Yes/No Questions)

Subject + Verb + if/whether (or not) + Subject of clause + Verb of clause

He doesn't care if they come.
Ask them whether they're buying the tickets now or not.

Verb + Subject + if/whether (or not) + Subject of clause + Verb of clause

Can you tell me whether or not flight 010 is on time?

Here are some expressions commonly used in the above patterns:

Do you know . . . ?	Could you tell me . . . ?	I can't tell you . . . .
I don't know	Can you tell me . . . ?	I can't explain . . . .
I know	Would you tell me . . . ?	I can't imagine . . . .
Do you remember . . . ?	Ask her	
I don't remember	Tell me	
I remember		
Are you sure . . . ?	I wonder	
I'm not sure	I don't care	

Complete the following exchanges with a clause beginning with *who, when, why, where, what,* or *which.*

> *Example:*   A: I don't understand these symbols on the flight schedule.
> B: I'm afraid I don't know *what they mean either.*

1.   A: Is she taking flight 409 or 609?

   B: I'm not sure _____ .

2.   A: His bags are brown, aren't they?

   B: I don't remember _____ .

3.   A: He's arriving at 3 P.M., isn't he?

   B: Actually, I don't know _____ .

4.   A: Is he sitting in the nonsmoking section or the smoking section?

   B: I don't know _____ .

5. A: Is he going to Chicago on business?*

    B: I don't know _____

*Note that the meaning of this question can change depending on intonation:
    Is he going *to Chicago* on business?
    Is he going to Chicago *on business*?
Thus, you can complete this exchange using *where* or *why*.

Change the following questions to questions beginning with "Do you know" or "Can you tell me." Then answer the question.

> ***Example:*** Where is Donald going?
>   A: Do you know *where Donald is going*?
>   B: *He's going to pick up his baggage.*

1. How can I get to the Lost and Found?

    A: Can you tell me _____

    B: _____

2. Why is he giving up his travel plans?

    A: Do you know _____

    B: _____

3. Where is gate 20?

    A: Do you know _____

    B: _____

4. When is the next available flight to San Francisco?

    A: Can you tell me _____

    B: _____

5.   How often does the airport bus run?

   A: Do you know _____

   B: _____

6.   How much is a round-trip ticket to Tokyo?

   A: Can you tell me _____

   B: _____

7.   Is the "red eye"[21] special from Los Angeles on time?

   A: Can you tell me _____

   B: _____

8.   Is the man paying by credit card?

   A: Do you know _____

   B: _____

9.   Are tomorrow's flights to Miami all booked?

   A: Can you tell me _____

   B: _____

Recall this sentence from the narrative:
Together they *spent about fifteen minutes filling* everything out.

PATTERN

spend + (amount of time) + Verb-ing

Pilots often *spend up to an hour taxiing*[22] on the runway.

---

[21]"red eye" special: refers to cross-country, all-night flights. Many people take these because they are usually the least expensive flights.
[22]taxi (refers to movement of an airplane): to go at low speed on the ground.

Complete the following exchanges with an appropriate response using the above pattern.

> **Example:** A: How much time do you usually spend *traveling out West*
> (travel out West)
>
> every summer?
> B: Oh, around a month.

1. A: Do you always do work when you travel on a plane?

   B: I usually do.

   A: Well, I _____ , so when I fly I like to relax.
   (eight hours a day-work in the office)

2. A: Artie always seems to find a cheap flight. How does he do it?

   B: Oh, he just _____ first, that's all.
   (a lot of time-check all the different rates)

3. A: I have to go over to Sunshine Travel to pick up my airline tickets.

   B: Oh, I hate that place. Every time I go there it seems like[23] I _____
   (over two hours-wait)

   to see someone.

4. A: I always fly standby.[24] It's really cheap.

   B: I know it's cheap, but I don't like hanging around[25] the airport waiting for a cancella-

   tion. It can take forever.[26]

   A: It doesn't take that long!

   B: Well, how much time do you usually _____ around the airport to
   (wait)

   get on a flight?

   A: I usually spend about an hour.

---

[23]seems like: colloquial form of *seems as if, seems as though.*
[24]stand by (to fly standby): to get on a flight without reservations by waiting for a cancellation.
[25]hang around: to wait.
[26]take forever: to take a very long time.

IV. EXPRESSIONS AND IDIOMS

● *had better*: the best thing to do.

> had better (not) + Verb (base form)

Note: We use *had better* in its contracted forms: I'd, you'd, he'd, she'd, they'd better.

Recall this sentence from the narrative:
> But *you'd better* go to the baggage claim area right away and speak to the supervisor.

Complete the following exchanges with an appropriate response using *had better*.

> ***Example:***   A: I think our flight is boarding now.
> B: Well, <u>*we'd better get to Departure Gate 12*</u> right away.
> (Departure Gate 12)

1.   A: The 4 o'clock flight is full. What should we do?

   B: _____ right   away.
   (another flight)

2.   A: I'm not sure which gate the flight is arriving at.

   B: _____
   (information desk)

3.   A: We are having air turbulence.

   B: _____
   (safety belts)

4.   A: My passport is missing!

   B: _____ right now!
   (Lost and Found)

● *give up*:   stop trying to do something.

> give up + <u>Verb-ing</u>
> Noun

Recall this sentence from the narrative:
> Mr. Lin had a hard time understanding them and was almost ready to *give up* when an American student came over . . . .

Complete the following exchanges with an appropriate response using *give up*.

   Example: A: He doesn't think he can pass the exam for a pilot's
                         license.
                    B: Oh, I'm sure he can pass it. Don't let him *give up*!

1.   A: Don't _____ .
                              (try to get a charter flight)[27]

         B: How come?

         A: Because we can't afford to take a regular flight!

2.   A: All the shuttle flights[28] to Boston this weekend are booked. I guess I can't go.

         B: Don't _____ . Why don't you take the train?
                              (so easily)

3.   A: I keep calling the travel agency, but the line is always busy.

         B: Well don't _____ . You have to get through[29] to them today.

4.   A: I don't think we can get on a flight today. I'm not waiting anymore.

         B: C'mon. Let's not _____ yet. Every time I fly standby I always get

              a seat at the last minute. Just be patient a little longer!

● have *a hard time*: to find something difficult to do.
       trouble

have a hard time / trouble	+	Verb-ing / with + Noun

Also, *give (someone) a hard time*: make something difficult for someone; give someone
trouble.

Recall these sentences from the narrative:
       Mr. Lin *had a hard time* understanding them.
       I always *have trouble* filling out forms.

---

[27]charter flight: A group or organization books (at a discount price) all the seats on a certain flight and
   then sells the tickets at a lower price than a regular flight.
[28]shuttle flight: short-distance flights with frequent departures.
[29]get through: reach, contact (on the phone).

Complete the following exchanges with an appropriate response using *have a hard time/ trouble*.

> ***Example:***   A: I always <u>*have a hard time getting through customs.*</u>
> (get through customs)
> B: Really? I never do. In fact, they hardly ever open my bags.
> A: Well, I guess that's because you have an honest face!

1.   A: I'm planning to go to Honolulu next month.

    B: Great! But isn't it quite expensive to fly there?

    A: Oh, I always fly standby, so it's not that expensive.

    B: I hate to fly standby. I always _____ .
                                                     (get on a flight)

2.   On board a plane:

    A: Call the flight attendant over the next time you see him, okay?

    B: What's the matter?

    A: I'm _____ . I can't tighten it.
                                   (my seatbelt)

3.   In an airport terminal:

    A: Where's Jack? Isn't he coming to pick us up?

    B: Yes, he is. I guess he's late.

    A: Jack late? He's never late. I bet he's _____ .
                                                 (find a parking space)

    B: You're right. He's probably out in the parking lot right now.

4.   A: Can you take me to the airport tomorrow night?

    B: Sure. What time is your flight?

    A: Midnight.

    B: Midnight! Why such a late flight?

A: Listen, it's the holiday season. It was the only flight available.

B: Oh, yeah. I usually _____ during the holidays, too.
     (book a flight)

5.   On board a plane:

A: Aren't you eating? The food isn't bad.

B: I never eat airline food.

A: Never?

B: No, I always _____ .
     (digest it)

V. SITUATIONAL DIALOGUES

1.   Sandy Burke, a Boston businesswoman, occasionally flies to Hawaii on business. She is calling to book a flight.

MS. BURKE: Hello. I'd like to book a flight to Honolulu and I'd like the lowest fare possible.

AGENT: When would you like to leave?

MS. BURKE: January 2nd.

AGENT: Let me check the computer to see what flights we have. Okay, we have two flights to Honolulu on the second of January. The first one leaves Boston at 9 A.M. and arrives in Honolulu at 12:30 P.M. local time. The second one departs at 12 midnight and arrives at 3:30 A.M. It is less expensive, but you have to fly all night. It's $595 one way, $895 round trip.

MS. BURKE: Is the night flight a nonstop flight or does it have stopovers?

AGENT: It has a two-hour stopover in San Francisco.

MS. BURKE: Do I have to change planes?

AGENT: No, but if you want, you can get off and stretch your legs.

MS. BURKE: Okay. I'd like a round-trip ticket on the night flight.

AGENT: Fine. How would you like to pay? We accept Visa, Mastercard, and American Express. We don't accept personal checks. Of course, we take cash, too.

MS. BURKE: I'll put it on my Mastercard. By the way, how many pounds of luggage can I take?

AGENT: The baggage weight limit is ninety pounds.

MS. BURKE: Oh, yes, what's the fare for a child? I may bring my daughter next time. She's dying to[30] see Hawaii.

AGENT: Children under eleven pay three-quarters of the normal fare.

MS. BURKE: Oh, that's not bad. Just one more thing. There isn't any chance the flight will be cancelled, right? I need to be in Honolulu by the third of January to attend an important meeting.

AGENT: It's unlikely, unless there is a problem with the weather.

MS. BURKE: Okay. Thanks for your help.

QUESTIONS

1. What is Ms. Burke's destination?
2. How many flights are there to Honolulu on the second of January?
3. Is the night flight a nonstop flight or does it have stopovers?
4. Does Ms. Burke want a one-way or a round-trip ticket?
5. How does Ms. Burke want to pay?
6. What's the luggage limit?
7. What's the fare for children? Why does Ms. Burke want to know it?
8. Under what conditions could the flight be cancelled?

2. Ms. Krakow, a college student, is returning home from school. She is checking in at the airport.

· CLERK: Your ticket, please.

MS. KRAKOW: Here you are. I'd like a seat in the nonsmoking section, please.

CLERK: Okay. Window or aisle seat?

MS. KRAKOW: I'd prefer a window seat.

CLERK: Fine. Put your bags on the scale, please. Your bags are several pounds over-weight.

MS. KRAKOW: Well, I have a lot of books.

CLERK: I'm afraid there's an additional charge.

MS. KRAKOW: All right. I also have this shoulder bag. Can I carry it on?

CLERK: Yes, you can carry one bag on the plane with you, but you must be able to fit it under your seat.

QUESTIONS

1. What section would Ms. Krakow like to sit in?
2. What seat does she prefer?
3. Why does she have to pay an additional charge?
4. How many pieces of luggage can she carry on board the plane?

---

[30]be dying to: to want to do something very much. Also, be dying for: to want something very much.

Customs declaration form

WELCOME
TO THE
UNITED STATES

DEPARTMENT OF THE TREASURY
UNITED STATES CUSTOMS SERVICE

CUSTOMS DECLARATION

FORM APPROVED
OMB NO. 1515-0041

Each arriving traveler or head of family must provide the following information (only **ONE** written declaration per family is required):

1. Name: --
   Last   First   Middle Initial

2. Number of family members traveling with you ---------------------

3. Date of Birth: ------/------/------ 4. Airline/Flight: -------------
   Month   Day   Year

5. U.S. Address: --

   ----

6. I am a U.S. Citizen   YES ☐   NO ☐
   If No,
   Country: --------------------------------

7. I reside permanently in the U.S.   YES ☐   NO ☐
   If No,
   Expected Length of Stay: ---------------

8. The purpose of my trip is or was
   ☐ BUSINESS   ☐ PLEASURE

9. I am/we are bringing fruits, plants, meats, food, soil,   YES ☐   NO ☐
   birds, snails, other live animals, farm products, or
   I/we have been on a farm or ranch outside the U.S.

10. I am/we are carrying currency or monetary   YES ☐   NO ☐
    instruments over $5000 U.S. or the foreign
    equivalent.

11. The total value of all goods I/we purchased
    or acquired abroad and am/are bringing
    to the U.S. is (see instructions under
    Merchandise on reverse side; visitors
    should report value of gifts only): $-------------------
                                              U.S. Dollars

SIGN ON REVERSE SIDE AFTER YOU READ WARNING.
(Do not write below this line.)

INSPECTOR'S NAME   STAMP AREA

BADGE NO.

Paperwork Reduction Act Notice: The Paperwork Reduction Act of 1980 says we must tell you why we are collecting this information, how we will use it and whether you have to give it to us. We ask for this information to carry out the Customs, Agriculture, and Currency laws of the United States. We need it to ensure that travelers are complying with these laws and to allow us to figure and collect the right amount of duties and taxes. Your response is mandatory.

Customs Form 6059B (051184)

WESTERN
Count on us

Boarding Pass
Connection/Return

FIRST CLASS   COACH
Flight Date *7-11*   Gate *4*
From *HNL*   To *LAX*
Seat Number *23a*

FIRST CLASS   COACH
Flight Date *7-11*   Gate *4*
From *HNL*   To *LAX*
Seat Number *23a*

Airline boarding pass

3. Mr. Coleman is returning to America from a trip overseas.

OFFICER: Open up your bags, please. Do you have anything to declare?

MR. COLEMAN: Yes. I have two bottles of whiskey.

OFFICER: That's all right. You're allowed two bottles of liquor.

MR. COLEMAN: I also have these two statues. They're gifts.

OFFICER: There's no duty on those either. Anything else?

MR. COLEMAN: Yes. This tape recorder.

OFFICER: You have to pay on that. [looking through the suitcase] What's this? Cigars?

MR. COLEMAN: Yes. I only have one box, though.

OFFICER: It doesn't matter how many you have. These are Cuban cigars. You can't bring them into the country.

MR. COLEMAN: Oh, I didn't know that.

OFFICER: Sorry, but I have to confiscate them. Now you have to go to the cashier. You can pay the duty on the tape recorder there.

QUESTIONS

1. How much liquor can Mr. Coleman bring into the country without paying duty?
2. What items are duty free?
3. What's the problem with the cigars?

VI. VOCABULARY BUILDER

bag	doggy bag/garbage bag/handbag/laundry bag/lunchbag/makeup bag/ paper bag/school bag/shopping bag/shoulder bag/travel bag
baggage	baggage claim area/baggage claim supervisor/baggage claim ticket
luggage	carry-on luggage/hand luggage/lightweight luggage/luggage rack
flight	day flight/direct flight/flight arrival gate/flight arrival time/flight attendant/flight departure gate/flight information counter/flight insurance/ flight number/flight reservation/flight schedule/night flight/nonstop flight
plane	plane fare/plane reservations/plane tickets
air	air freight/airline/air mail/airplane/airport/airsick/air terminal/air traffic/air travel

VII. ROLE PLAY SUGGESTIONS

1. Your passport, wallet, or some other item is lost. Find out what to do.
2. Ask how to get to the information counter or Lost and Found.

3. Describe your lost bag, wallet, or handbag, including size, color, contents, and identification markings.
4. Book a flight.

VIII. PREPOSITION PRACTICE

A. Prepositions of Space: IN   ON   AT

USE **IN** FOR:

a city or town	O'Hare Airport is **IN** Chicago.
a county	Chicago is **IN** Illinois.
a state	The state of Illinois is **IN** the Mid-West.
a region	The Mid-West is a region **IN** the United States.
a country	

USE **ON** FOR:

a street without an address number	Sunshine Travel Agency is **ON** Palifax Road.
a direction + side (east side, west side, etc.)	The airport is **ON** the east side of town.
a direction + coast (South Coast, North Coast, etc.)	This is the largest car rental agency **ON** the East Coast.

USE **AT** FOR:

a street with an address number	Alpine Airways is located **AT** 1322 Kirk Avenue.
a specific location	Your luggage is **AT** Gate 4.

Fill in the following exchanges with the appropriate preposition:

1. A: Is L.A.'s International Airport _____ Burbank?

    B: No, silly, it's _____ West L.A.

    A: Are you kidding? There's an airport _____ the west side of town?

    B: Sure.

2. A: How many shuttle flights are there _____ the East Coast?

    B: Well, there are the New York-Washington and the New York-Boston shuttles.

A: Does the shuttle to D.C. land _____ Virginia?

B: Yes, it lands _____ Washington National Airport

_____ Virginia.

3.   In the customs area of an airport:

A: Sir, I'm sorry but we have to inspect your luggage thoroughly.

B: Does the inspection take a long time?

A: Not usually. The inspector is over there _____ that special

counter. The inspection only takes about fifteen minutes.

4.   At a travel agency:

A: Can I pick up my tickets now?

B: No, I'm sorry. They're not ready yet. Can we mail them to you?

A: Yes, I'm _____ 446 South Shore Drive.

B: Is that _____ La Jolla or _____ Del Mar?

A: Neither. It's _____ Solana Beach.

5.   In the baggage claim area at Newark Airport:

A: Miss, your baggage is somewhere _____ the Mid-West.

B: What? How come?

A: Well, it was a mix-up[31] I guess.

B: That's incredible! Is your customer relations office still _____

Lexington Avenue _____ New York?

---

[31]mix-up: mistake.

A: No, it's now _____ West Orange Blvd. _____

Newark.

B: Where _____ West Orange Blvd.?

A: It's _____ 4188 West Orange.

B: Thanks.

6.   A: Pardon me, do you know where the duty free shop is?

B: Yes, it's located _____ the south side of this terminal.

A: Is it near the rest rooms?

B: That's right.

7.   Announcement over a public address system:

Flight 910 is delayed because of bad weather. Since it cannot land _____

Miami _____ Miami International, it will land _____

Fort Lauderdale _____ Broward Airport.

B. Additional Preposition Combinations

Verb + Preposition Combinations can be separable (S) or inseparable (IS).

For inseparable forms, the verb and preposition must be kept together.
For separable forms, we can place an object noun or pronoun between the verb and preposition:
   Bill *picked up* his wife at the airport.
   Bill *picked* his wife *up* at the airport.

When we use a pronoun, we must place it between the verb and the preposition.

   Correct: Bill *picked* her *up* at the airport.
   Incorrect: Bill *picked up* her at the airport.

pick up (S):

   to meet (someone)   My friend usually *picks* me *up* at the airport.

   to get (something)   Mr. Lin *picked up* his baggage at Gate 5.

help out (S):

   to help (someone) with (something)   He *helped* me *out* with the forms.

Complete the following exchanges with one of the foregoing preposition combinations.

1.   In the baggage claim area of an airport:

    A: Gosh, Dan, I see you have six suitcases. Let me _____ you

         _____ .

    B: No problem. They're all light. You can help, though, if you go to the baggage area

        and _____ my other three bags. They all have ID tags on them.

2.   In a taxi:

    A: What time is it?

    B: Half past one.

    A: Oh, wow! Can you step on it?[32] I have to be at the airport by two o'clock.

    B: Do you have to catch a flight?

    A: No, I have to _____ my boss there.

3.   Two flight attendants on board a flight:

    A: The woman in seat 23C can't open the overhead compartment.

    B: Well, let me go _____ her _____ then.

---

[32]step on it: to go faster.

4. Talking with a ticket agent:

A: What? You mean you overbooked[33] this flight, and now you're bumping[34] me!

B: Yes, I'm afraid so.

A: Well, what can I do?

B: I'm sure the supervisor can _____ you _____ .

He'll get you on another flight.

---

[33]overbook: to sell more tickets than the actual number of seats.
[34]to be bumped: not to get a seat because of overbooking.

2 HE TOOK A TAXI, DIDN'T HE?

I. NARRATIVE

Mr. Lin finally collected all his baggage and found his way to the air terminal exit. He walked over to a taxi stand and waited there. After about fifteen minutes, he **got tired of** waiting and decided to take a bus instead of a taxi. Just at that moment, an independent cab[1] pulled up and the driver shouted to him, "Get in! I can take you to the city."[2] Since Mr. Lin had a reservation at the Excelsior Hotel in the city, he got in the cab. Meanwhile, the driver jumped out and put Mr. Lin's bags in the trunk. The whole thing happened so quickly that Mr. Lin forgot to ask how much the fare was. That was a big mistake.

After a half hour, Mr. Lin finally asked the cabbie, "How much longer before we get there?" The cab driver shrugged his shoulders and said, "**At least** another half hour." Suddenly, Mr. Lin remembered reading that the hotel was only twenty minutes from the airport. He said to himself, "This cabbie wants to take me for a ride."[3] He felt helpless in a foreign country, however, and didn't know what to say. Finally, he got up the nerve[4] to ask the cab driver, "Could you drop me off at the next corner?" The driver mumbled something and then said to Mr. Lin, "You know, I had to put your bags in the trunk, so there's a special luggage charge. Five dollars extra."

Mr. Lin was very angry, but he simply paid the man fifteen dollars for the ride plus five for his luggage. Fortunately for Mr. Lin, there was a subway station nearby. "I suppose that I can get there by subway," he thought. He struggled with his bags for ten minutes before he arrived at the token booth. He asked the woman in the booth if she could tell him how to get to the Excelsior Hotel on Forty-third Street. She smiled, took out a subway map, and carefully explained to Mr. Lin how to get to the hotel.

[1]independent cab: a taxi operated by an individual, not a taxi company.
[2]the city: for New Yorkers this term means Manhattan, one of five boroughs that make up the City of New York.
[3]take someone for a ride: to cheat someone.
[4]get up the nerve: to become brave enough to do something.

QUESTIONS

1. Why did Mr. Lin decide to go over to the bus stop and catch a bus?
2. How come Mr. Lin forgot to ask about the fare?
3. Where did Mr. Lin have a reservation?
4. Where did the cabbie put Mr. Lin's bags?
5. How far is it from the airport to the Excelsior Hotel?
6. When did Mr. Lin finally realize the cab driver was "taking him for a ride"?
7. Why did the cabbie make Mr. Lin pay a "special luggage charge"?
8. How did Mr. Lin feel about paying the extra charge?
9. How did Mr. Lin finally get to the hotel?
10. What kind of attitude did the woman in the token booth have?

II. DIALOGUES

1.   Mr. Lin is in the airport terminal. He'd like to find out how to get to his hotel. He walks over to the information counter.

LIN: Excuse me, can you help me?

CLERK: Of course. What can I do for you?

LIN: Can you tell me how I can get to the Excelsior Hotel from here?

CLERK: The Excelsior? Let's see, that's in the city, right?

LIN: Yes, it is. On Forty-third Street, just off Eleventh Avenue.

CLERK: Well, you can take a bus to the city. Just go out the front door of the terminal and cross the street. There is a sign that says, "Airport-City Bus." Otherwise, you can take a taxi. You can catch one right in front of the terminal.

LIN: Thank you. Oh, do you know how much the bus fare is?

CLERK: It's five dollars. A taxi runs[5] about fifteen to twenty dollars.

LIN: I'd better take a bus then. How often do the buses run?

CLERK: I think you just missed one. There is a schedule printed on the sign outside. I think that they run every half hour or so.[6]

LIN: On second thought,[7] I'd better take a cab. I have a lot of luggage and it's late. Thank you!

QUESTIONS

1. What does Mr. Lin want to find out?
2. Where is the Excelsior Hotel located?

---

[5]run: to cost.
[6]or so: about.
[7]on second thought: after reconsidering.

3. Where can Mr. Lin catch a bus to the city?
4. Where can Mr. Lin find a bus schedule?
5. Why does Mr. Lin change his mind and decide to take a cab?

2. Mr. Lin is at a token booth in a subway station.

LIN: Can you tell me how to get to the Excelsior? It's on Forty-third Street just off Eleventh Avenue.

CLERK: Sure. Just a second. I have to check the map first. Okay, first take the GG train one stop to Queens Plaza. Then transfer to the E train. Get off at Forty-second Street and then walk from there. It's only a few blocks.

LIN: I got it.[8] Oh, I'd better buy two tokens.

CLERK: Here you are. And here is a subway map; it's free.

LIN: Thank you again. I really appreciate your help!

CLERK: No problem. Have a good day, now.

QUESTIONS

1. What does Mr. Lin ask the clerk in the token booth?
2. Does the clerk know offhand[9] how to get to the Excelsior Hotel?
3. Describe how to get to the Excelsior Hotel by subway.

III. GRAMMAR

A. Past Tense

Use the Past Tense to talk about what happened at a specific time in the past.

FORM: REGULAR VERBS | Subject + Verb-ed

Affirmative: She *missed* the bus last night.

Negative: She <u>did not</u> *miss* the bus last night.
          didn't

Question: Did she *miss* the bus last night?

Wh- Questions: When *did* she *miss* the bus?

Who/What/Which as Subject: Who *missed* the bus last night?

---

[8]get it: to understand; be clear about something.
[9]offhand: to know without checking or consulting anyone or anything; to know immediately.

FORM: IRREGULAR VERBS | Subject + Verb (Past Tense form)

Affirmative: Jane *took* a taxi home yesterday afternoon.

Negative: Jane *did not take* a taxi home yesterday afternoon.
                      didn't

Question: *Did* Jane *take* a taxi home yesterday afternoon?

Wh- Questions: Why *did* Jane *take* a taxi home yesterday afternoon?

Who/What/Which as Subject: Who *took* a taxi home yesterday afternoon?

FORM: VERB "TO BE" | Subject + $\dfrac{\text{was}}{\text{were}}$

Affirmative: They *were* late this morning.

Negative: They *were not* late this morning.
                      weren't

Question: *Were* they late this morning?

Wh- Questions: Why *were* they late this morning?

Who/What/Which as Subject: Who *was* late this morning?

Note: Use *was* instead of *were* for *I, he, she, it.*

TIME EXPRESSIONS

These time expressions are often used with the Past Tense:

yesterday	last night	a few minutes ago
yesterday morning	last week	a little while ago
yesterday afternoon	last month	a week ago
the day before yesterday	last year	a year ago
	last March	

USED TO

Use *used to* to talk about (a) something you did repeatedly in the past, but no longer do now [past habit]; (b) a past state or condition.

Example: Subway tokens *used to* cost twenty-five cents.

FORM: | Subject + used to + Verb (base form)

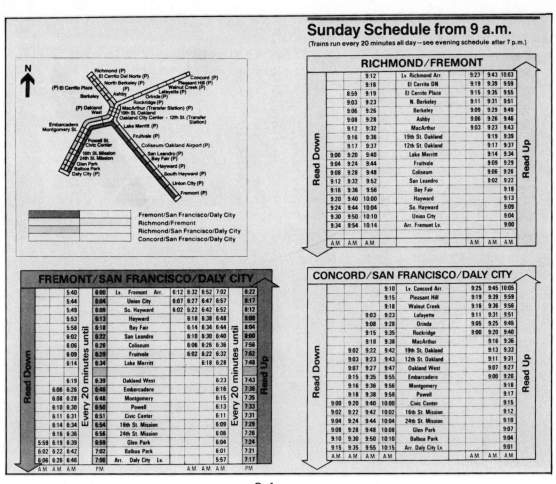

Legend:
- Fremont/San Francisco/Daly City
- Richmond/Fremont
- Richmond/San Francisco/Daly City
- Concord/San Francisco/Daly City

Sunday Schedule from 9 a.m.

(Trains run every 20 minutes all day—see evening schedule after 7 p.m.)

RICHMOND/FREMONT

Read Down →   ← Read Up

			Station			
		9:12	Lv. Richmond Arr.	9:23	9:43	10:03
		9:16	El Cerrito DN	9:19	9:39	9:59
	8:59	9:19	El Cerrito Plaza	9:15	9:35	9:55
	9:03	9:23	N. Berkeley	9:11	9:31	9:51
	9:06	9:26	Berkeley	9:09	9:29	9:49
	9:08	9:28	Ashby	9:06	9:26	9:46
	9:12	9:32	MacArthur	9:03	9:23	9:43
	9:16	9:36	19th St. Oakland		9:19	9:39
	9:17	9:37	12th St. Oakland		9:17	9:37
9:00	9:20	9:40	Lake Merritt		9:14	9:34
9:04	9:24	9:44	Fruitvale		9:09	9:29
9:08	9:28	9:48	Coliseum		9:06	9:26
9:12	9:32	9:52	San Leandro		9:02	9:22
9:16	9:36	9:56	Bay Fair			9:18
9:20	9:40	10:00	Hayward			9:13
9:24	9:44	10:04	So. Hayward			9:09
9:30	9:50	10:10	Union City			9:04
9:34	9:54	10:14	Arr. Fremont Lv.			9:00
A.M.	A.M.	A.M.		A.M.	A.M.	A.M.

CONCORD/SAN FRANCISCO/DALY CITY

Read Down →   ← Read Up

				Station			
			9:10	Lv. Concord Arr.	9:25	9:45	10:05
			9:15	Pleasant Hill	9:19	9:39	9:59
			9:18	Walnut Creek	9:16	9:36	9:56
		9:03	9:23	Lafayette	9:11	9:31	9:51
		9:08	9:28	Orinda	9:05	9:25	9:45
		9:15	9:35	Rockridge	9:00	9:20	9:40
		9:18	9:38	MacArthur		9:16	9:36
	9:02	9:22	9:42	19th St. Oakland		9:13	9:33
	9:03	9:23	9:43	12th St. Oakland		9:11	9:31
	9:07	9:27	9:47	Oakland West		9:07	9:27
	9:15	9:35	9:55	Embarcadero		9:00	9:20
	9:16	9:36	9:56	Montgomery			9:18
	9:18	9:38	9:58	Powell			9:17
9:00	9:20	9:40	10:00	Civic Center			9:15
9:02	9:22	9:42	10:02	16th St. Mission			9:12
9:04	9:24	9:44	10:04	24th St. Mission			9:10
9:08	9:28	9:48	10:08	Glen Park			9:07
9:10	9:30	9:50	10:10	Balboa Park			9:04
9:15	9:35	9:55	10:15	Arr. Daly City Lv.			9:01
A.M.	A.M.	A.M.	A.M.		A.M.	A.M.	A.M.

FREMONT/SAN FRANCISCO/DALY CITY

Read Down →   ← Read Up — Every 20 minutes until

				Station					
	5:40		6:00	Lv. Fremont Arr.	6:12	6:32	6:52	7:02	8:22
	5:44		6:04	Union City	6:07	6:27	6:47	6:57	8:17
	5:49		6:09	So. Hayward	6:02	6:22	6:42	6:52	8:12
	5:53		6:13	Hayward		6:18	6:38	6:48	8:08
	5:58		6:18	Bay Fair		6:14	6:34	6:44	8:04
	6:02		6:22	San Leandro		6:10	6:30	6:40	8:00
	6:06		6:26	Coliseum		6:06	6:26	6:36	7:56
	6:09		6:28	Fruitvale		6:02	6:22	6:32	7:52
	6:14		6:34	Lake Merritt			6:18	6:28	7:48
	6:19		6:39	Oakland West				6:23	7:43
6:06	6:26		6:46	Embarcadero				6:16	7:36
6:08	6:28		6:48	Montgomery				6:15	7:35
6:10	6:30		6:50	Powell				6:13	7:33
6:11	6:31		6:51	Civic Center				6:11	7:31
6:14	6:34		6:54	16th St. Mission				6:09	7:29
6:16	6:36		6:56	24th St. Mission				6:06	7:26
5:59	6:19	6:39	6:59	Glen Park				6:04	7:24
6:02	6:22	6:42	7:02	Balboa Park				6:01	7:21
6:06	6:26	6:46	7:06	Arr. Daly City Lv.				5:57	7:17
A.M.	A.M.	A.M.	PM		A.M.	A.M.	A.M.		PM

Subway map

Affirmative: He *used to go* to work by subway.

Negative: He *didn't used to go* to work by subway.

Question: *Did* he *used to go* to work by subway?

Wh- Question: How *did* he *used to go* to work?

Who/What/Which as Subject: Who *used to go* to work by subway?

Dialogues

Complete the following dialogues using either *Past Tense* to show what happened at a specific time in the past or *Present Tense* to show what happens regularly or in general.

1.   Alberto arrives at the office late. His colleague, Armand, asks him what happened.

ARMAND: Morning, Alberto. How come you're so late? _____ any-

thing _____ ?
$\qquad\qquad\qquad\qquad\quad$ (happen)

ALBERTO: No, not really. It just _____ me longer than usual to get
$\qquad\qquad\qquad\qquad\qquad\quad$ (take)

here today.

ARMAND: How long _____ it _____ you?
$\qquad\qquad\qquad\qquad\qquad\qquad\qquad\qquad\quad$ (take)

ALBERTO: An hour and a half!

ARMAND: How long _____ it usually _____
$\qquad\qquad\qquad\qquad\qquad\qquad\qquad\qquad\qquad\qquad$ (take)

you?

ALBERTO: Most of the time it _____ about an hour. Yesterday it
$\qquad\qquad\qquad\qquad\qquad\qquad$ (take)

only _____ forty-five minutes.
$\qquad\qquad\quad$ (take)

ARMAND: Oh? Well, what _____ today?
$\qquad\qquad\qquad\qquad\qquad\qquad\qquad$ (happen)

ALBERTO: The subway _____ really slow. Usually I only
$\qquad\qquad\qquad\qquad\qquad\qquad$ (be)

_____ to wait four or five minutes for a train. This morning
(have)

I _____ to wait twenty minutes!
$\qquad\qquad\qquad\qquad$ (have)

QUESTIONS

1. How long did it take Alberto to get to the office today?
2. How long does it usually take him?
3. Why did it take him so long this time?
4. How long does he usually wait for a train?

2. Susan and Maria are classmates in high school.

SUSAN: How _____ you _____ to school yes-
(come)

terday? I _____ you on the bus yesterday morning as
(see; negative)

I usually _____ .

MARIA: My father _____ me.
(drive)

SUSAN: Oh? He _____ usually _____ you.
(drive; negative)

How come he _____ yesterday?
(do)

MARIA: Usually he _____ enough time to drive me. But
(have; negative)

since the weather _____ so bad yesterday and we live far from the
(be)

bus stop, he _____ me.
(take)

QUESTIONS

1. How did Maria get to school yesterday?
2. How does Maria usually go to school?
3. How come her father drove her yesterday?

3. Laura and Debbie are co-workers. Debbie is already in the office when Laura enters.

LAURA: Good morning, Debbie. You know, a funny thing[10] _____
(happen)

to me this morning. I _____ a taxi to work every morning and it
(take)

always _____ me $3.75. Today, though, it _____
(cost)   (cost)

$4.25. I can't understand it.

---

[10]funny thing: a strange or unusual thing or incident.

DEBBIE: _____ the driver _____ you?
                              the driver   (tell; negative question)

LAURA: Tell me what?

DEBBIE: That the fare _____ up[11] fifty cents as of[12] midnight last night.
                                    (go)

LAURA: The fare _____ up again? It seems like it
                              (go)

_____ up every few months or so.
        (go)

QUESTIONS

1.   How does Debbie usually get to the office?
2.   How much does the fare usually run?
3.   How much was the fare this morning?
4.   When did the fare go up?
5.   How much did the fare go up?

Complete the following dialogues using *Present Tense*, *Past Tense*, or *Past Tense with used to*:

4.   Ed is planning to go to Central City, Colorado. He asks Roberto about the fare.

ED: _____ you know how much it _____ to
                                                          (cost)

go to Central City by bus?

ROBERTO: I'm not sure how much it _____ now. It
                                                (be)

_____ fifteen dollars, but the fare _____
        (cost)   (go up)

a few months ago.

QUESTIONS

1.   How much did it used to cost to go to Central City by bus?
2.   When did the fare increase?

5.   Alexine is surprised to run into[13] her friend, Jamie, on the Metroliner express train from New York to Washington, D.C.

ALEXINE: Jamie! What a surprise! _____ you usually

_____ down to Washington?
        (fly; negative question)

---

[11]go up: to increase.
[12]as of: starting from (a time or date).
[13]run into: to meet unexpectedly.

Long-distance bus ticket

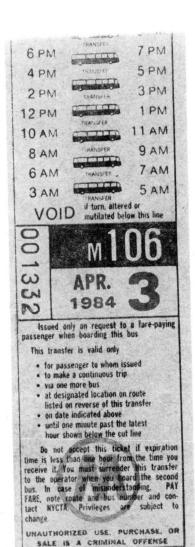

P.O.S. FORM 2

Greyhound Lines
PASSENGER TICKET

ISSUING CARRIER WILL BE RESPONSIBLE ONLY FOR TRANSPORTATION ON ITS OWN LINES, in accordance with tariff regulations and limitations. AND ASSUMES NO RESPONSIBILITY FOR ANY ACTS OR OMISSIONS OF OTHERS OCCURRING WITHIN OR OUTSIDE THE UNITED STATES except as imposed by law with respect to baggage. Seating aboard vehicles operated in interstate or foreign commerce is without regard to race, color, creed or national origin. ONE WAY FARES LIMITED TO 2 MONTHS ROUND TRIP FARES LIMITED TO 1 YEAR SPECIAL FARES LIMITED AS ENDORSED.

GOOD FOR ONE TRIP AS SHOWN

VALIDATION

GLI SAN DIEGO   CA 8946
AGENT 09-01 03:29:83 14:16 0865

SAN DIEGO   CA RT 02

FROM LOS ANGELES   CA GL
TO   SAN DIEGO   CA GL

CLASS FULL FARE $ 20.65 FARE
TRANSACTION NO. 0865
PAYMENT TYPE CASH
ENDORSEMENTS 45595714

PRINTED IN USA   VOID IF DETACHED   PUNCH   BOGEE
1 2 3 4   5 6 7 8

Ticket Number 2 2 45595714 12

---

6 PM TRANSFER 7 PM
4 PM TRANSFER 5 PM
2 PM TRANSFER 3 PM
12 PM TRANSFER 1 PM
10 AM TRANSFER 11 AM
8 AM TRANSFER 9 AM
6 AM TRANSFER 7 AM
3 AM TRANSFER 5 AM

VOID if torn, altered or mutilated below this line

001332 M106
APR. 1984 3

Issued only on request to a fare-paying passenger when boarding this bus

This transfer is valid only

- for passenger to whom issued
- to make a continuous trip
- via one more bus
- at designated location on route listed on reverse of this transfer
- on date indicated above
- until one minute past the latest hour shown below the cut line

Do not accept this ticket if expiration time is less than one hour from the time you receive it. You must surrender this transfer to the operator when you board the second bus. In case of misunderstanding, PAY FARE, note route and bus number and contact NYCTA. Privileges are subject to change.

UNAUTHORIZED USE, PURCHASE, OR SALE IS A CRIMINAL OFFENSE

New York City Transit Authority
S U R F A C E

City bus transfer

JAMIE: I _____ , but not anymore. Not since my brother

_____ the Metroliner to me.
(recommend)

ALEXINE: Your brother _____ in Washington now,
(live)

_____ he?
(do)

JAMIE: No, he _____ . He _____ there while
(do)   (live)

he was in college, so he _____ the train back home all the time.
(take)

QUESTIONS

1.   How does Jamie go to Washington now?
2.   How did he used to go to Washington?
3.   When did Jamie's brother live in Washington?
4.   How did Jamie's brother used to go back home?

6.   Phil and John are talking in the office.

JOHN: _____ you _____ to work everyday?
(drive)

PHIL: No, I _____ public transportation. But
(use)

I _____ to work when I _____ in Ozone Park.
(drive)   (live)

At that time I _____ to a car pool[14] with Maurice and a few of the
(belong)

other guys in the neighborhood. How _____ you
_____ to the office?
(get)

JOHN: Well, I _____ my car, too. But now that[15]
(take)

I _____ in Woodside, I just _____
(live)   (ride)

the commuter railroad. It's only a twenty minute ride.

QUESTIONS

1.   How does Phil get to work?
2.   How did Phil used to get to work?
3.   How does John get to work?

---

[14]car pool: a group of car owners who take turns driving each other to work.
[15]now that: since, because.

B. Can/Could

We use *can* and *could* to show ability, permission, possibility, and request.

CAN: We use *can* to show

Ability:
He *can* fix automobile engines, but I can't.

Note: Use *be able to* to show future, learned ability. Do not use *can*.
When you finish this course, you'll *be able to* drive quite well.

Permission in the Present or Future:
You *can* smoke on this bus.
Can I leave early today?

Note: We also use *may* to show permission. It is more formal than *can*.

Possibility in the Present or Future:
Even a good driver *can* have an accident.
She *can't* pick you up tomorrow because she'll be out of town.

Request:
Can you please meet me at the station?

COULD: We use *could* to show

Ability in the Past:
I *could* drive an automobile very well when I lived in Long Beach. [But I can't drive one very well now.]

Permission in the Present or Future:
A: *Could* I leave early today?
B: No, you *can't*.

Note: Use *can* to answer.

Possibility in the Present or Future: We use *could* to show that
(1) the possibility is not very definite or
(2) we are not sure about a situation.
She *could* be planning to take a later bus. [It is possible, but you are not very sure about it.]

The negative of *could* shows
(1) impossibility in the present or future. It is the same as *can* in this case.
He <u>*couldn't*</u> be at the terminal now!
    can't
(2) impossibility in the past
A hundred years ago people *couldn't* fly across the country. There were no planes!

Request: *Could* is more formal than *can.*
Could you please meet me at the station?

Suggestion or Solution: We often use *could* to offer a suggestion or a possible solution to a problem.
   A: Mark can't take me to the airport tomorrow. I don't know what to do.
   B: Well, you *could* take the airport bus. It's not very expensive.

Complete the following exchanges using *can, could,* or *be able to.* In some cases, more than one answer is possible.

1.   A: I don't know what to do. I went to both the train station and the bus terminal this

morning, but I _____ a seat on any of the trains or buses to
       (get)

Philadelphia tomorrow night.

   B: Well, you _____ .
         (fly)

   A: I know I _____ , but I really dislike flying.

   B: Well, it looks like you don't have any other choice if you want to get to Philly

tomorrow night.

2.   A: How are your driving lessons coming along?[16]

   B: Just fine. In a few more weeks, I'll _____ quite well.
                                             (drive)

3.   A: _____ you _____ me up at the
                                    (pick)

station tomorrow evening?

   B: What time?

   A: About 6 P.M.

   B: Oh, I'm sorry. I _____ .

   A: Do you think Dan _____ me then?
                              (meet)

---

[16]be coming along: to make progress; improve.

B: Maybe he _____ , if he has time.

A: _____ you _____ him for me?
(ask)

B: Sure.

4. A: How are you getting to Saratoga?

B: I don't know yet. _____ I _____
(take; question)

a train there?

A: Well, at one time you _____ , but no longer.[17] That line stopped

running a long time ago.

5. A: _____ I _____ your new motorcycle?
(try; question)

B: Are you sure you _____ it?
(ride)

A: Of course. When I was a teenager I had my own cycle. I _____
(ride)

one then, so I'm sure I still _____ now.

C. Sentence Patterns

Recall this sentence from the narrative:
The whole thing happened *so quickly that* Mr. Lin forgot to ask how much the fare was.

PATTERNS

Subject + Verb + so + Adverb + *that* + Subject + Verb
of clause of clause

The driver drove *so recklessly that* we almost had an accident.

Subject + Verb + so + Adjective + *that* + Subject + Verb
of clause of clause

The train was *so late that* everyone complained.

---

[17]no longer: not anymore.

Complete the following exchanges with a *so + adverb + that* or a *so + adjective + that* pattern.

> ***Example:***   A: Why was Lawrence late for the meeting this morning?
> Did he have to wait for the bus?
> B: Yes. *He had to wait so long for a bus that he finally had to take a taxi.*

1.   A: Why was Monique so angry at that taxi driver? Did he drive too fast?

     B: He sure did. _____ .
                                   (almost have-accident)

2.   A: Was the subway slow this morning?

     B: Yes. _____ .
                         (school-late)

3.   A: Was the bus very crowded last night?

     B: Yes. _____ .
                       (stand the whole way)

4.   A: I'm glad we're finally out of that taxi. The driver talked so loudly, didn't he?

     B: Yes. _____ .
                           (headache)

5.   A: I refuse to set foot[18] in Mario's car again.

     B: How come? He's not that bad[19] a driver.

     A: Oh yes he is. Last night _____ .
                                           (recklessly)

6.   A: Don't forget to pick up our train tickets on your lunch hour today!

     B: Don't worry!

     A: Well, you forgot yesterday.

     B: No, I didn't. Yesterday I _____ .
                                         (busy-not have time)

---

[18]set foot: (in) enter; (out of) leave.
[19]that (adjective) a: such a.

7.   On a train:

A: The next time the conductor walks by, you'd better ask him if we have to change

trains at Huntington Station.

B: I know. I tried to ask him a few minutes ago, but I couldn't get his attention. He

walked by _____ .
                                   (quickly-not hear)

Recall this sentence from the narrative.
I suppose that I can get there by subway.

PATTERN

Subject + Verb + (that) + Subject of clause + Verb of clause

She is sure (that) the fare isn't expensive.

We use this pattern with the expressions listed in Chapter 1, page 12.

Complete the following exchanges with an appropriate response.

Example: A: Is there a 4:30 bus to Boston?
                   B: I'm not sure. *But I know (that) there is a 4:45 bus.*

1.   A: Which train stops at Eighty-sixth Street?

B: I believe (that) _____ .

2.   A: It's 9:15 already. How come Michael isn't here yet?

B: I suppose (that) _____ .

3.   A: How often do the buses to the airport run?

B: I think (that) _____ .

4.   A: How do you think she went to Chicago?

B: I imagine (that) _____ .

5.   A: Why does he want to take Amtrak[20] instead of Greyhound[21] to Boston?

     B: I'm not really sure. I suppose (that) _____ .

6.   A: When did Jeff buy the tickets?

     B: I believe (that) _____ .

7.   A: Do you think that we can still make[22] the seven o'clock express to Westchester?

     B: No sweat![23] I'm sure (that) _____ .

8.   A: Do you know when they raised the fare?

     B: I believe (that) _____ .

IV. EXPRESSIONS AND IDIOMS

● *get tired of*: to not want to do something any longer.
be

get tired of +	Verb-ing
be	Noun

Recall this sentence from the narrative:

After about fifteen minutes, he *got tired of waiting* and decided to go to the bus stop across the street.

Complete the following exchanges with an appropriate response using *get/be tired of*.

Example: A: He took a taxi.
            B: Why?
            A: He *got tired of waiting* for the bus.

1.   A: C'mon. Here comes the local.[24] We'd better take it.

---

[20]Amtrak: name of the only national passenger railroad line.
[21]Greyhound: Greyhound and Trailways are two of the largest long-distance bus companies in the U.S.
[22]make: to catch; to have enough time to get to; to be able to go to.
[23]no sweat: no problem; easy.
[24]local (train): refers to subways or trains which make all the stops on a particular line.

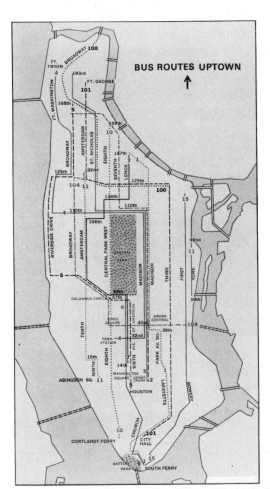

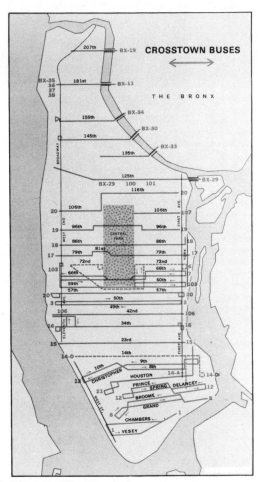

City bus route map

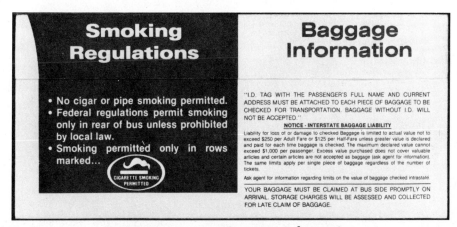

Long-distance bus baggage information

B: Don't you want to wait for the express train a little longer?

A: No. _____

2. A: Does Alfred commute from the suburbs every day?

B: Not any more. He moved to the city last month.

A: Really! Why?

B: _____

3. A: I took the bus to work every day last week.

B: What happened? You always used to ride the subway.

A: _____

4. Two people in a car:

A: Would you take the wheel for a while?

B: Why? _____ you _____ ?
                                    (drive)

A: Yes. My eyes are beginning to hurt.

5. At a train station:

A: What are you doing here? Are you having trouble with your car again?

B: Yes. And I _____ really _____ take it to the
                              (have to)

mechanic all the time.

A: Why don't you sell it and just take the train every day?

B: Well, I could _____ the train every day, too!
                            (ride)

● *instead of*: in place of.

> instead of + Noun
>   Verb-ing

Recall this sentence from the narrative:

After about fifteen minutes, he got tired of waiting and decided to take a bus *instead of* a taxi.

Complete the following exchanges with an appropriate response using *instead of*.

Example: In a taxi:
A: Where to?
B: El Cajon Boulevard and Fifty-sixth Avenue.
A: Okay.
B: Oh, on second thought, drop me off at University Avenue *instead of* El Cajon.

1. A: What took you so long? You're a half hour late.

   B: I got lost.

   A: How'd that happen?

   B: I got off the freeway at _____ .
                                (Rose Blvd. South – Rose Blvd. North)

2. A: Do you know where Jessica is?

   B: She left for the train station.

   A: Already? It's only two o'clock and her train isn't until five-thirty.

   B: Oh, didn't she tell you? She decided to take the _____ .
                                                        (three o'clock train – five-thirty)

3. A: I'm so tired of taking the bus to work every day. It's always packed.

   B: Well, you could _____ . It's not very far to the office from
                        (walk – take the bus)

   your place.[25]

_____

[25]one's place: one's apartment or house.

4. An employee is talking to her boss:

> A: Ms. Lewis do you think I could leave at _____
>
> (four o'clock-five o'clock)
>
> today? I've got to catch the early train.
>
> B: Sure, no problem.

● *at least*:

no less or fewer than

> Subject + Verb + at least + (amount of time, money, etc.)

It will take *at least* another half hour.

anyway

> at least + Subject + Verb

A: There's no heat in this bus.
B: Well, *at least* we got a seat.

Recall this sentence from the narrative:
The cabbie shrugged his shoulders and said, "*At least* another half hour."

Complete the following exchanges with an appropriate response using *at least*.

> ***Example:*** A: I hated riding the subway when I lived in the city. It was always so crowded.
>
> B: *Well, at least most of the trains were air conditioned.*

1. A: Say, how long do I have to wait for a bus?

> B: _____ . You just missed one.

2. A: How much did it cost Jonathan to take a taxi from the airport to the city?

> B: I don't know exactly, but I'm sure it was _____ .

3. A: How long do you think it took them to get to the amusement park?

> B: It depends. How did they go?
>
> A: By subway.
>
> B: _____ .

4. A: The traffic was very bad this morning.

B: What are you complaining about? _____ . Try riding the subway

(have a car)

every morning and see how that is!

5. A: Carlton bought a new Mercedes last week.

B: No kidding? I wonder how much it cost?

A: _____ , I guess.

B: He's always spending money. Last month he bought a boat, now a new car. How

does he do it?

A: Well, listen, he earns _____ a year.

V. SITUATIONAL DIALOGUES

1. In a subway station. A train comes into the station. Mr. Lin sticks his head in the door and asks:

LIN: Excuse me, does this train stop at Eighth Street?

PASSENGER: No. Take the local. This is the express.

LIN: (to a person on the platform) Does the local stop here?

PERSON ON PLATFORM: The local stops over there. You see? Across the platform, on the track against the wall.

LIN: Thanks a lot.

QUESTIONS

1. Which train stops at Eighth Street?
2. On what track does the local run?

2. In a bus terminal. Mr. Lin wants to go to Philadelphia by bus. He walks up to the information desk.

LIN: Hello. I want to go to Philadelphia. Where can I buy a ticket?

CLERK: Greyhound Lines, Window 10.

LIN: (at Window 10) What buses are there to Philadelphia this afternoon?

SECOND CLERK: There's one at 2:30, 3:45, and 5:00.

LIN: Okay. I'd like a ticket for the 2:30 bus.

SECOND CLERK: That's $27.50.

LIN: Can you tell me how long it takes to get there?

SECOND CLERK: It takes about two hours, depending on traffic.

LIN: Okay. Oh, where's the platform for that bus?

SECOND CLERK: Philadelphia buses leave from Platform 5 on the upper level. You can take the escalator over to the right.

LIN: Thanks very much.

QUESTIONS

1.   Which bus line goes to Philadelphia?
2.   What's the fare to Philadelphia?
3.   How long does it take to get there?
4.   Which platform do the buses to Philadelphia leave from?

VI. VOCABULARY BUILDER

bus   bus driver/bus fare/bus lane/bus route/bus schedule/bus station/bus stop/bus terminal/bus ticket

train   auto train/express train/local train/train fare/train platform/train schedule/train station/train ticket/train tracks

subway   subway car/subway map/subway station/subway stop/subway token

taxi   taxicab/taxi driver/taxi fare/taxi meter/taxi stand

VII. ROLE PLAY SUGGESTIONS

1.   Pick someplace to go. Ask someone how to get there by (a) subway, (b) bus, (c) walking.
2.   Ask how to get to the nearest subway station or bus stop.
3.   Buy a train ticket in a train station.

VIII. PREPOSITION PRACTICE

A. More on Prepositions of Space

USE **ON** FOR:

Location

the island   There isn't a bus stop **ON** this island.

the beach   We parked our Jeep **ON** the beach.

Next to
the ocean
the river
the lake   You can't get to their summer house **ON** the lake by train.

On top of
the mountain   He had to leave his car **ON** the mountain.
the ocean
the river
the lake   There are several sailboats **ON** the lake.

USE **IN** FOR:

Location
the mountains   Last year we spent a week hiking **IN** the mountains.

the desert   The year before last we went camping **IN** the desert.

Specific Enclosed Space   First, she put the luggage **IN** the trunk of her car.
                               She put the coats **IN** the hall closet.

Specific Room/Apartment   Mr. Lin stayed **IN** Room 410 when he was at the Excelsior Hotel.

Inside
the ocean   We went swimming **IN** the ocean.
the river   There aren't any fish **IN** that river.
the lake

USE **ACROSS** FOR:

movement from one side to the other   That type of jeep can go **ACROSS** a shallow river, and it has no trouble traveling **ACROSS** deserts or mountains.

location on the opposite side   They live **ACROSS** the street from us.

Complete the following exchanges with the appropriate preposition.

1.   A: The bike trail ends just before the river.

      B: Why's that?

      A: The old bridge collapsed last winter. But don't worry, I know another way

                                              _____ the river.

B: I'm not worried. You got us _____ the Mohave Desert and

_____ the Canadian Rockies so this little river doesn't worry me.

2.   A: Now that the car broke down[26] again, can we give it back to your brother?

B: Sure, but where can we find a Hertz or Avis[27] here _____ the

desert?

A: Well, what's up that way?

B: Mountains, and there certainly aren't any car rental agencies _____

the mountains.

3.   A conductor and a passenger:

A: May I have your ticket please?

B: Let's see now. I can't seem to find it _____ my wallet. Maybe it's

_____ my briefcase.

A: Well, there's no problem. I can sell you another one now.

4.   A policeman and a motorist:

A: You know I clocked you on my radar,[28] and you were going fifty-five in a thirty-five-

mile-an-hour zone.

B: Well, I didn't realize it, but if you say so.

A: Say, I can't read the address on your license. Where do you live?

B: I live _____ Block Island. I mean the address is 14 Shelter

Rock Road.

---

[26]break down: to stop working.
[27]Hertz and Avis: two of the largest car-rental companies in the United States.
[28]clock on radar: to measure car speed by using radar.

5.   Calling a gas station:

A: Hello. I have a flat[29] and I don't have a spare tire.

B: Okay. We can tow you into the station. Where are you?

A: We're parked in front of the Seaside Club. That's the old Spanish-style club right

_____ the ocean.

B: Yes, I know where that is. We'll be there in ten minutes.

B. Additional Preposition Combinations

wait for (someone/something) (IS):
      (an amount of time)

We never have to *wait for* the bus. It's always on time.
I usually have to *wait for* ten minutes.

wait on (someone) (IS):
    to serve

She likes to fly with Mid-West Airways because the flight attendants *wait on* her hand and foot.[30]

wait up (IS):
    to delay going to bed because you are waiting for someone or something.

The plane will be five hours late. I can't *wait up* any longer. I have to go to bed.

Complete the following exchanges with the appropriate preposition combination.

1.   A: Did you hear the news?

B: What happened?

A: The 10 P.M. out of Toledo had an accident.

B: Was anyone hurt?

A: The radio reporter didn't have the details.

---

[29]flat (tire): a tire that does not have air in it.
[30]wait on someone hand and foot: to take care of a person's every need.

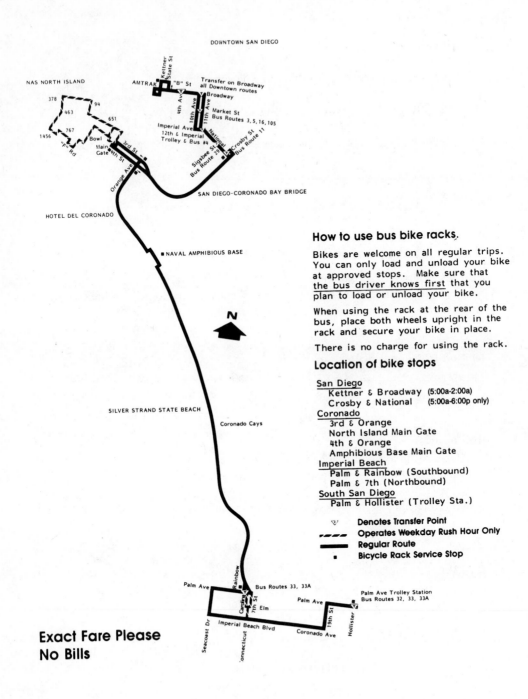

DOWNTOWN SAN DIEGO

NAS NORTH ISLAND

AMTRAK

Kettner State St
"B" St
Transfer on Broadway
all Downtown routes
Broadway
4th Ave
10th Ave
2nd Ave
11th Ave
Market St
Bus Routes 3, 5, 16, 105
National
Imperial Ave
12th & Imperial
Trolley & Bus #4
Crosby St
Bus Route 11
Sigsbee St
Bus Route 29

378
94
463
651
767
1456
"F" Rd
Bowl
Main
Gate
3rd St
4th St
Orange Ave

SAN DIEGO-CORONADO BAY BRIDGE

HOTEL DEL CORONADO

■ NAVAL AMPHIBIOUS BASE

N

How to use bus bike racks.

Bikes are welcome on all regular trips. You can only load and unload your bike at approved stops. Make sure that the bus driver knows first that you plan to load or unload your bike.

When using the rack at the rear of the bus, place both wheels upright in the rack and secure your bike in place.

There is no charge for using the rack.

Location of bike stops

San Diego
    Kettner & Broadway (5:00a-2:00a)
    Crosby & National   (5:00a-6:00p only)
Coronado
    3rd & Orange
    North Island Main Gate
    4th & Orange
    Amphibious Base Main Gate
Imperial Beach
    Palm & Rainbow (Southbound)
    Palm & 7th (Northbound)
South San Diego
    Palm & Hollister (Trolley Sta.)

SILVER STRAND STATE BEACH

Coronado Cays

▽   Denotes Transfer Point
━━ Operates Weekday Rush Hour Only
━━ Regular Route
■   Bicycle Rack Service Stop

Palm Ave
Rainbow
Bus Routes 33, 33A
Cardiga
7th St
Elm
Palm Ave
Palm Ave Trolley Station
Bus Routes 32, 33, 33A
Seacoast Dr
Connecticut
Imperial Beach Blvd
Coronado Ave
19th St
Hollister

Exact Fare Please
No Bills

City bus route map

B: Well, I'm going to _____ until I hear the complete report,

because that's the train my nephew always takes.

2. On a shuttle flight:

A: Why didn't we take a train? We had to _____ two hours to get

on this flight.

B: Why don't you sit back and relax? We'll be there before you know it.[31]

A: Can you believe there's only one flight attendant on this flight? Who knows when

he'll _____ us. And I'm starving!

B: I hate to tell you this, but they don't serve meals on shuttle flights.

A: Oh, I give up. Wake me up when we get there.

---

[31]before (one) knows it: very quickly.

3 THE EXCELSIOR EXPERIENCE

I. NARRATIVE

Mr. Lin expected the Excelsior Hotel to be a first-class hotel located in a good part of town. He was wrong. It was run-down[1] and located in a seedy[2] part of the city. As he stood outside the hotel's front door, he remembered the words of his travel agent, "I don't know much about the hotel, but its name sounds good and its rates are reasonable. It must be okay." Mr. Lin hesitated a moment and then entered the hotel lobby. He was surprised because it was clean and neat inside, and the manager and his staff seemed eager to help him. Mr. Levine, the manager, had a bell-boy assist him with his luggage and then personally showed Mr. Lin to his room. When Mr. Levine asked Mr. Lin what he thought of New York, Mr. Lin replied that he didn't have a very good impression **so far**. When he asked why, Mr. Lin told him about the incident with the cabbie. "No wonder," he exclaimed. "Well, why don't you drop by[3] my office later **so that** I can set you straight on[4] the 'do's and don'ts'[5] of city life." Two hours later, when Mr. Lin came back downstairs, Mr. Levine introduced him to Mr. and Mrs. Murphy, a friendly couple from St. Louis, Missouri. They chatted for a while and then Mrs. Murphy said to Mr. Lin, "Listen, since you haven't seen the city yet, **how about** coming sightseeing with us tomorrow?" At first, Mr. Lin felt too embarrassed to accept the invitation, but the Murphys were so friendly and sincere that he decided to accept their offer.

That night, when Mr. Lin returned to his room, he thought about the difference between the shabbiness of the hotel and the friendliness of the people in it. He then realized the truth of the expression, "You can't judge a book by its cover."[6]

---

[1]run-down: in poor condition.
[2]seedy: dirty, run-down.
[3]drop by: to visit.
[4]set (someone) straight on (something): to give someone the correct information.
[5]do's and dont's: what you should do and should not do.
[6]You can't judge a book by its cover (proverb): You cannot judge something just by its appearance.

QUESTIONS

1. What did Mr. Lin expect the Excelsior Hotel to be like?
2. What kind of neighborhood is the Excelsior Hotel located in?
3. Why was Mr. Lin surprised when he entered the hotel?
4. How did the manager and staff act?
5. Why did Mr. Levine ask him to drop by later?
6. How come Mr. Lin felt he couldn't refuse Mr. and Mrs. Murphy's invitation to go sightseeing with them?
7. What did Mr. Lin realize that night?

II. DIALOGUES

1. Mr. Lin enters the lobby of the hotel and speaks to Mr. Levine, the manager, who is at the front desk.

   MR. LEVINE: Good afternoon, may I help you?

   MR. LIN: Yes, my name is Lin. I have a reservation for a single room.

   MR. LEVINE: Fine, sir. Would you spell your last name please?

   MR. LIN: L-I-N, Lin.

   MR. LEVINE: I don't seem to have your name listed. When did you make the reservation?

   MR. LIN: My travel agent made it for me some time last week.

   MR. LEVINE: Okay, let me check again. Oh, yes, here it is. I'm sorry. How long do you plan to stay, Mr. Lin?

   MR. LIN: At least three or four days until I find a permanent place to stay.

   MR. LEVINE: Fine. Just fill out this form. Then sign your name here. The rate for a single room is $38.50 per[7] night. (He hands Mr. Lin the key.) Room 355. Let me show you up there myself. The bellboy will assist you with your bags.

   MR. LIN: Thank you.

QUESTIONS

1. What kind of room does Mr. Lin have a reservation for?
2. Who made Mr. Lin's reservation for him?
3. How much is a single room?
4. How long does Mr. Lin plan to stay at the hotel?

2. Mr. Lin is in his room and dials the operator.

   OPERATOR: Hello, operator. May I help you?

   MR. LIN: Yes. Do you think I can have some extra towels sent up?

---

[7]per: each. We also use "a."

OPERATOR: Of course. I can have someone in housekeeping bring them up to you right away. Anything else?

MR. LIN: No. I don't think so. Oh, wait a second. I just realized that I don't have an alarm clock with me. Can you give me a wake-up call at six o'clock tomorrow morning?

OPERATOR: All right, sir. Six o'clock.

MR. LIN: Thanks. Oh, one more thing. How late do you have room service?

OPERATOR: We can send up meals until 1 A.M.

MR. LIN: Thank you.

QUESTIONS

1.   What would Mr. Lin like to have sent up to his room?
2.   How come he needs a wake-up call?
3.   What time does room service close?

III. GRAMMAR

A. Present Perfect Tense

Use the Present Perfect Tense to talk about something that happened at an indefinite time in the past. [No specific time is mentioned.]

FORM: | have + Verb (Past Participle) |

Affirmative: He *has traveled* to Europe.

Negative: He <u>has not</u> *traveled* to Europe.
         hasn't

Question: *Has* he *traveled* to Europe?

Wh- Question: Where *has* he *traveled* in Europe?

Who/What/Which as Subject: Who *has traveled* to Europe?

Use the Present Perfect Tense to talk about something that has happened many times in the past. [No specific time is mentioned.]

Example: They *have been* to California many times.

Note: There is a difference between *have* + *been* and *have* + *gone*:
He *has been* to California. (He has already returned from California.)
He *has gone* to California. (He is on the way to California or is in California now.)

Use the Present Perfect to talk about something that started in the past and is still happening now.

Example: He *has lived* in Boston since 1968.

Note: We almost never use certain verbs in the Present Perfect when talking about something that started in the past and has continued up to now. These verbs are actions that occur in a moment, not over a period of time:

begin	finish
come	go
end	start

Incorrect: I *have come* here for two months.

Correct: I *came* here two months ago. I *have been* here for two months.

B. Present Perfect Continuous Tense

Use the Present Perfect Continuous Tense to talk about something that started in the past and is still happening now.

FORM: have + been + Verb-ing

Affirmative: They *have been staying* at the hotel since last Monday.

Negative: They *have not been staying* at the hotel for long.
            haven't

Question: *Have* they *been staying* at the hotel for a long time?

Wh- Question: Where *have* they *been staying* since Monday?

Who/What/Which as Subject: Who *has been staying* at the hotel since last Monday?

Notes:

a. We use the Present Perfect Continuous Tense to talk about actions (e.g., working, fixing, reading, talking, waiting) which started in the past and are still happening *at this moment* (i.e., the action is not completed):

Correct: I *have been standing* in this line since noon.

Incorrect: I *have stood* in this line since noon.

Correct: He *has been reading* those travel brochures for hours.

Incorrect: He *has read* those travel brochures for hours.

b. When we want to show that an action started in the past and is still happening *nowadays*, instead of emphasizing *at this moment*, we can use either the Present Perfect Continuous or the Present Perfect:

Correct: He *has been living* in Pensacola since 1968.

Correct: He *has lived* in Pensacola since 1968.

c. With some verbs we can only use the Present Perfect to talk about something that started in the past and has continued up to now. (Do not use the Present Perfect Continuous.) You can find a list of these verbs in Chapter 1 on page 6.

Correct: We *have known* each other for a long time.

Incorrect: We *have been knowing* each other for a long time.

TIME EXPRESSIONS

We often use the following time expressions with the Present Perfect and Present Perfect Continuous Tenses:

already	lately	up to now	for (a length of time)
before	recently	for a long time	since (a specific time)

We use the following time words only in Negative Sentences or Questions:

ever   never   yet

1. A: Have you *ever* been to Richmond?
    B: No, I've *never* been there.

2. A: Have you seen the new hotel on Main Street *yet*?
    B: No, I haven't seen it *yet*.

Dialogues

Complete the following dialogues using either *Present Perfect Tense* or *Past Tense*.

1. George and Dick are in town on business; they are staying at the same hotel. They met each other a few days ago and are now talking in the hotel coffee shop.

GEORGE: _____ you _____ a chance to do any
                                    (have)

sightseeing yet?

DICK: Not yet. I just _____ any free time. What about you?
                          (have; negative)

GEORGE: I _____ to a few places. Yesterday I _____
                (be)   (go)

to the aquarium; the day before I _____ a walk through Golden
                                          (take)

Gate Park.

DICK: I _____ never _____ to either of those
(be)

places. I guess I should find the time to go.

QUESTIONS

1. Why hasn't Dick been able to go sightseeing?
2. Has George done any sightseeing?
3. What places did George go to?
4. Has Dick ever been to either of those places?

2. Danny is talking with his friend Roderick.

DANNY: You _____ a lot of skiing, _____ you?
(do)

RODERICK: No. I _____ only _____ once.
(go)

DANNY: How _____ you _____ it?
(like)

RODERICK: Well, I _____ the skiing that much, but we
(enjoy; negative)

_____ at a fantastic lodge.
(stay)

QUESTIONS

1. How many times has Roderick gone skiing?
2. What did he like about the ski trip?

3. Beth is asking her friend, Janet, about hotels in Atlanta.

BETH: I know you _____ to Atlanta many times. Can you recom-
(be)

mend a decent hotel there?

JANET: _____ you _____ to Atlanta before?
(be)

BETH: I _____ only _____ there a few times.
(be)

JANET: Where _____ you _____ the last time
(stay)

you were there?

BETH: I _____ a room at the Empire Hotel, but it _____
(have)   (be)

very expensive.

JANET: I _____ never _____ there. The last time
                                    (stay)

I _____ in Atlanta I _____ a room at the
          (be)   (book)

Rosewood Hotel.

BETH: Oh, I _____ never _____ of it. How is it?
                                               (hear)

JANET: Well, it's not exactly the[8] Empire, but it's clean, safe, and relatively inexpensive.

BETH: Sounds good to me.

QUESTIONS

1. Has Beth ever been to Atlanta?
2. Where did she stay the last time she was there?
3. Has Janet ever stayed at the Empire?
4. What hotel did Janet recommend?
5. Why did she recommend it?

4. Mr. Sakamoto and Ms. Ido are guests at a hotel in Minneapolis.

SAKAMOTO: How long _____ you _____ here at
                                                      (be)

the hotel?

IDO: I _____ here since Monday. And you?
                   (be)

SAKAMOTO: I _____ only _____ here for two
                                               (be)

days. I _____ in[9] Wednesday night. _____ you
              (check)

_____ in Minneapolis before, or is this your first time here?
       (be)

IDO: I _____ here a few times before. How about you?
                   (be)

SAKAMOTO: I _____ here on business once about five years ago.
                       (come)

This is only my second visit.

QUESTIONS

1. How long has Ms. Ido been at the hotel?
2. How long has Mr. Sakamoto been there?

---

[8](A) is not exactly the (B): (A) is not as good as (B).
[9]check in: to register at a hotel.

3.   When did he check in?
4.   How long has it been since Mr. Sakamoto's last visit to Minneapolis?
5.   Why did Mr. Sakamoto come to Minneapolis five years ago?

Complete the following dialogues using the *Present Perfect, Present Perfect Continuous* or *Past Tense*.

5.   Hank has been trying to book[10] a hotel room all morning. Kenny enters and sees him on the phone:

KENNY: How long _____ you _____ to call the hotel?
                                                                         (try)

HANK: I _____ all morning. I _____ calling at
                         (try)   (start)

seven-thirty. They _____ and _____ me on hold.
                              (answer)   (put)

Then I _____ disconnected. The line _____
                  (get)   (be)

busy ever since.[11]

KENNY: _____ you _____ the operator to have
                                                  (call)

the line checked yet?

HANK: Yes, I _____ a few moments ago. There's no trouble on
                         (call)

the line.

KENNY: Well, _____ you _____ calling any of
                                                       (try)

the other hotels in town?

HANK: Sure I _____ . But they're all booked.

QUESTIONS

1.   How long has Hank been trying to get through to the hotel?
2.   When did he start calling?
3.   Why hasn't he been able to get through?
4.   Why did he call the operator?
5.   Why hasn't he made a reservation at another hotel?

6.   Brianne is sitting in a hotel lobby. She has been waiting for her cousin Julia for half an hour and is now annoyed. Julia finally arrives.

---

[10]book: to make a reservation at a hotel.
[11](ever) since: (from the time referred to) up to now.

BRIANNE: Well, it's about time[12] you showed up.[13]

JULIA: How long _____ you _____ ?
                                                    (wait)

BRIANNE: I _____ here at six o'clock. I _____
                        (get)   (sit)

here for a half hour. What _____ to you?
                                              (happen)

JULIA: I thought[14] we _____ to meet at six-thirty. I'm sorry.
                                    (agree)

QUESTIONS

1.   How long has Brianne been waiting?
2.   What time did Julia think the appointment was?

7.   Rick and Terry are traveling together. Rick is in the lobby of a youth hostel. He is standing in line to register. Terry enters.

TERRY: What are you doing? _____ you _____
                                                            (check in; negative question)

yet?

RICK: No, I obviously _____ .

TERRY: Well, how long _____ you _____ in this
                                                            (stand)

line?

RICK: I _____ for about twenty minutes. Where the hell[15]
                    (wait)

_____ you _____ ?
                                                      (be)

TERRY: Outside on the porch. There's no need for[16] both of us to stand in line, right?

QUESTIONS

1.   Why hasn't Rick been able to check in yet?
2.   How long has Rick been standing in line?
3.   What has Terry been doing?

---

[12]about time: finally, but later than it should have been.
[13]show up: to come, to appear.
[14]thought: to think mistakenly.
[15]hell: We use this word to express anger or annoyance; it is not considered polite.
[16]there is no need: it is not necessary for someone to do something.

8.   George and Ira are talking about their vacation plans.

IRA: _____ you _____ where to go on vacation
                                        (decide)

    yet?

GEORGE: Yes. Last week Martha and I finally _____ on Lake Tahoe.
                                                        (agree)

IRA: Oh? We're planning to go there, too. _____ you

_____ hotel reservations yet?
                        (make)

GEORGE: No, we _____ . Why?

IRA: Well, we _____ to get a room for weeks. Every place
                        (try)

    I _____ so far is booked solid.[17]
                (call)

QUESTIONS

1.   When did George and Martha decide to go to Lake Tahoe?
2.   Have they made a reservation yet?
3.   What has Ira been trying to do?
4.   How come Ira hasn't been able to reserve a room?

C. May/Might

We use *may/might* mainly for permission and possibility.

PERMISSION

We use *may* for permission in the present and future.

A: *May* I leave my luggage here for a few moments?
B: Yes, you *may*.

We also use *can* for permission. It is less formal than *may* (see Chapter 2).

POSSIBILITY

Both *may* and *might* show present and future possibility. They have the same
meaning in this case.

---

[17]booked solid: full.

She *may* be staying at the Regency Hotel. (present)
   might

I *may* pay the bill by credit card. (future)
  might

Notes:
a. Do not use contractions with *may/might* + not.
b. Do not use *may/might* for questions when talking about possibility in the present or future. We can use *may/might* for short answers.

    Example: (present)
          A: Is Connie staying at the Hewlit Hotel? (*Not*: Might Connie be staying at the Hewlit Hotel?)
          B: She *may* be.
              might

    Example: (future)
          A: Are you going to check out of the hotel tomorrow? (*Not*: Might you check out of the hotel tomorrow?)
          B: I *may*.
            might.

D. Have to/Must

We use *have to/must* to show necessity and logical conclusion.

NECESSITY

   Must: shows necessity in the present and future.
     I *must* find a reasonable hotel.

   Have to: shows necessity in the present and future. It is the same as *must* in this case.
     I *have to* find a reasonable hotel.

Notes:
a. We use *have to* for questions and negatives showing necessity. *Do not use must.*
     Do we *have to* check out by noon?
     We don't *have to* check out by noon.

b. *Had to* shows necessity in the past. *Do not use must.*
     He *had to* leave town late last night.

LOGICAL CONCLUSION

We use *must* to indicate what we think is a logical conclusion or deduction.

> A: I couldn't get a table at the hotel's restaurant last night.
> B: Oh, that restaurant is always packed.[18] The food *must* be excellent.

PROHIBITION

We use the negative of *must* to show that something is not permitted. When we use *must not* we are usually talking about rules.

> Hotel doormen *must not* eat while they are working.

Complete the following exchanges using *may, might, must,* or *have to*. In some cases, more than one answer is possible.

> ***Example:*** A: What hotel is Pearl staying at?
> B: She <u>might be staying</u> at the Plaza, but I don't know for
> (stay)
> sure.

1. A: Why don't we stay at the Grand Regency Hotel?

   B: You _____ ! Do you know how expensive that place is? There is
      (joke)

   no way we can afford to stay there.

2. In a hotel restaurant:

   A: Where are Bill and Jane? We've been waiting for quite a while now.

   B: I just called their room a few minutes ago and no one answered. They

   _____ on their way[19] down here now.
        (be)

3. A: I know Peggy wanted to stay at the "Y,"[20] but I called and she's not there.

   B: I don't know where she is then. She _____ at the Youth Hostel.
                                            (stay)

   A: I doubt it. She doesn't have an International Youth Hostel card.

---

[18]packed: very crowded.
[19]on the way: to be coming or going to a place.
[20]the "Y": YMCA (Young Men's Christian Association); YWCA (Young Women's Christian Association). These are comparatively low-cost hostels located in all major cities in the U.S.

B: I can think of only one other place—the Wavecrest Motel. That's where her uncle works.

A: You're right. She _____ there.
                                    (be)

4.   In a boarding house:

A: _____ we _____ the kitchen facilities
                                      (use)
     after 10:00 P.M.?

B: Yes, but at that hour you _____ a problem with the hot water.
                                      (have)
     Sometimes they turn it off around that time.

A: Oh, that's no problem. We don't _____ hot water.
                                            (use)

5.   A: Could you get into the Cambridge Hotel last night?

B: No, it was all booked up. We _____ to the Walden Arms. It
                                         (go)
     was the only place that had rooms. By the way, let me tell you what happened
     there last night.

A: Oh, tell me about it later. I _____ now.
                                         (run)²¹

6.   A: Hurry up! We _____ by 11:00 A.M.
                              (check out)

B: What are you talking about? We _____ till²² noon.
                                          (check out; negative)

A: Noon? No, the man at the front desk said eleven o'clock.

B: Well, then I _____ wrong. I'd better call the front desk and
                        (be)
     check, just to be sure.

---

²¹have to run: to have to go, leave.
²²till: until.

E. Sentence Patterns

Recall this sentence from the narrative:

At first Mr. Lin felt *too embarrassed* to accept the invitation.

PATTERN

too + Adjective (+ for + Object) + to + Verb (base form)

He felt *too* shy *to* ask.
That hotel is *too* expensive for us *to* stay in.
They have been *too* sick *to* leave their hotel room.

Complete the following exchanges with a *too + Adjective + Verb* pattern.

Example: A: Why don't you and Bill join us for dinner at the hotel nightclub tonight? The four of us haven't gone out[23] together for a long time.
B: Bill doesn't like to have dinner at nightclubs. He says *it's always too noisy to enjoy the meal.*

1.   A: Why haven't you called the hotel and made a reservation yet?

   B: _____
                                                (busy)

2.   A: How about dinner at the hotel's restaurant tonight?

   B: I'd like to, but _____
                                         (late-get a table)

3.   A: How can I get in touch with[24] Mr. Nordby?

   B: He's been in Phoenix for the past few weeks. He's staying at the Phoenix Belmore.

   Why don't you call him long distance?

   A: No, I'll send him a mailgram. It's _____ .
                                                (expensive)

4.   A: What happened to Jane last night? Don't tell me you forgot to invite her!

   B: I did invite her, but she said _____ .
                                                (tired)

---

[23]go out together : to spend leisure time with someone.
        with someone
[24]get in touch with: to contact someone. Compare *keep in touch with:* to maintain contact with someone.

5. In a hotel lobby:

A: Let me have someone help you with your bags.

B: That's okay. I can manage.

A: Oh, no. Those bags are really _____ by yourself. One second
(heavy for you-carry)

and I'll get a bellboy to take them up for you.

Recall this sentence from the narrative:
Mr. Levine, the manager, *had a bellboy help* him with his luggage.

PATTERN

> Subject + have + (somebody) + Verb (base form)

Have the maid straighten up[25] the room immediately.
We can have room service send up some ice.

> Subject + have + (something) + Verb (Past Participle)

Have the room straightened up immediately!
We can have some ice sent up.

Complete the following exchanges using one of the preceding patterns.

Example: A: Hello, room service. May I help you?
B: *Yes, have some ice sent up to room 355, please.*

1. A: Hello, front desk. May I help you?

B: I'd like to speak to the manager, please.

A: I'm sorry. He stepped away for a few moments.

B: _____ .
(call me back)

2. A: Hello, front desk. May I help you?

B: I've lost my key. What should I do?

---

[25]straighten up: to put in order.

A: Don't worry. We can _____ .
(new one-send up)

3. A: Hello, operator. May I help you?

B: Yes. This is Mr. Feinstein in room 1210. The bathroom sink has been leaking all

evening. Can you _____ ?
(fix)

4. A: Hello, operator. May I help you?

B: Yes, this is Ms. de los Santos in the penthouse suite. The TV doesn't seem to work.

Please _____ .
(repair)

IV. EXPRESSIONS AND IDIOMS

- *so far*: up to now; until now.

Recall this sentence from the narrative:
. . . [he] replied that he didn't have a very good impression *so far*.

Complete the following exchanges with an appropriate response using *so far*.

Example: A: Haven't you made our hotel reservations yet?
B: *No. I haven't found any available rooms so far.*

1. A: I'm expecting a Mr. Van Dyck to arrive soon. I'd like to know if he has checked in

yet.

B: _____ .

2. A: Hello, Chicago Ambassador Hotel. May I help you?

B: Yes, do you have any available rooms for tonight?

A: I'm sorry. We're all booked.

B: Do you think there may be some cancellations?

A: Perhaps, but _____ .

3. A: Have you encountered any difficulties since you arrived in the city?

B: _____ .

4. A: Has the hotel management found your missing bag yet?

B: _____ .

● *no wonder*: not surprising.

Recall this sentence from the narrative:
"*No wonder*," she exclaimed.

Complete the following exchanges with an appropriate response using *no wonder*.

> *Example:* A: Why are you still calling room service? Meals aren't available after 1 A.M.
> B: Oh, is it after one already?
> A: It sure is.
> B: *No wonder I haven't gotten any answer!*

1. A: I can't believe there isn't a room available in the whole city!

B: Well, there's a convention in town this weekend.

A: _____ .

2. A: How come you checked out and went to another motel?

B: How come? Because the sheets didn't look clean, the TV didn't work, and I thought the rates were too high in the first place![26]

A: Oh, _____ .

3. A: I haven't seen Mr. Angus in the coffee shop lately. He usually reads his morning newspaper there.

---

[26]In the first place: from the beginning.

B: Oh, he checked out of the hotel early last week.

A: _____   .

4.   A: Which hotel did Mr. Kim recommend?

   B: He suggested the Imperial Hotel.

   A: Why the Imperial?

   B: He said the rooms were luxurious, the food fabulous, the service fantastic, and the

      rates reasonable!

   A: _____   .

● *so that*: in order that; for the purpose of.

Subject + Verb + so that + Subject of clause + Verb of clause

Recall this sentence from the narrative:
   "Well, why don't you drop by my office later *so that* I can set you straight on the 'do's and don'ts' of city life."

Complete the following exchanges with an appropriate response using *so that*.

   Example: A: Why are you booking our hotel room now? We still
               have over two months before we go on vacation.
            B: I'm reserving a room now *so that we won't have to worry about it later.*

1.   In a hotel room:

   A: What should I do with these dirty towels? The maid didn't change them yesterday.

   B: Just leave them on the dresser _____   .
                                      (can see them)

2.   A: Do you think we should pay the hotel bill with cash or put it on our credit card?

   B: I think we should charge it _____ cash.
                                 (run short of;[27] negative)

---

[27]run short of: not to have enough.

Hotel registration form

ROOM #	NAME			RATE	DEPART	
NO. ROOMS	ADDRESS				ARRIVE	ROOM TYPE
CLERK	CITY	STATE	ZIP		GUESTS	CIT/AMOUNT

060499

REMARKS:

☐ WE HAVE CONFIRMED THE ABOVE GUARANTEED RESERVATION FOR YOU.

☐ WE HAVE MADE THE ABOVE TENTATIVE RESERVATION FOR YOU. YOUR DEPOSIT OF $ _____ MUST BE RECEIVED BY _____ IN ORDER TO CONFIRM THESE ACCOMMODATIONS.

☐ YOUR RESERVATIONS ARE CONFIRMED UNTIL 4 P.M. ON THE ARRIVAL DATE. IF YOU PLAN TO ARRIVE LATER A DEPOSIT OF $ _____ MUST BE RECEIVED PRIOR TO THE ARRIVAL DATE.

PLEASE CHECK THE ABOVE RESERVATION CAREFULLY. ALL CHANGES AND CANCELLATIONS MUST BE RECEIVED 48 HOURS PRIOR TO CHECK-IN. OUR CHECK-IN TIME IS 2 P.M. AND CHECK-OUT IS NOON.

WE ARE LOOKING FORWARD TO HAVING YOU AS OUR GUEST

SIGNED _____

The Westgate Hotel
1055 Second Ave.
San Diego, CA 92101
Tel. (714) 238-1818

GUEST'S SIGNATURE X

I REQUEST THAT YOU SEND THIS BILL TO THE NAME AND ADDRESS LISTED FOR PAYMENT. IF THE BILLING IS TO ANYONE OTHER THAN MYSELF AND IT IS NOT PAID I UNDERSTAND THAT I SHALL BE PERSONALLY LIABLE FOR PAYMENT. I FURTHER AGREE TO PAY INTEREST AT THE RATE OF 1½% PER MONTH (18% PER ANNUM) ON THE UNPAID BALANCE AND AGREE TO PAY REASONABLE COLLECTION AND ATTORNEY'S FEES INCURRED

CHARGE TO

ADDRESS

CITY   STATE   ZIP

The Westgate Hotel
1055 Second Avenue
San Diego, California 92101
Tel. (714) 238-1818

SB SUPERIOR BANK

5412 3456 7890 1230 MC

MasterCard

VOID   00/00   MC
LEE M CARDHOLDER
WB0048   VOID   VOID

Credit card

75

3.   A: Let's go to the Bear Rug Lodge this weekend. I could use[28] a rest.

      B: Okay. But we'd better call first and see if they have a room _____

_____

                     (make the trip for nothing;[29] negative)

4.   A: What time do you plan to leave for the country[30] next weekend?

      B: We haven't decided yet, but we want to leave early _____ .
                                        (avoid–traffic)

5.   In a hotel:

      A: Do you think my jewelry is safe in this room?

      B: No. You'd better put it in the hotel safe _____ .
                                (worry)

● *how about:*

We use this phrase to make a suggestion, request or invitation.

how about + Noun
Verb + ing

How about giving me a ride to work?

Note: *How about* and *how* have different meanings.
    How about a movie tonight? [Would you like to see a movie tonight?]
    How was the movie? [Was the movie good or bad?]

We use both *how about* and *what about* to mention something or someone:
A: I bought my train ticket this morning.
B: *How* about mine? [Did you buy my ticket, too?]
    What
A: Didn't you buy your own ticket yesterday?
B: No, I didn't.

Recall this sentence from the narrative:
    Listen, since you haven't seen the city yet, *how about* coming sightseeing with us tomorrow?

Complete the following exchanges with an appropriate response using *how about*, *what about*, or *how*.

---

[28]could use: to need.
[29]for nothing: with no result.
[30]the country: the area beyond the city and suburbs.

Example: A: *How about* going out tonight?
          B: No, I want to go back to our hotel room and relax. I'm
              exhausted.

1. A: You just got back from Seattle this morning, didn't you?

       B: That's right.

       A: _____ was it?

       B: Oh, I had a very nice trip.

2. A: Did Werner give a talk at the conference?

       B: Yes, he did.

       A: _____ was it?

       B: Excellent!

       A: _____ Stewart? Did he speak, too?

       B: No, he didn't.

3. A: What hotel do you think we should stay at?

       B: _____ the Milwood?

       A: Oh, I stayed there the last time I was in Houston.

       B: Well, _____ did you like it?

       A: It was adequate. Listen, _____ booking a room at the new

       Century Hotel. It's expensive, but I've heard that it's really fabulous.

       B: Okay, I'm willing.

V. SITUATIONAL DIALOGUES

1. Mr. Olsen, a jewelry salesman, is checking in at a hotel.

       OLSEN: I'd like a room for tonight, please.
       CLERK: Single or double?

OLSEN: Single.

CLERK: Do you have a reservation?

OLSEN: No, I don't.

CLERK: Okay, we still have some rooms available.

OLSEN: I'd like a private bath, if possible.

CLERK: All right. Room 811.

OLSEN: What is the price of the room?

CLERK: $57.50 a day.

OLSEN: You wouldn't happen to have anything cheaper, would you?

CLERK: We have some rooms on the top floor, but the bathroom is in the hall. They're $20.00 a night.

OLSEN: No, I'll take the $57.50 room.

CLERK: Fine. How long do you plan to stay?

OLSEN: Just three or four days. Probably until Monday.

CLERK: Just sign the register, and I'll have someone help you with your luggage and show you to your room.

OLSEN: Oh, by the way, I have some jewelry with me. Do you think it will be safe in my room?

CLERK: Well, the hotel is not responsible for valuables. You'd better leave your valuables in the hotel safe.

OLSEN: I guess I'd better, just to be on the safe side.[31] One more thing, when is check-out time?

CLERK: 12 noon, sir.

QUESTIONS

1.   What kind of room does Mr. Olsen want?
2.   Is the hotel booked up or are there rooms available?
3.   What's the rate for a single room with a private bath?
4.   How long does Mr. Olsen plan to stay at the hotel?
5.   Why does Mr. Olsen decide to put his valuables in the safe?

VI. VOCABULARY BUILDER

hotel   hotel bar/hotel booking/hotel cafe/hotel conference room/hotel entrance/hotel gift shop/hotel intercom/hotel kitchen/hotel laundry service/hotel lobby/hotel manager/hotel reservation/hotel restaurant/hotel room/hotel rules and regulations/hotel safe/hotel staff

room   ballroom/bedroom/dining room/double room/game room/rest room/room reservation/room service

---

[31]be on the safe side: to be safe; to avoid trouble; to make sure nothing goes wrong.

VII. ROLE PLAY SUGGESTIONS

1. Make a hotel reservation (a) in person (b) over the phone.
2. Call up room service and request (a) a meal or something to drink (b) a wake-up call.

VIII. PREPOSITION PRACTICE

A. Prepositions of Time

DURING (an event in progress)

DURING his brief stay at the Excelsior, Mr. Lin was happy.

FOR (a length or appointed time)

He stayed at the Sands Hotel **FOR** two weeks.

SINCE (a specific time in the past)

She has been here **SINCE** last week.

Other prepositions of time: **IN   ON   AT**

USE **IN** FOR:

a month

She arrived here **IN** May, 1983.

a year

IN 1981 she lived in the dormitory.

a time of day (i.e., the morning, the afternoon, the evening)

I checked into the hotel **IN** the morning.

USE **ON** FOR:

specific dates

ON May fifteenth we checked out of the motel.

days of the week

She made reservations **ON** Tuesday.

USE **AT** FOR:

midnight, noon, night

One couple checked in **AT** noon.

specific times

The other couple came **AT** two-thirty in the afternoon.

Complete the following exchanges with the appropriate preposition.

1. A: It's two-thirty _____ the afternoon and they haven't fixed the

   shower yet.

   B: What! I called the front desk _____ eight o'clock

   _____ the morning. Where the hell are they?

2. A: _____ six o'clock _____ the morning

   _____ Monday, we are taking off[32] for the Canadian Rockies.

   B: Oh, that's too early. Why don't we leave _____ noon?

3. A: He hasn't slept _____ eight o'clock yesterday morning.

   B: You mean he has not slept all night?

4. A: Mary says the motel wrote her a letter _____ October. They

   asked her to pay the same bill twice.

   B: That's nerve.[33]

5. A: Have you turned in[34] the hotel key?

   B: Not yet. Why do it now? We're not leaving _____ another two

   hours.

6. A: Have you found our missing bags yet?

   B: Yes, they are on the way. You can pick them up _____ seven

   o'clock _____ the evening _____ Tuesday.

7. A: This youth hostel is clean and inexpensive.

   B: I know, but you can only stay here _____ three nights.

8. A: _____ this past week, I've spent a lot extra on sightseeing.

   B: Don't worry. I always bring extra cash with me just to be on the safe side.

---

[32]take off: to leave.
[33]nerve: too bold; pushy. Also *have a lot of nerve*; *What nerve!*
[34]turn in: to return (something).

9. A: Let's go over to that antique shop across the street from the hotel. I'd like to see

   what they have.

   B: I think we'd better stay away from that place, I've heard bad things about it

   _____ the first moment I arrived here. It must be a tourist trap.[35]

10. A: How long have you been trying to get in touch with Mr. Jacovo?

    B: _____ at least two hours, but his line has been busy the whole time.

11. A: Is there a Jack Dolan staying here?

    B: Not any more.

    A: What do you mean?

    B: Well, sir, he checked in _____ Thursday, May eighth and he

    checked out _____ noon _____ Thursday,

    the fourteenth.

B. Additional Preposition Combinations

go on (+ Verb-ing)   (IS):
     (+ with + Noun)

to continue	I can't *go on* spending money like this. You can *go on* with your vacation now that you've found your tickets.
to happen, occur	What's *going on*?
"I don't believe it!"	A: I won ten thousand dollars in Atlantic City last week! B: Go on!

go along with (IS):

agree with	We always *go along with* his decisions. After all, he is the boss.
accompany (*also*, come along with)	Do you want me to *go along with* you?

---

[35]tourist trap: a place or business that cheats tourists.

go for (IS):

to desire; like; be interested in (*also*, go in for)	I don't *go for* fancy hotels.
to apply; to include	What I told Laurie *goes for* you, too!
to do one's best; to try; attempt	A: I don't know if I can do it. B: Just *go for* it.
to go to get <u>something</u> someone	Let's *go for* a hamburger. You'd better *go for* the hotel manager.

Complete the following exchanges with the appropriate preposition combination.

1.   Two hotel employees are arguing. The manager comes over and asks:

A: What _____ here?

B: Oh, nothing.

A: Well, _____ your work then.

2.   A: I'd like to take you and Tom out to dinner tonight. There's a new Chinese restaurant

in the Oxford Inn, and I've heard that their food is fabulous.

B: Well, I'd love to go, but I'm afraid Tom doesn't _____ Chinese

food.

A: _____ ! Everybody likes Chinese food.

B: Not Tom.

A: Well, okay. I'll take you someplace else instead.

3.   A: I'm going out for a while.

B: Where are you going?

A: I just want to take a walk.

B: Can I _____ you?

A: Of course. Hey, I have an idea. Why don't we _____ some

ice cream?

B: Sounds good to me.

4. A: Listen, if you finish your work today, we can leave for the country a day early.

B: Oh, I don't think I can.

A: Well, just _____ it! You can do it.

5. Two hotel employees are talking:

A: Our new manager certainly has a lot of new ideas.

B: I know, but I can't _____ all of them.

A: Well, I think most of his ideas are pretty good.

6. An employee is talking with his manager:

A: I don't understand why we have to write you a note when we're out a day.

B: Well, it's a rule and all employees have to follow the rules. That _____

you, too!

4 THE SUPERMARKET SCENE

I. NARRATIVE

One morning, Mr. Lin decided to have breakfast in the hotel coffee shop. Shortly after he sat down at the counter, the woman next to him struck up[1] a conversation. Her name was Janet Watkins. When she learned that Mr. Lin was new to this country, she asked, "Have you done much sightseeing yet?" She was surprised to find out that he **had yet to** see a shopping mall. She said, "Well, you must go to the one on Sixty-seventh Avenue. It's fantastic. It's bigger and more attractive than the Queens Plaza Mall, and it's not as crowded. Also, it has the largest and best supermarket in the city. You really must go! In fact, why don't you let me take you there today, if you're free?" Janet's straightforwardness[2] surprised Mr. Lin a little, but he accepted her offer.

The mall was an extraordinary place. There were at least fifty stores; each one was more beautiful than the next. Mr. Lin remembered that he needed some toothpaste and shampoo, so he told Janet he wanted to find a drugstore. "Those items are almost always cheaper at a supermarket," she replied.

After they entered the supermarket, Mr. Lin couldn't stop asking questions. He asked about pet foods, frozen foods, the "deli counter"[3] and the coupons in the hands of so many shoppers. Janet was pleased when they got to the aisle with the toothpastes and shampoos. She thought, "No more questions for a while." She was wrong. Mr. Lin immediately asked, "Why is this brand of toothpaste more expensive than that one?" Janet explained the difference between store brands[4] and national brands.[5] She told him that the advertising costs of national brands

---

[1]strike up: to begin (a conversation).
[2]straightforwardness: direct manner.
[3]deli counter (delicatessen counter): the section of a supermarket where you can buy cooked meats, cheeses, and other prepared foods.
[4]store brand: products which are sold under the name of a store.
[5]national brand: products which are produced by large manufacturers and sold throughout the nation.

have a lot to do with their higher price. Mr. Lin decided to buy the cheaper of the two.

Now Mr. Lin asked the most difficult question of the day, "How do I choose a shampoo? I've never seen so many kinds of shampoo." Janet agreed that this section had many more bottles of shampoo than other supermarkets, but she said, "Look, we can do this easily. First, your hair is drier than mine, so I suggest one of these shampoos for normal to dry hair. Next, among these shampoos for dry hair, we simply look for the best buy."[6] She then showed Mr. Lin how to read the unit price labels[7] and compared two bottles of shampoo. She said, "This bottle costs more, but when you compare the unit price, or price per ounce, you see that you are getting more shampoo for your money." Mr. Lin was pleased to learn the unit pricing method. It helped him to select the bottle with the most shampoo for the least money.

Mr. Lin then paid for his purchases. After they left the store, Janet had to return to her law office so she wished Mr. Lin good luck with his studies. Mr. Lin thanked her for her patience and for helping him become a wiser consumer.

QUESTIONS

1. Where did Mr. Lin meet Janet Watkins?
2. What was Janet surprised to find out?
3. Which shopping mall did Janet recommend? Why?
4. What did Janet offer to do?
5. Why was Mr. Lin a little surprised?
6. Why did Mr. Lin want to find a drugstore?
7. Why did Janet tell Mr. Lin that he should buy toothpaste and shampoo in a supermarket instead of a drugstore?
8. Why was it difficult for Mr. Lin to choose a shampoo?
9. What did Janet show Mr. Lin how to do?

II. DIALOGUE

Janet and Mr. Lin enter the shopping mall:

LIN: Wow! This place is really something![8] It's just as big as you said.

JANET: Well, it is the largest mall in the city. C'mon. Let's do a little browsing.

LIN: Okay. Oh, I just remembered. I need toothpaste and shampoo. Do you think we can find a drugstore here?

JANET: I'm sure we can, but those items are often cheaper in a supermarket. Let's go down to the other end of the mall; the supermarket is over there.

---

[6] a good buy: something purchased at a reasonable price; to get a lot for your money.
[7] unit price label: a label that tells you the price per unit of measure, such as ounce or pound.
[8] be something: to be great, wonderful.

QUESTIONS

1. What does Mr. Lin think of the mall?
2. What does Janet want to do?
3. What does Mr. Lin need?

III. GRAMMAR

A. Count and Non-Count Nouns

Count Nouns can be counted; a number can be placed in front of them. The plural is formed by adding -s or -es.

Examples: two gallons   six pounds

              several peaches   three apples

Non-Count Nouns cannot be counted. There is no plural form.

Examples: milk   money

              bread   air

The following quantifiers are often used with nouns:

For Count Nouns	For Non-Count Nouns
lots of	lots of
a lot of	a lot of
many	much
a great many	a great deal of
quite a few	quite a bit of
not many	not much
(very) few	(very) little
a few	a little
$\frac{just}{only}$ a few	$\frac{just}{only}$ a little

B. There + Be

FORM:

Affirmative and Negative:

There <u>is</u> (not) + <u>singular Count Noun.</u>
      was   Non-Count Noun

There <u>are</u>   (not) + plural Count Noun.
   <u>were</u>

Questions:

<u>Is</u>   there + <u>singular Count Noun.</u>
<u>Was</u>   Non-Count Noun

<u>Are</u>   + there + plural Count Noun.
<u>Were</u>

C. Some/Any

Use *some* for Affirmative Sentences.

> **Plural Count Noun:**   There are *some* peaches in the bowl.
>
> **Non-Count Noun:**   There is *some* milk on the table.

Notes: We can also use *some* in questions:
a.   when we expect, or want to suggest, an affirmative answer.
Isn't there *some* sugar left in the bowl?
b.   when the question is a request, offer, or invitation.
Would you like *some* coffee?

Use *any* for Negative Sentences and Questions.

> **Plural Count Noun:**   Are there *any* peaches in the bowl?
> There aren't *any* peaches in the bowl.
>
> **Non-Count Noun:**   Is there *any* milk on the table?
> There isn't *any* milk on the table.

Note: We often omit the noun in conversations when it is clear from the context.

> **Example:**   A: You'd better buy some milk.
> B: You mean there isn't any (milk) left?
> A: No, not a drop.
> B: Oh, okay. I thought there was still some (milk) left.

Complete the following exchanges using *some* or *any*.

> **Example:**   A: We'd better buy another watermelon. We have to serve
> twenty people.
> B: There aren't *any* (watermelons) left. We bought the last
> one!

1.   A: I'm going to the corner grocery store. I need to buy _____ razor

blades.

B: Oh, I think I still have _____ . Take one of mine.

A: I've already checked. You don't have _____ either.

2.   In a supermarket:

   A: Do you carry _____ generic[9] products?

   B: Yes, we have _____ in aisle 4, near the back of the store.

3.   In a supermarket:

   A: Look at all the beer and soda you have!

   B: Well, I'm expecting a lot of people to come over tomorrow.

   A: Can you pay for all of this?

   B: That's the problem. Can you lend me _____ cash?

   A: I don't have _____ with me.

   B: Well, I guess I'd better put a few bottles of soda back[10] then.

4.   A: See if you can[11] pick up _____ fresh strawberries when you go

   to the market.

   B: I doubt if they have _____ this time of year.

   A: Well, if not, just get _____ frozen ones.

5.   A: Don't we have _____ butter?

   B: Look in the fridge.[12] I'm sure we have _____ .

   A: I just looked. There isn't _____ .

   B: Okay. Remind me to get _____ later then.

---

[9]generic: products which do not have a brand name. They are usually cheaper than national and store brands.
[10]put back: to return.
[11]see if one can (do something): to try.
[12]fridge: short form for refrigerator.

Complete the following exchanges with *there + be* and a quantifier (*many, a lot of, quite a few*, etc.). Do not use *some* or *any* in this exercise.

> ***Example:*** A: You didn't buy very much fruit. How come?
> B: Well, there *wasn't much* (fruit) left to choose from at the supermarket.

1. A: Look at all these cereals! I never know which one to buy.

B: You're right. _____ really _____ to choose
(brands)

from. Why don't you just buy the cheapest one and be done with it?[13]

2. A: Is the west side of town a nice area to live in?

B: Well, it's kind of[14] run-down, but _____
(food stores and wholesale markets)

there, so shopping is quite convenient.

3. A: _____ left in the sugar bowl. There's enough for your coffee this
(sugar; negative)

morning, but that's it.[15]

B: Okay. I can buy some on my way home from work tonight.

4. A: I heard you went to that new mall last weekend. How was it?

B: It's fabulous! In addition to all the shops, _____ , too. The only
(nice restaurants)

problem is that _____ .
(parking space; negative)

5. A: _____ in yesterday's newspaper?
(food coupons; question)

B: Sure. In fact, there were several pages of ads, so I'm sure you can find lots of

coupons.

D. Comparison of Adjectives and Adverbs

Recall this sentence from the narrative:
> It's *bigger* and *more attractive* than the Queens Plaza Mall.

---

[13]be done with it: to do something or make a decision about something so that you don't have to worry about it any longer.
[14]kind of: rather, somewhat.
[15]that's it: to be finished; to have no more left.

PATTERNS

```
(a lot)    + one-syllable Adjective + -er + than
(a little)
(much)
```

Chicken was (much) *cheaper than* usual.

```
(a lot) + more + two-or-more-syllable Adjective + than
          less                Adverb
```

Milk is *less expensive than* half-and-half.[16]
She always shops *more quickly than* I do.

Notes:
a. Irregular Adjectives

good   *better*
bad   *worse*
far   *farther*

b. We use -ier with two-syllable adjectives that end in *y*.

   Example: happy — happier

c. We do *not* use -er with adjectives with an *ed* ending.

   Example: tired — more tired

d. Some adverbs do not end in -ly, such as fast, hard, late. To make a comparison use the first pattern above.

   Example: She shops *faster* than I do.

```
(not) + as + Adjective + as
             Adverb
```

I'm just *as concerned* about rising food prices *as* you are.

Complete the following exchanges using one of the preceding patterns.

   Example: A: Why did you buy this imported cheese? It's *a lot more expensive than domestic cheese*.
   (expensive — domestic)
   B: I know, but it *tastes better than domestic*.
   (tastes — domestic)

---

[16]half-and-half: half cream, half milk.

1. A: When you go to the supermarket, pick up some plums, okay?

    B: No, they cost too much.

    A: Oh, c'mon. They're not _____ and, besides,[17] you know
                                    (expensive — you think)

         how much I like them.

2. A: I'm going to the supermarket. Do you want to go with me?

    B: Do you still go to Green's?

    A: No, I don't. I go to Savemark now. It's not only _____ but also
                                                               (big)

         a lot _____ Green's.
                    (clean)

3. A: When you go out shopping later, be sure to pick up some beer.

    B: All right. What kind do you want?

    A: Tak Beer.

    B: Why Tak? It's _____ domestic beer.
                            (expensive)

    A: So what? It's a lot _____ domestic beer.
                                 (good)

4. A: Why did you buy this white bread?

    B: What do you mean? What's the matter with it?

    A: It's not _____ whole wheat bread.
                      (nutritious)

    B: It's not?

    A: No, it's really not _____ for you _____
                                (good)

         wheat bread is.

5. A: I'm sorry I didn't ask Joan to go grocery shopping for me instead of you.

    B: Why?

---

[17]besides: in addition, furthermore.

A: Because she does things _____ you do. You know, you

(thoroughly)

forgot to get three of the items on the list.

6. A: Who told you to buy this brand of detergent?

B: What are you angry about? It's _____ than the one you always

(expensive)

buy. I saved you money!

A: Yes, but I've tried this brand before and it's not _____ the one I

(effective)

always use.

E. Superlatives of Adjectives

Recall this sentence from the narrative:
> Also, it has *the largest* and *best* supermarket in the city.

PATTERNS

> the + one-syllable Adjective + -est (+ Noun)

This is *the cheapest* brand available.

> the + <u>most</u> + two-or-more-syllable Adjective (+ Noun)
>   <u>least</u>

This is *the most expensive* product in the store.

Notes:
a. Irregular Adjectives

good	better	*best*
bad	worse	*worst*
far	farther	*farthest*

b. We use -iest with two-syllable adjectives that end in *y*.

    Example: happy — happier — *happiest*

Complete the following exchanges using one of the preceding patterns.

    Example: A: I'm going to Christie's to do some food shopping. Want to come with me?

B: Christie's Gourmet Shop![18] Are you kidding? They have *the highest* prices in town.

1. A: Did you do all your shopping yesterday?

    B: No. Do you know what happened? I lost my wallet.

    A: Oh, no! Did you have a lot of cash in it?

    B: Around $40, but the money is really _____ thing. The
          (important)

          _____ part of it is that I lost my credit cards, driver's license, and
          (bad)

          supermarket courtesy card.[19]

2. A: Are these paper towels okay?

    B: No, don't buy national brand towels. They're _____ . Here, buy
          (expensive)

          this store brand. It's _____ one in the store.
          (cheap)

3. A: Why are you buying those Grade B eggs? You should only buy Grade A eggs;

          they're _____ .
          (good)

    B: Listen, I can't make ends meet[20] as it is[21] and you want me to spend more? Give me

          a break![22]

4. A: You'd better buy a bigger bag of potato chips than that one.

    B: This is _____ one they have.
          (big)

5. A: What kind of cereal should I get?

    B: This one is _____ .
          (good)

---

[18]gourmet shop: a store which sells a variety of special foods.
[19]supermarket courtesy card: a special identification card which a supermarket issues to its customers so that they can cash checks at the supermarket.
[20]make ends meet: to have enough money to pay one's bills.
[21]as it is: the way it is now.
[22]give (one) a break: don't be so demanding, strict; give (one) a chance.

```
$3.15OREO ICE CRM ASTD FLVRS
4.9¢ PER OUNCE  3.15
`D913896 004
                              64Z
```

Unit price label

DOUBLE COUPON

Present this coupon along with any one manufacturer's "cents off" coupon and get double the savings when you purchase the item. Not to include "retailer", "free grocery" purchase, coupon greater than one dollar or exceed the value of the item. Excludes alcoholic beverages, tobacco and dairy products. Limit one coupon per item. Limit two coupons per customer. Good June 21-27 at Safeway Stores. **Sample copy.**

AMT _____ TAX _____

DOUBLE COUPON

Present this coupon along with any one manufacturer's "cents off" coupon and get double the savings when you purchase the item. Not to include "retailer", "free grocery" purchase, coupon greater than one dollar or exceed the value of the item. Excludes alcoholic beverages, tobacco and dairy products. Limit one coupon per item. Limit two coupons per customer. Good June 21-27 at Safeway Stores. **Sample copy.**

AMT _____ TAX _____

Food coupons

A: Well, it may be _____ , but it's also _____
                          (nutritious)   (high)

priced.

F. Comparison of Nouns

Recall this sentence from the narrative:

Janet agreed that this section had *more bottles* of shampoo than other supermarkets . . . .

PATTERNS

> more + plural Count Noun + than
> fewer

She always eats *more* cookies *than* her brother.
There were *fewer* items on sale this week *than* last week.

> more + Non-Count Noun + than
> less

He has *more* money to spend *than* I do.
There is *less* fresh fruit available now *than* during the summer.

> (not) + as + many + plural Count Noun + as
>   much + Non-Count Noun

I didn't buy *as many* cans of soda *as* you wanted.
He doesn't buy *as much* junk food[23] *as* you do.

Complete the following exchanges with one of the preceding patterns.

Example: A: What kind of ham should I buy?
             B: Get boiled ham; it has <u>less salt than</u> Virginia ham.
                                              (salt)

1.   A: Why are you buying diet soda? I don't think it tastes as good as regular soda.

     B: I know, but I'm on a diet and it has _____ .
                                                           (calories)

2.   A: Don't buy those hot dogs. They don't have _____ some of the
                                                              (flavor)

          other brands.

---
[23]junk food: food that is not nutritious.

B: But they're the cheapest.

A: Forget about the price! You shouldn't skimp[24] when it comes to[25] food.

3.   A: I need to pick up some tuna this afternoon.

B: Oh, go over to A and D's for it. They have _____ most
(brands of tuna)

of the other supermarkets.

4.   A: Do you want me to buy some sugar when I go shopping?

B: No, we still have plenty in the cabinet.

A: Boy, you're using a lot _____ now than you used to.
(sugar)

B: Well, everyone says it's not healthy to use too much sugar.

5.   A: Why don't we buy some ice cream for Jim? You know how he loves it.

B: No, we'd better not; he's trying to lose weight. Buy him some frozen yogurt instead;

it doesn't have _____ ice cream.
(calories)

G. Superlatives of Nouns

Recall this sentence from the narrative:

Mr. Lin was pleased to learn the unit pricing method. It helped him to select the bottle
with *the most shampoo* for *the least money.*

PATTERNS

| the + most + plural Count Noun |
| fewest |

This store carries *the most* brands of ice cream.
This brand of margarine has *the fewest* calories.

| the + most + Non-Count Noun |
| least |

This one costs *the most* (money).
Which one of these steaks has *the least* fat?

---

[24]skimp: to try to save money; to be cheap.
[25]when it comes to: in regard to.

Complete the following exchanges with one of the preceding patterns.

> **Example:** A: Don't forget to buy coffee. And check the newspaper for coupons.
>
> B: Do you bother with coupons?
>
> A: Of course. That way I get <u>*the most coffee*</u> for the
>   (coffee)
>
>   *least amount of money.*
>   (amount of money)

1. A: When you go to the supermarket, make sure you only buy Butler's rye bread. Don't get any other brand.

   B: What's the difference?

   A: Listen, Butler's has _____ of any brand bread.
                                (additives)

   B: Well, if you're that picky,[26] why don't you go to the health food store? I'm sure you can find bread without any additives at all.[27]

2. A: There are so many cereals here!

   B: You're right. I think this store carries more cereals than any supermarket in the area. Which one should we get?

   A: Well, let's read the list of ingredients and then get the one with _____
   _____ .
                     (nutritional value)

3. A: Do you want me to buy steak or roast beef for tonight?

   B: Do we have to have beef again? How about some other meat?

   A: Well, beef has _____ doesn't it?
                            (protein)

   B: I don't know about that.[28] I think chicken and fish have just as much protein. Besides, everyone says too much red meat[29] isn't good for you.

---

[26]picky: to be very careful about choosing; fussy.
[27]at all: (used in negative sentences), not even a little.
                              one
[28]I don't know about that: We use this phrase to express disagreement.
[29]red meat: beef.

4. A: Why did you buy Jones' bacon?

B: You told me to! You said it has _____ .
(fat)

A: You're impossible![30] I never told you that. I told you not to buy Jones' bacon

because it has _____ . So what I told you went in one ear and out
(fat)

the other[31] as usual.

B: Well, at least it's the cheapest brand, so you're getting _____
(bacon)

for your money.

A: Wrong again. This package may be the least expensive one in the store, but it also

has _____ in it. So it's not really the best buy.
(slices of bacon)

IV. EXPRESSIONS AND IDIOMS

● *have yet to*: never to have done something.

```
Subject + have yet to + Verb (base form)
```

Recall this sentence from the narrative:
 She was surprised to find out he *had yet to* see a shopping mall.

Complete the following exchanges with an appropriate response using *have yet to*.

   Example: A: Are you still using that same brand of soap?
          B: Well, *I've yet to find a better brand*.
            (find a better brand)

1. A: I see you did all the grocery shopping. Did you go by yourself?

B: No, Henry went with me. He helped me to carry the packages.

A: Did he help you pay?

B: You must be kidding! I _____ .
(see Henry fork out[32] money for groceries)

---

[30]impossible (referring to a person): unreasonable; difficult to deal with.
[31]go in one ear and out the other: to not pay attention to what a person is saying.
[32]fork out (up, over): to pay.

2.   A: Which supermarket do you want to go to?

   B: I always shop at Green's.

   A: You still go there? There are so many newer and bigger supermarkets in the area

   now.

   B: Yes, but I _____ .
   (cleaner one–Green's)

3.   A: Be sure to buy Hanley's bread.

   B: Oh, how about getting some other bread for a change?[33] Aren't you tired of eating

   the same kind of bread every day?

   A: Not really, and I _____ .
   (find a more nutritious bread–Hanley's)

   B: You know, you're beginning to sound like a commercial.

4.   A: The new supermarket on Main Street has a great deli. You have to try it.

   B: I've been there. I'll stick to[34] Lundy's Deli. I _____ .
   (taste better cold cuts[35]–they have)

5.   A: I've tried so many different brands of ice cream, but I _____ .
   (find one without additives)

   B: Well, let's go over to that new health food store on Maple Street. They have "all-

   natural" ice cream. It doesn't have any preservatives or additives, and it tastes great.

6.   A: Why don't we buy TV dinners for tonight's supper?

   B: No way! I hate those frozen dinners.

   A: Have you tried some of the newer TV dinners? They're not bad at all!

   B: I _____ .
   (taste a decent TV dinner)

---

[33]for a change: something different from the usual.
[34]stick to: not change.
[35]cold cuts: cooked meats served cold.

Supermarket advertisement

- *have (something) to do with*: to be related.
     (nothing)
     (a lot)

Recall this sentence from the narrative:
> Janet explained the difference between store brands and national brands. She told him that the advertising costs of national brands *have a lot to do with* their higher price.

Complete the following exchanges with an appropriate response using *have to do with*.

Example: A: I just came back from the supermarket. Beef prices have skyrocketed![36]

B: *Well, I'm sure that has something to do with the drought in the Mid-West this summer.*

1.   A: You bought the wrong kind of meat. I wanted veal, not pork.

     B: Don't blame me! I _____ . I didn't do the shopping; Jill did.
                                   (it)

2.   In the produce[37] section of a supermarket:

     A: The fruit has been terrible this year.

     B: I know. Either there's not enough, or what they have is really poor quality. I wonder what happened?

     A: I imagine that all the rainy weather we had this summer _____ .
                                                             (the poor crop)

3.   A: When you go to the store make sure to get Flakman's margarine. Don't get any other brand.

     B: Listen, there's really no difference among all those brands. You've been listening to too many commercials!

     A: I want Flakman's because I like its taste. It _____ . In fact, I've
                                                     (their advertisements)
          never even seen any of their T.V. spots.[38]

---

[36]skyrocket: to quickly increase by a large amount.
[37]produce: fruits and vegetables.
[38]T.V. spot: T.V. commercial.

V. SITUATIONAL DIALOGUE

Mr. Lin is shopping in a supermarket.

LIN: Excuse me, do you carry bean sprouts?

CLERK: No, I'm sorry. We don't carry them.

LIN: Do you have cherries?

CLERK: No, they're not in season right now.

LIN: Okay. Oh, where is the delicatessen section?

CLERK: Down the aisle, on your left.

LIN: (at the deli counter) How much is your Virginia ham?

2ND CLERK: $2.79 a pound. We also have a special on[39] imported Danish ham; it's only $2.39 a pound.

LIN: Okay. Let me have a quarter pound of the Danish ham.

2ND CLERK: Here you are. Please pay up front, sir. Since you don't have too many items, you can go to the express checkout lane.[40]

QUESTIONS

1.   How come the store doesn't have any cherries?
2.   How much is Virginia ham?
3.   What do they have a special on?
4.   Where can Mr. Lin pay for his purchase?

VI. VOCABULARY BUILDER

shopping	clothes shopping/food shopping/grocery shopping/shopping basket/ shopping cart/shopping center/shopping mall
food	baby food/canned food/diet food/ethnic food/frozen food/health food/high or low calorie food/high or low cholesterol food/kosher food/pet food/preserved foods/snack food

VII. ROLE PLAY SUGGESTIONS

1.   Ask where to find an item or section in a supermarket.
2.   Return some food product because it is spoiled or stale. Ask for your money back.

---

[39]have a special on (something): something is on sale.
[40]express checkout lane: usually for shoppers with ten or fewer items to buy.

VIII. PREPOSITION PRACTICE

A. More Prepositions of Time

AFTER (later than)	He went shopping **AFTER** work yesterday.
BEFORE (earlier than)	Can you get here **BEFORE** noon?
UNTIL (to the time of)	The supermarket is open **UNTIL** midnight.
IN (after a period of time)	I'll return **IN** a few days.

Complete the following exchanges with the appropriate preposition.

1. A: Are you ready? It's 8:40 already!

    B: What's the rush? The supermarket doesn't even open _____

    nine o'clock.

    A: I know, but I want to get back _____ one o'clock.

2. Two college students:

    A: I'm starving. How about going to the deli for a sandwich _____

    our next class? We still have a half hour.

    B: No, I need to look over my notes first.

    A: Well, when do you plan to eat lunch?

    B: _____ class.

    A: Well, I can't wait _____ then. I'm going for something now.

3. A: That deli never closes. It's open twenty-four hours a day!

    B: That's not so. It only stays open _____ five o'clock on Sundays.

4. A: Have you seen Andrea? I've been looking for her all morning.

    B: Oh, she'll be back _____ an hour.

Delicatessen advertisement

B. Additional Preposition Combinations

buy up (IS):
to buy all or as much as possible

Don't *buy up* all the bananas. Leave some for me!

buy out (S):
to buy a business or property from another person

My partner has been trying to *buy* me *out* for years.

sell out (S):
to sell completely
(*also* be sold out)

It rained yesterday, so we *sold out* all our umbrellas.
The tickets are *sold out*.

sell out (S):
not be true to (your ideals, country, etc.)

Don't *sell out*! Be true to your ideals!

Complete the following exchanges with the appropriate preposition combination.

1.   A: Look at all these cans of sardines! Why did you buy so many?

      B: They were on sale.

      A: Okay, but did you have to _____ every can in the store?

      B: Listen, stop exaggerating! There aren't that many cans here.

2.   A husband and wife are talking. The husband has just gotten off[41] the phone.

      A: That was my mother. Guess what she told me.

      B: What?

      A: Somebody wants to _____ their business.

      B: Really? Do your folks want to sell?

      A: Maybe. They've been thinking of retiring for a while now.

3.   Customer and supermarket clerk:

      A: Where is the Red Leaf apple juice? I believe it's on sale.

      B: I'm sorry, but we're all _____ .

---

[41]gotten off: stopped talking and hung up the receiver.

4. A: You've always eaten health food and now you're buying that junk food!

    B: It's only a bag of potato chips.

    A: How can you _____ like that.

REVIEW CHAPTER AND POPULAR EXPRESSIONS

I. CREATE A DIALOGUE

Create a dialogue using the words and expressions listed.

> **Example:**   At an airport ticket counter:
>
> A: round-trip ticket to
>   four-thirty flight
> B: sorry
>   booked solid
>   six o'clock flight
>   available seats
> A: put on one's credit card
>
> A: I'd like a *round-trip ticket* to Boston. Can I get on the *four-thirty flight* today?
> B: I'm *sorry*. That flight is *booked solid*. The *six o'clock flight* has some *available seats* though.
> A: That's fine. I'll *put this on my credit card.*

1.   Two people are in a hurry to catch a flight:
    A: leave for the airport
        run late
    B: ready
    A: be about time

_____

_____

_____

_____

_____

2. Two people are at the baggage claim area:
   A: look like
        have a hard time
        help out
   B: could use
        a hand with
        too heavy for me to

   _____

   _____

   _____

   _____

   _____

3. A person is waiting at a bus stop. When the bus comes, he asks the driver a question.
   PERSON: stop at?
   DRIVER: no
             had better
             taxi

   _____

   _____

   _____

   _____

   _____

4. In a taxi:
   PASSENGER: step on it
   DRIVER: as fast as I can
             after all
             traffic
   PASSENGER: have to
                pick up my boss at the airport
                had better
                show up on time
                for a change

_____

_____

_____

_____

_____

5. Mr. Jones is making reservations at a hotel:
   A: how much
        single room
        with a view
   B: per night
   A: more than last time
   B: rates
        go up
        as of

_____

_____

_____

_____

6. A guest and the hotel manager:
   GUEST: try
            get in touch with Mr. Perlman
            since yesterday morning
   MANAGER: no longer
   GUEST: no wonder

_____

_____

_____

_____

7. A couple is checking into a motel:
   A: get tired of
      stay in motels
   B: at least
      cheap
   A: have yet to
      a good night's sleep

   _____

   _____

   _____

   _____

   _____

8. Two friends are talking on the phone:
   A: we can't
      go out
      car break down
   B: see if (one) can
      have Donald take us
   A: already
      think of that
      get in touch with
      so far

   _____

   _____

   _____

   _____

   _____

9. A couple is shopping in a supermarket:
   A: potato chips
      good buy
   B: give (one) a break
      make ends meet
      as it is
      junk food

_____

_____

_____

_____

_____

10. In a supermarket:
    A: generic canned vegetables
    B: skimp
        when it comes to
    A: picky

_____

_____

_____

_____

_____

11. A husband and wife in a butcher shop:
    A: more meat
        so that
        run short
        during the holidays
    B: there is no need
        more meat
        already have
        frozen meat
    A: buy some more
        to be on the safe side

_____

_____

_____

_____

_____

12. A customer talking to the owner of a fruit stand:
CUSTOMER: anymore
                         melons?
OWNER: no
                so cheap that
                sell out
                as soon as
                get them

_____

_____

_____

_____

_____

13. In the house:
A: buy wrong kind of coffee
B: dirty look
       have nothing to do with
       Sarah
       do the shopping

_____

_____

_____

_____

14. Two people at a bus stop:
A: take a taxi
       be tired of
       wait
B: not give up
       buses must be
       run late
       a little while longer

_____

_____

_____

_____

_____

II. POPULAR EXPRESSIONS FROM SPORTS

Sport	Expression	Definition	Example
Baseball	strike out	to fail	I don't know why, but when it comes to exams I always *strike out*.
Golf	par for the course	expected	A: Tim's late again. B: That's *par for the course* for him; he's never on time.
Track	start from scratch	to start from the beginning	He lost everything in the fire; now he'll have to *start from scratch*.
Horse racing	lay odds	to bet someone	Listen, I'll *lay odds* that nobody comes tonight.
Horse racing	a tip	advice on something	Let me give you a *tip* on how to pass the course.
General	(give someone) a pep talk	to inspire; to encourage	They're not doing very well. You'd better give them a *pep talk*.

Complete the following exchanges with an appropriate expression from the preceding list.

1. A: Where's Lily?

   B: She's up in her room. She's down in the dumps[1] because she failed her road test[2] again.

   A: Oh, let me go up and give her a little _____ .

2. A: Didn't Steve come to the meeting last night?

   B: No, he didn't show up again.

---

[1] in the dumps: depressed; in a bad mood.
[2] road test: a driving test; you have to pass this test to get a driver's license.

A: Well, that's _____ . He never keeps his appointments. I'll

_____ he doesn't show up for tomorrow's meeting either.

3. A: I'm really upset. I left my briefcase in the taxi. I lost all the notes for my paper!

B: Then you'll just have to _____ again.

4. A: I'd love to go to the Super Bowl[3] next week, but I don't have a way to get to New

Orleans. Oh well, I don't think there are any more tickets available anyway.

B: Why don't you talk to Laura? She's a big football fan. She might be able to give you

a _____ on how to get a ticket. And I know she is planning to go

herself, so maybe you could go with her.

5. A: I just couldn't find a way to do it.

B: Well, I guess you _____ again.

III. GRAMMAR REVIEW

A. Tenses

Present; Present Continuous; Past; Present Perfect; Present Perfect Continuous.
Complete the following exchanges using the appropriate tense.

1. A: _____ you _____ to the Yankee game last
                                    (go)

   night?

   B: Yes, I _____ . I _____ a great time.
                                              (have)

   A: Who _____ ?
                              (win)

   B: The Yankees.

---

[3]Super Bowl: the championship game of professional football.

A: No wonder you _____ the game so much. You may not believe
              (enjoy)

this, but I _____ never _____ to Yankee
                                          (be)

Stadium.

B: No?

A: No. In fact, I _____ never _____ a baseball
                                              (see)

game in person.⁴ I _____ only _____ a few
                                          (watch)

games on T.V.

B: I guess I _____ to hundreds of games. I'd love to take you
                      (be)

sometime.

2.   In a college cafeteria:

A: Where's Terrence? How come he _____ lunch with us now?
                                        (have; negative)

B: He _____ to the gym to work out⁵ instead.
                (go)

A: During his lunch hour? _____ he always

_____ in the morning?
        (exercise; negative question)

B: Yes, he usually _____ . But he _____
                                                  (have; negative)

a chance to this morning. He _____ here too late to go to the
                                    (get)

gym before his first class.

3.   Two people are jogging:

A: You _____ too fast! I can't keep up with⁶ you!
              (go)

B: Oh, you _____ always _____ .
                                        (complain)

---

⁴in person: actually present.
⁵work out: to exercise.
⁶keep up with: to maintain the pace; stay even with.

A: That's because you always _____ too fast for me. Slow down a
(run)

little!

B: Listen, I _____ slower than I usually do. Just run!
(go)

4. A: I _____ Arthur out on the tennis courts this morning. I
(see; negative)

wonder what _____ to him?
(happen)

B: Why? _____ he _____ a lot of tennis lately?
(play)

A: Yes, he _____ every morning for the last three weeks.
(practice)

B: Well, maybe he _____ to take a break this morning.
(need)

5. A: Where _____ you _____ ?
(go)

B: I'm headed for the gym. I have to meet Brad there.

A: What _____ he _____ there?
(do)

B: He _____ weights. I want him to give me a few pointers.[7]
(lift)

He _____ at it[8] for quite a while now and he really
(be)

_____ what he _____ .
(know)   (do)

A: Oh, _____ you _____ these days, too?
(work out)

B: I _____ weights twice a week since October.
(lift)

A: Lately I _____ about starting to work out myself, but I
(think)

_____ much free time since I _____ my new
(have; negative)   (begin)

job last month.

B: Well, there's no time like the present. Why don't you come with me right now?

---

[7]pointer: a tip.
[8]be at it: to be doing something.

B. Modals

Complete the following exchanges using the following modals.

can	be able to	might	have to
could	may	must	

1. A: Alberto has become quite a[9] runner. He _____ run a mile in less

    than four minutes!

    B: Alberto? I _____ see it before I _____ believe it.

    A: Then why don't you go to the track meet[10] this Saturday and watch him run?

    B: Are you planning to go?

    A: Yes, I am.

    B: _____ I go with you? I don't have a way to get to the stadium

    by myself.

    A: Of course you _____ .

2. A: How many push-ups _____ you do?

    B: Well, when I was younger, I _____ do fifty at a time,[11] but no

    longer. I haven't exercised for years.

    A: Why don't you start exercising again? Who knows? It _____

    make you feel a lot younger.

3. A: Aren't you having breakfast?

---

[9]quite a (noun): a very good (noun).
[10]track meet: a competition for running and other track events.
[11]at a time: at one time; together; as a unit.

B: No, I'm in a hurry to get to the track. I _____ do without[12] it.

A: No, you _____ . You _____ eat properly now

that you're exercising every day.

4. A: Have you seen Sonia?

B: No, I haven't. Oh, she _____ be at the ice skating rink. She

_____ practice for the competition next week.

A: I just came from the rink. She's not there.

B: Then I'm not sure where she is. Try the library; she _____ be

over there studying now.

5. On a tennis court:

A: I give up!

B: What's the matter?

A: I just _____ play this game well.

B: Don't give up. After a few more weeks of practice you'll _____

play much better.

C. Comparative and Superlative Forms

Complete the following exchanges with an appropriate response using the comparative or superlative.

1. A: I give up. I'm never playing tennis with Jimmy again.

B: What's the matter? Are you tired of losing?

A: Yes. He's _____ . I just can't beat him.

(player-I)

_____

[12]do without: to not need.

2. A: Would you like to learn how to ski? I can teach you.

   B: Oh, no thank you. I don't think I can learn.

   A: C'mon. It's not _____ . In fact, it's really
      (difficult–you think)

      quite simple.

3. A: Do you want to go jogging with me?

   B: Well, I don't think I can keep up with you. You're in _____ .
      (shape[13]–I am)

4. A: Why don't we walk to work today? It's a nice day and, besides, we need some

      exercise.

   B: It's too far.

   A: It's _____ .
      (far–you think)

5. A: How did you like the game?

   B: It was very exciting.

   A: I thought so, too. In fact, it was _____ I've ever seen in my
      (game)

      whole life!

6. A: Are you still eating health food?

   B: Yes, and I'm jogging every day, too.

   A: Well, do you feel better?

   B: I feel _____ .
      (strong–ever)

7. A: I'd like to start going to the gym regularly.

   B: Why don't you? I go every day.

[13]shape: physical condition.

A: But I don't have _____ .
                                 (free time-you do)

B: Well, you have to make time then.

8. A: Is Katie a good bowler?

     B: She's _____ I've ever seen, even _____ you!
                    (bowler)   (good)

9. A: Why do you always seem to have _____ ?
                                        (energy-I do)

     B: Maybe it's because I eat properly and take vitamins.

10. A: Which team do you think is _____ in the league?
                                  (good)

     B: Well, of all the teams, Greenwood has _____ so far. So
                                         (wins)

       I guess they're _____ .
                              (good)

5 THE NEW APARTMENT

I. NARRATIVE

Although Mr. Lin liked living at the Excelsior Hotel, it was rather expensive, and now that he **was running out of money**, he really had **to cut down on** his expenses. One possibility was to move in with some distant relatives. The more he thought about sharing a room with two teenage cousins, however, the more he began to consider other options. He could either rent a room in a private home or get his own apartment.

One morning, while he was thinking about what to do, he decided to start looking through the classified section[1] of the newspaper. He saw two advertisements for apartment sharing. One read, "Elderly woman looking for another woman to share an apartment"; the other advertised an apartment in the suburbs. As he leafed[2] through the pages, he noticed that there were several ads[3] for apartments near the university. One, in particular, caught his eye.[4] "Two room apartment, low rent, convenient location. Contact Super."[5] Mr. Lin decided to go and have a look at it, so he called and made an appointment to see the apartment the next day.

Mr. Bacci, the superintendent, met him at the front door of the apartment building and took him to the vacant apartment. While Mr. Lin was looking around the apartment. Mr. Bacci **kept on** repeating, "You can walk to class, and don't worry, you can make new friends around here, 'cause there are lots of students in the building. It's nice and clean, but listen, you'd better decide soon 'cause it won't last long." Mr. Lin really liked the apartment. The rent seemed a little too high, but after he **took into account** all the advantages, especially the convenient location, he gave the super a deposit. While Mr. Bacci was pocketing the money, he said, "By the way, you know you can't make any noise here; you can't

---

[1]classified section: the section of a newspaper with advertisements listed in different categories, such as apartments, help wanted, houses, etc.
[2]leaf: to turn over pages.
[3]ads: advertisements.
[4]catch one's eye: to attract one's attention.
[5]super (superintendent): the person who takes care of an apartment building.

leave trash in the hallways, in the basement, or on the sidewalk; and you've got to[6] be on time with your rent."

Before he returned to the Excelsior, Mr. Lin took a stroll around his new neighborhood. He liked the many small shops and the crowded streets. He felt at home[7] here. On the way back to the hotel, he kept thinking about how he was going to transform his empty apartment into a comfortable home.

QUESTIONS

1. Why was Mr. Lin considering moving out of the Excelsior Hotel?
2. Why didn't he want to move in with his relatives?
3. What other choices did Mr. Lin consider?
4. Why weren't the apartments to share suitable for Mr. Lin?
5. How come Mr. Lin decided to take the apartment even though he thought the rent was a little too high?
6. What did Mr. Lin do before he went back to the Excelsior?
7. What was he thinking about on his way home?

II. DIALOGUES

1. Mr. Lin calls in response to an ad. The superintendent, Mr. Bacci, answers.

LIN: Hello. I'm calling about your ad for an "apartment for rent" in today's newspaper.

SUPER: Oh, yes. I'm Frank Bacci, the super. Do you want to come over and take a look?

LIN: Yes, I do, but the ad didn't mention the rent. How much is it?

SUPER: $270.00 a month.

LIN: Does that include utilities?[8]

SUPER: Nope.[9] You pay the gas and electricity. We supply hot water and heat.

LIN: Okay. When can I come over?

SUPER: Anytime you want. It's up to you. Actually, evenings are best though.

LIN: How about this evening?

SUPER: Fine. What time?

LIN: Seven-thirty, okay?

SUPER: All right. The address is 32 Bleecker Street. Just ring the bell for apartment 1A.

LIN: Okay. See you at seven-thirty.

---

[6]have got to: have to; must.
[7]feel at home: to feel very comfortable, as if you were in your own home.
[8]utilities: gas, water, heat.
[9]nope: no.

QUESTIONS

1. Where did Mr. Lin see the ad?
2. How much is the rent?
3. Does the rent include utilities?
4. When is the best time for Mr. Lin to go and see the apartment?

2.   Mr. Lin arrives to take a look at the apartment. Mr. Bacci, the super, answers the doorbell.

LIN: Hello. My name is Lin. I called earlier today about coming to see the apartment for rent.

BACCI: Oh, yes. I'm Frank Bacci; I'm the super here. Come on in[10] and let me show you around. This is the living room. Spacious, huh?

LIN: Yes, it's big. Is there a telephone outlet?

BACCI: Sure, but it's not hooked up yet.[11] Here's the kitchen. It's got a built-in range[12] and a new fridge. C'mon. Let me show you the bathroom. Look, all new fixtures.

LIN: Yes, very nice. By the way, how much does the electric bill run?

BACCI: It depends on how much you use, of course. I live on the second floor and mine usually runs around twenty dollars a month.

LIN: That's not bad. Is this neighborhood fairly quiet?

BACCI: It's so quiet that at night you can hear a pin drop.

LIN: Well, I like the apartment very much. How much is the deposit?

BACCI: One month's rent, plus you've got to pay me the first month's rent now, too.

LIN: No problem. When can I move in?

BACCI: After you pay and sign the lease, it's all yours.

LIN: How long a lease can I get?

BACCI: You can sign a one-, two-, or three-year lease. I'll have Mr. Wade, the land-lord, call you tomorrow. You can make an appointment and discuss it with him.

QUESTIONS

1. Who showed Mr. Lin around the apartment?
2. What appliances are in the kitchen?
3. How much does the super's electric bill usually run?
4. How much deposit is required?
5. When can Mr. Lin move in?
6. What lease options does Mr. Lin have?

---

[10]come on in: come in.
[11]hooked up: connected.
[12]range: stove.

III. GRAMMAR

A. Past Continuous Tense

We use the Past Continuous Tense to show
(1) what was happening when another action interrupted.

FORM: $\boxed{\dfrac{\text{was}}{\text{were}} + \text{Verb-ing}}$

Affirmative:

She found her ring while she *was cleaning* the apartment.
She *was cleaning* the apartment when she found the ring.

Negative:

She didn't find her ring while she *was cleaning* the apartment.
She *wasn't cleaning* the apartment when she found her ring.

Question:

Did she find her ring while she *was cleaning* the apartment?
Was she *cleaning* the apartment when she found her ring?

Wh- Questions:

What did she find while she *was cleaning* the apartment?
What *was* she *doing* when she found her ring?

Who/What/Which as Subject:

What happened while she *was cleaning* the apartment?

(2) what was happening over a given period of time in the past.

Example: I *was looking* for an apartment all morning.

(3) two things that were happening at the same time in the past.

Example: While you *were looking* at ads in the newspaper, he was checking in those magazines.

(4) what was happening at an exact time in the past.

Example: What *were* you *doing* at 10 o'clock last night?

Dialogues

Complete the following dialogues using *Past Tense* or *Past Continuous Tense.*

1. Philip and John are talking about their friend, Maurice. Both Philip and Maurice have been looking for apartments.

PHILIP: _____ Maurice _____ an apartment
                                                    (find)

last week?

301
Apts. for Rent

3 Bedroom, 2 Bath, carpet, drapes, fenced yard. Balboa Ave. No pets. 555-6207.

2 bedrooms $650. 417 B Ave. Open now

EXCELLENT FOR ENTERTAINING 3 bedroom, 2 bath, formal dining, encircled with sun decks, patios, and flower gardens. 2350 sq. ft. with with 600 sq. ft. garage. Like new. $1200. 555-3518.

$475. Small 2 bedroom suitable for couple or family with infant. No pets. Available July 1st. 555-6961 after 4:00 p.m.

3 bedroom 1 3/4 bath and den unfurnished, long term or furnished, short term. 1300 9th or 555-6066.

$350. 1 bedroom plus den duplex, near beach, quiet area. 555-3226.

4 bedroom charming designers home; furnished completely. Village & beach convenient. 555-2703.

Home across from beach.
UNOBSTRUCTED OCEAN VIEW. 3 bedroom, 2 decks. Owner/Broker 555-6083.

Charming beach house - 1 bedroom, den, large balcony, private. 1038 Isabella. $1200. July 19-August 21. 555-9145.

Beautifully furnished 2 bedroom apartment. View of bay. Call after 5:00. 555-1821.

3 bedroom, 2 bath, garage, covered patio, washer, dryer. 555-6335.

Large 3 bedroom, 3 plus bath, sauna and hot tub and lofts. 1 family only. No smoking. No waterbeds. Shown by appointment. $1300. 555-1420.

3 bedroom and 1 bedroom on 75 ft. corner. Call 555-8915.

Available July & August 3 bedroom, 2 bath, fully furnished home $2000.

3 bedroom, family room, jacuzzi, near beach, maid and gardener. $2000/month. Available July 7 - August 17. 555-1394.

Professional, commercial property for rent. 900 sq. feet. 1020 Isabella. Inquire Judy, 555-8333.

305
Home Services

Hedges- small trees trimmed, yard clean-ups, etc. Reasonable, experienced. Student, 555-3969

House sitter: available for month of July. Ph.D. Harvard University. Relative/references, call 555-8846.

Housekeeping - $5 hour. Reliable, hard-working. Good references. After 3, 555-1427, Maria.

We will: Clean your garage, attic, basement. Organize a garage/sidewalk sale. Housesit, plant and animal care. Wall washing and painting. Dave and Yvonne. 555-8039.

Classified ads for apartment and house rentals
Classified ads for home services

JOHN: No, he _____ . He _____ still

_____ through the classified ads when I _____
(look) (call)

him last week.

PHILIP: Well, guess what. I _____ a place yesterday.
(find)

JOHN: Really!

PHILIP: Yep![13] While Maurice _____ out ads on bulletin boards in
(check)

supermarkets, I _____ all the rental agencies in town. One of them
(call)

_____ me back yesterday, and now I have a new apartment.
(call)

QUESTIONS

1. What was Maurice doing last week?
2. What did Philip find yesterday?
3. What was Philip doing while Maurice was checking out bulletin boards in super-markets?
4. How did Philip find his new apartment?

2. Beverly is talking with her friend, Joan.

BEVERLY: Where _____ you yesterday? I _____
(be) (try)

to call you all afternoon.

JOAN: I _____ all over town. I _____
(run) (look)

at apartments.

BEVERLY: _____ you _____ one?
(find)

JOAN: No, I _____ .
(do)

BEVERLY: Well, good, because while you _____ around,
(run)

I _____ an apartment for you.
(find)

JOAN: Oh, great! You're a real friend.

_____
[13]yep: yes.

QUESTIONS

1. What was Joan doing yesterday afternoon?
2. Why was Beverly trying to call her?

3. Walt and Hart are roommates. Walt enters their apartment.

WALT: Hart? Where are you?

HART: In the kitchen. I'm on the phone. (Walt enters the kitchen. Hart is now off the

phone.)

WALT: Who _____ you _____ to?
(talk)

HART: The landlord. I _____ the new rent increase with him.
(discuss)

WALT: What _____ he _____ ?
(say)

HART: Not much. Just that we have to pay it.

WALT: Oh, I _____ that we could get out of it.[14]
(hope)

QUESTIONS

1. Who was Hart talking to when Walt came home?
2. What were they talking about?
3. What was Walt hoping?

4. Oscar and Ernest are neighbors. They are talking on the telephone.

ERNEST: What _____ you _____ at this time
(do)

yesterday afternoon?

OSCAR: I don't remember. Why?

ERNEST: I _____ over to see you. I _____
(come) (ring)

your doorbell, but no one answered. That was around three-thirty.

---

[14]get out of something
doing something : to avoid doing something.

OSCAR: Oh, I remember. I _____ in the basement; it's a lot cooler
            (take a nap)

than the rest of the house. But I can't hear the doorbell when I'm down there. I'm

sorry. What _____ you _____ to see me about?
                                              (want)

ERNEST: I _____ to use your phone. Mine _____
                      (want)   (work; negative)

yesterday afternoon.

QUESTIONS

1. What was Oscar doing at three-thirty yesterday afternoon?
2. Why couldn't Oscar hear the doorbell?
3. Why did Ernest want to use Oscar's phone?

5. Josephine and William are a married couple. Josephine has just come home from work.
William has been home all day.

JOSEPHINE: _____ the plumber _____
                                                           (come; negative question)

to fix the shower today?

WILLIAM: Yes, but I _____ out in the backyard when he
                              (work)

_____ and I _____ the doorbell.
        (come)   (hear; negative)

JOSEPHINE: I don't believe it!

WILLIAM: Don't worry. I just _____ a few minutes ago and
                                          (call)

_____ for him to come back tomorrow.
        (arrange)

JOSEPHINE: But I _____ to take a shower tonight!
                              (hope)

QUESTIONS

1. Why did they need a plumber?
2. What was William doing when the plumber rang the doorbell?
3. What was Josephine hoping to do?

B. Should/Ought to

We use *should/ought to* to show obligation, advisability and expectation.

OBLIGATION

Both *should* and *ought to* show obligation. We seldom use *ought to* in negative sentences.

You *should* pay your rent on time.
  ought to

He *shouldn't* leave trash in the hallway.

ADVISABILITY

Both *should* and *ought to* show that it would be a good idea to do something.

You *should* go to a rental agency to find an apartment.
  ought to

EXPECTATION

Both *should* and *ought to* show that you expect, think or assume that something is true.

She's a real estate agent. She *should* know whether that house is for sale or not.
There are a lot of apartments available. It *shouldn't* take you long to find one.

C. Be supposed to

We use *be supposed to* to show obligation and expectation.

OBLIGATION

Be supposed to shows that
(1) someone may not be doing (or did not do) what a rule, custom, or another person *requires* him/her to do.

She was *supposed to* sign a new lease. [She was required to sign a new lease, but she did not.]

(2) You don't know whether the person is doing what is required.

He is *supposed to* pay his rent on time. [He is required to pay his rent on time, but you think he may not be paying on time.]

EXPECTATION

Be supposed to shows one of the following:
(1) that someone may not be doing (or did not do) what another person expects or wants him/her to do.

She's a real estate agent. She *is supposed* to know whether that house is worth the money. [You expect her to know, but she doesn't know.]
You *were supposed to* call me about the apartment yesterday. [I expected you to call me, but you did not call.]

(2) that you don't know what is expected of you or another person.
    What time *are we supposed to* meet them?

Complete the following exchanges using *should, ought to,* or *be supposed to*:

> *Example:*   A: Have you rented your spare room[15] yet?
>   B: No. A student <u>*was supposed to come and look at it*</u> last
>   (come and look at it)
>   night, but he never showed up.

1.   A: C'mon, James. Aren't you ready yet?

       B: What time _____ we _____ ?
                                                    (be there)

       A: No special time; it's an open house.[16] But we _____ too late.
                                                           (get there; negative)

2.   A: Don't you think we _____ that cracked window?
                                              (fix)

       B: The landlord _____ yesterday. I'd better call him and find out
                                   (repair it)

            why he didn't come.

3.   A: Do you think we can sell our house quickly?

       B: It _____ . Mortgage rates are low now, so a lot of people
                (take long; negative)

            are buying.

4.   A: Do you think Colleen can come over tomorrow and help us redecorate the

            apartment?

       B: Well, she _____ . Tomorrow is her day off.
                                  (be able to)

         _____ she _____ last week?
                                     (come over; negative question)

       A: Yes, but she couldn't make it.

5.   A: Have you paid the electric bill yet?

---

[15]spare room: extra room.
[16]open house: (1) a house or apartment open for viewing;
                     (2) a party where guests can come and go at any time.

B: No, not yet. I don't think we _____ it right away. They over-
(pay)

charged us last month.

A: You mean we _____ until they send us a credit?
(pay; negative)

B: Right.

6. A: I called up the telephone company and they require a $100 deposit to install a

phone.

B: O.K. Each of the four roommates _____ $25 then.
(pay)

A: _____ we buy our own phone or rent one from the telephone

company?

B: Let's buy it; it's a lot cheaper in the long run.[17]

7. A: I thought that the telephone service person _____ our
(install)

phone today.

B: Well, no one showed up!

8. A: I plan to move next month, but my landlord hasn't given me my $500 deposit back.

B: Do you know that in this state a landlord _____ you interest on
(give)

your deposit.

A: Really? My landlord never mentioned that. What do you think I _____
(do)

if he just hands me a check for exactly $500?

B: Well, you _____ now and remind him that he
(call)

_____ four years' interest on your original deposit. It's
(include)

yours by law, so he can't refuse.

_____

[17]in the long run: over a long period of time.

D. Sentence Patterns

Recall this sentence from the narrative:

> . . . *the more* he thought about sharing a room with two teenage cousins, however, *the more* he began to consider other options.

PATTERN

> the more + Subject + Verb + the more + Subject + Verb
>   less   less

The *more* he thought about the problem the *more* he worried.
The *more* I see him the *less* I like him.

SIMILAR PATTERNS

In general, follow the rules for making the comparative forms of adjectives, adverbs, and nouns.

Adjectives

>   more + two-syllable Adjective
>   less
> the +   + Noun (+be) . . . .
>   one-syllable Adjective + -er

The more spacious the apartment (is), *the more expensive it is.*
The bigger the apartment (is), *the more I like it.*

Adverbs

>   more + Adverb
>   less
> the +   + Subject + Verb
>   Adverb + -er

The more carefully you work, the faster you can finish.
The longer I live here, the more I like it.

Nouns

>   more + Non-Count Noun
>   less
> the +   + Subject + Verb
>   more + Count Noun
>   fewer

The more money I have, the more I spend.
The fewer rooms you have, the less time you spend house cleaning.

Complete the following exchanges with an appropriate response using one of the above patterns.

> *Example:* A: Aren't you satisfied with your present apartment?
> B: I don't know. The neighborhood isn't that safe, and the rent keeps going up. In fact, I was sitting at home last night and seriously thinking about moving.
> A: Well, do you think you'll move, then?
> B: I'm not sure, but *the more I consider it the more I*
> _____
> (consider-want to)
>
> *want to.*

1. A: Are you going to try to fix the pipes yourself or have a plumber come in and do it?

   B: I was planning to[18] do it myself, but there's so much to do that _____

   _____ .
   (think about it-feel like[19] doing it myself)

2. A: Are you still thinking about subletting[20] your apartment again this summer?

   B: Well, to tell you the truth, I was planning to, but now I'm having second thoughts.[21]

   _____ .
   (think of all the trouble I had last year-want to)

3. A: I thought you were planning to move to the suburbs.

   B: I was. When I first moved into the city I hated it, but _____
   (longer)

   I live here _____ .
   (like it)

   A: Well, I'm glad to hear it. I don't like to lose a good neighbor.

4. A: I see you've moved back into the city. Didn't suburban life agree with[22] you?

   B: It's not that, it's just that I couldn't take[23] the daily commute. The traffic was

   murder![24]

---

[18]was planning to: We use the verb "plan" in the Past Continuous to express original or former intention.
[19]feel like: to want to; have a desire for.
[20]sublet: to rent an apartment (1) from the original tenant, or (2) to another tenant.
[21]have second thoughts: to reconsider; to have doubts; to think about something again.
[22]agree with (one): to be suitable for.
[23]can (not) take: to stand, endure.
[24]murder: used as an adjective to mean very bad (traffic, hot weather); difficult (test).

A: That's why I live in the city myself. _____ I spend
                                              (time)

commuting _____ .
                    (good)

5. A: Wow! It's cold in here. Why don't you ask your super to send up a little more heat?

    B: Well, you know how it is in these old buildings. It seems that _____
                                                                              (cold)

    it is outside _____ we get.
                          (heat)

    A: Listen, you can call the city's Heat Complaint Office and complain. There's a special

    number to call. Just look it up in the phone book.

    B: When do you think I should call?

    A: _____ . Before we both freeze to death!
              (soon-good)

6. A: I don't know how you can live in that new high rise.[25]

    B: What do you mean?

    A: None of those new apartment buildings are soundproof. The _____
                                                                          (new)

    the building _____ it is.
                          (noisy)

    B: Well, I don't know how you can live in an old tenement[26] like this one. The

    _____ the building _____ it has.
            (old)   (cockroaches)

IV. EXPRESSIONS AND IDIOMS

- *cut down on*: to reduce the use of; to use less.

Subject + cut down on + $\frac{\text{Noun}}{\text{Verb-ing}}$

Recall this sentence from the narrative:
    . . . he really needed to *cut down on* his expenses.

[25]high rise: a very tall apartment building.
[26]tenement: low-rent housing, usually crowded and in poor condition.

169486127006	8020 EL PS GRANDE LJ	091582	$23.00
ACCOUNT NUMBER	SERVICE ADDRESS	DATE PAST DUE	TOTAL AMOUNT DUE

TYPE OF SERVICE·RATE	SERVICE DATES AND METER READINGS		THERM MULTIPLIER	USAGE	AMOUNT
	PRESENT	PREVIOUS			
GAS/GR	08-23 8703	07-23 8680	1.050	24 THERMS	11.73
ELEC/DR	08-23 14632	07-23 14535		97 KWHR	10.92

SAN DIEGO 1.0% GAS FRANCHISE FEE DIFFERENTIAL   .12
SAN DIEGO 1.9% ELECTRIC FRANCHISE FEE DIFFERENTIAL   .21
STATE SURCHARGE TAX 0.00020 PER KWHR   .02

ITEMIZED BILLING	GAS	ELECTRIC
LIFELINE ALLOWANCE	26 THERMS	240 KWHR
LIFELINE USAGE	24 THERMS a $.41771	97 KWHR a $.08990
NON-LIFELINE USAGE		
CUSTOMER CHARGE	$1.70	$2.20

YOUR ENERGY CONSERVATION HISTORY

THIS MONTH	BILLING DAYS	GAS		ELECTRIC	
		THERMS BILLED	THERMS PER DAY	KWHR BILLED	KWHR PER DAY
THIS YEAR	31	24	0.8	97	3.1
LAST YEAR					
PERCENT INCREASE + OR DECREASE -					

*** IMPORTANT ***

WE SHOW YOU RECEIVE
LIFELINE ALLOWANCES
FOR NATURAL GAS
BASIC AND WATER
HEATING AND HOME
HEATING AND ELECTRIC
BASIC.

WHEN MAKING INQUIRIES CONTACT OUR OFFICE AT:

SATELLITE OFFICE - LA JOLLA FEDERAL
1100 WALL ST   LA JOLLA   239-7511

PLEASE READ ENCLOSED
LITELINES FOR DETAILS

Electric bill

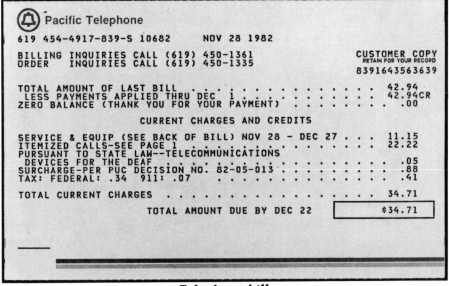

Telephone bill

Complete the following exchanges with an appropriate response using *cut down on*.

> *Example:* A: I'm so broke[27] that I can hardly[28] pay my bills anymore.
> B: Well, don't you think it's about time you *cut down on your expenses?*

1. A: Our last electric bill was $85.

   B: Well, don't look at me! You're the one who was turning on the air conditioning every day last month.

   A: You're right. I'd better _____ .

2. A: Do you realize that you made eleven long distance calls to Miami last month? Who were you calling anyway?

   B: My sister. How much was the phone bill?

   A: $137.

   B: What! I guess I'd better _____ .

3. A: I'm afraid I spent so much last month that I can't pay the rent by the first of the month.

   B: It's the same story every month! I even warned you last month that you were spending too much again. You really have to _____ .

● *run out (of)*: to have no more left.

Recall this sentence from the narrative:
> . . . he was *running out of* money . . . .

Complete the following exchanges with an appropriate response using *run out of*.

> *Example:* A: Why are you in such a hurry to find a new apartment?
> B: Because my lease is up[29] next month and I can't afford the rent increase, so I'm *running out of time.*
> (time)

---

[27]be broke: to not have money.
[28]hardly: barely; not likely.
[29]be up: expired; at an end.

1.   A: I have to stop painting for today.

        B: Why don't you finish the rest of the room now? You don't have much to do.

        A: I can't, I've _____ .

                                          (paint)

2.   A: I like your new fridge. Where did you buy it?

        B: I spotted[30] it on sale while I was shopping at Macy's the other day. I've decided to

              re-do[31] the whole kitchen, so I also bought floor tiles and new cabinets.

        A: Why didn't you buy a new stove while you were at it?[32] You really need one.

        B: I know, but _____ .

                                         (money)

3.   A: Did you move into your apartment last weekend?

        B: Yeah. It took us all day Saturday.

        A: Did you unpack everything?

        B: No. We couldn't finish. There was so much to do that we finally _____

        _____ .

                                         (energy)

● *take into account*: to consider various facts when making a decision.

Recall this sentence from the narrative:
> The rent seemed a little high, but after he *took into account* all the advantages, especially the convenient location, he gave the super a deposit.

Complete the following exchange with an appropriate response using *take into account*.

> ***Example:***   A: Why did you decide to buy a co-op[33] instead of renting?
>   B: When I *took into account all the advantages*, it seemed
>   like the best thing to do.

---

[30]spot: to notice
[31]re-do: to do again. In this case, to decorate again.
[32]while one is at it: during the time that.
[33]co-op (cooperative apartment): apartments owned jointly by the residents.

1. A: How come you didn't take that apartment? I know you were considering it. Couldn't

   you afford the rent?

   B: I thought I could, but I forgot to _____ .
   (utilities)

2. A: Didn't they make a big profit when they sold their co-op?

   B: Not as much as they expected. They weren't _____ .
   (all the fees)

3. A: Why don't you buy the house you want? You have enough cash for the down

   payment.

   B: Yes, but the problem is getting a mortgage.

   A: I'm sure you can get a mortgage.

   B: Yes, but can I afford it?

   A: Of course you can. Why not?

   B: I don't think you're _____ .
   (high interest rates)

● *keep (on)*: to continue.

Subject + keep (on) + Verb-ing

Recall this sentence from the narrative:
. . . Mr. Bacci *kept on* repeating . . . .

Complete the following exchanges with an appropriate response using *keep* or *keep on*. See if
you can add a phrase beginning with *until*.

Example: A: Are you still looking for a roommate?
          B: I'm afraid so. I haven't found anyone so far.
          A: *Well, you just have to keep on looking until you do.*

1. A: I've been trying to call the movers all day.

B: You mean you haven't gotten hold of[34] them yet? You'd better _____

_____ .

2.   A: I've been searching for an apartment for weeks now.

B: No luck yet, huh? Well, you just have to _____ .

3.   A: Who were you talking with this morning? I was calling all morning, but your line was

busy.

B: I was trying to get through to the landlord because I didn't have any hot water. But

his line was busy.

A: So what happened? Did you finally get hold of him?

B: Yes, I just _____ .

V. SITUATIONAL DIALOGUES

1.   Ms. Dow is going to look at an apartment.

MS. DOW: Hello. I'm here about the apartment you have for rent. I called this morning.
SUPER: Oh, yes. Ms. Dow?
MS. DOW: Yes.
SUPER: Come in. Come in. The apartment is on the fourth floor. The stairs are this way.
MS. DOW: Oh, you mean there's no elevator?
SUPER: This building is a four-floor walk-up. Don't worry. The exercise is good for you.
MS. DOW: I live on the fifth floor now, but we have a self-service elevator. Well, okay, let's go up and take a look.
(They enter the apartment)
MS. DOW: How much is the rent?
SUPER: This apartment is $345 a month, not including utilities. We're in the entrance hall here. On your right is the living room. It's nice and bright, isn't it?
MS. DOW: Yes, it sure is. I guess that's one advantage of living on the top floor. May I have a look at the bedroom?

---

[34]get hold of: to reach, contact.

SUPER: Yes, right this way. You see, it has windows on two sides, so you've got good cross ventilation.[35]

MS. DOW: How about the bathroom?

SUPER: Right here on the left. It's completely modern. It's got a new tub and toilet. The kitchen is also completely modern.

MS. DOW: Well, the apartment is small, but I think it's big enough for us.

SUPER: How many people?

MS. DOW: Just my husband and me.

SUPER: Okay. By the way, we don't allow pets.

MS. DOW: That's okay, we don't have any. I suppose you repaint the apartment when a new tenant moves in?

SUPER: We paint every three years. This apartment was just painted last year.

MS. DOW: I see. Do you require a deposit?

SUPER: Yes, there is a one-month deposit required.

MS. DOW: Well, I have to discuss it with my husband first. I'll let you know what we decide as soon as possible.

QUESTIONS

1.   What floor is the apartment on?
2.   What kind of building is the apartment in?
3.   How much is the rent?
4.   What's one advantage of living on the top floor?
5.   How often does the super repaint the apartment?
6.   How much deposit is required?
7.   What does Ms. Dow want to do before she decides about the apartment?

2.   On the telephone. Armand would like to make a long-distance call.

OPERATOR: May I help you?

ARMAND: Yes, I'd like to make a person-to-person, collect call.

OPERATOR: What is the person's name and number, please?

ARMAND: Andrea DiCarlo. Area code 615-921-1289.

OPERATOR: What's your name and number?

ARMAND: Armand DiCarlo, 212-765-6764.

OPERATOR: Thank you. (puts call through)

ANDREA: Hello.

OPERATOR: I have a person-to-person call for Andrea DiCarlo from Armand DiCarlo. Will you accept the charges?

---

[35]cross ventilation: air flowing through (a room).

ANDREA: Yes, I will.

OPERATOR: Okay. Go ahead.

QUESTIONS

1.   What kind of call does Armand want to make?
2.   What information does the operator need in order to make the call?

3.   On the telephone. Priscilla dials a wrong number.

HELEN: Hello.

PRISCILLA: Hello. Is Cindy there, please?

HELEN: Cindy? There's no Cindy here. You have the wrong number.

PRISCILLA: Oh, I'm sorry. Did I dial 778-9876?

HELEN: No. This is 778-8876.

PRISCILLA: Oh, sorry to bother you.

HELEN: That's okay.

QUESTIONS

1.   Who does Priscilla want to talk to?
2.   What mistake did Priscilla make?

4.   On the telephone. Oded is calling his wife at her office.

BETH: Hello. W.E. Enterprises. May I help you?

ODED: Hello. May I speak to Janet, please?

BETH: I'm sorry, but she isn't here now. She stepped out for a few moments. Can I take a message?

ODED: Yes, please. Tell her Oded called and to please call me at home this afternoon.

BETH: Does she have your number?

ODED: Yes, I hope so. I'm her husband!

QUESTIONS

1.   Who is Oded calling?
2.   What message does he leave?

5.   On the telephone. Rob is trying to reach his friend, Hayden.

JAYNE: Hello.

ROB: Hello. May I speak to Hayden, please?

JAYNE: I'm sorry, he's not here now. May I ask who's calling?

ROB: This is his friend, Rob. Do you know what time he'll be back?

JAYNE: Well, I'm not sure. Probably after 10 P.M.

ROB: Would you mind taking a message?

JAYNE: No problem.

ROB: Just tell him I called and that I'll call him back tomorrow.

JAYNE: Okay. I'll be sure that he gets the message.

ROB: Thank you.

QUESTIONS

1.   What time will Hayden get back?
2.   What message does Rob leave for him?

6.   On the telephone. Tom wants to get some information. He dials 411:

OPERATOR: Directory Assistance.

TOM: I'd like the number of James Mayer on Northern Boulevard.

OPERATOR: Is that in Manhattan?

TOM: No, it's in Nassau County.

OPERATOR: You have to dial the area code and 555-1212. The area code for Nassau County is 516.

TOM: Okay. Thank you.

QUESTIONS

1.   What information does Tom want?
2.   What does the operator tell him to do?

VI. VOCABULARY BUILDER

apartment   apartment building/apartment complex/apartment dweller/apartment house/apartment hunting/apartment lease/apartment living/apartment sharing/apartment super/co-op apartment/low-income apartment/luxury apartment/rent-controlled apartment

VII. ROLE PLAY SUGGESTIONS

1.   Call up and inquire about an ad you saw in the newspaper for (a) an apartment to rent, (b) an apartment to share, (c) an apartment to sublet.
2.   Go to look at an apartment. Ask about (a) rent, (b) utilities, (c) deposit.

VIII. PREPOSITION PRACTICE

A. Prepositions That Show Logical Relationships

USE **OF** TO SHOW:

relationship of a part to the whole

One of + Plural + Singular Verb
Noun

*One **OF** the doors doesn't lock.*

One of + Plural + Singular Verb
Pronoun

*One **OF** them doesn't lock.*

<u>much</u> of + Singular Non- + Singular
some   Count Noun   Verb
none
all

*Some **OF** the money is missing.*

origin   Maria is a citizen **OF** Chile.
Jane is a native **OF** Ohio.

material   These appliances are made **OF** steel.

content   He has a box **OF** keys.

kind   My agent has a list **OF** available apartments.
The new tenant is a doctor **OF** internal medicine.

USE **FROM** TO SHOW:

origin   Maria is **FROM** Chile.
Jane is **FROM** Ohio.

source   We got our apartment **FROM** an ad in the Times.

Complete the following exchanges with the appropriate preposition.

1. Two movers:

   A: Can you give me a hand with these things? They are made _____

   heavy wood and I can't carry them by myself.

   B: Sure, no problem, but just a minute. First, I have to put down this box _____

   _____ books and then put that bag _____

   clothes in the trunk. Then I can help.

2. Real estate agent and a client:

    A: I'd like to see a one-bedroom or studio[36] on the top floor.

    B: I'm sorry, we've rented all _____ them. We still have some apartments on the first floor, though. They are large and airy.

    A: Well, I prefer top floor apartments because they are usually brighter. Tell me, do the apartments on the first floor have large windows?

    B: Most _____ them do. In fact, one _____ them has floor to ceiling windows facing south, so it gets a lot of sunshine. Why don't you let me show it to you?

    A: Okay. Let's have a look.

3. Real estate agent and a client:

    A: I'm looking for a two-bedroom apartment with a nice view of the lake, and I can't spend more than $200 a month.

    B: What! Where are you _____ ?

    A: I'm _____ Newtown, Nevada.

    B: Well, around here you can't even get a one-bedroom basement apartment for that price!

4. Real estate agent and client:

    A: I'm interested in buying that condominium,[37] but I don't know if I can.

---

[36]studio: a one-room apartment.
[37]condominium: an apartment complex where each tenant owns his/her apartment.

B: Is the mortgage a problem?

A: No, I have the money, but I don't know if they will allow me to buy it.

B: Why?

A: You see, I'm not a resident _____ the United States. I'm a

citizen _____ Pakistan and here on business.

B: There's no problem if you have the cash.

B. Additional Preposition Combinations

look for (IS):
to search

We are *looking for* a larger apartment.

look at (IS):
to view

They *looked at* over ten apartments before they found the one they liked.

look up (S):
to search for (as in a dictionary)

You'd better *look up* those words if you don't understand them.

look over (S):
to examine

When you have a chance, just *look over* the lease.

look out (for) (IS):
to be careful of

Look out for apartments with no fire exits.
Look out! A car is coming!

talk about (IS):
to speak on a subject; to discuss

She seldom *talks about* her problems.
Let's *talk about* that before you go.

talk on (IS):
to speak on the radio, T.V., or telephone

He *talks on* the radio about consumer protection.

talk over (S):
to discuss

We have to *talk over* this problem before we make a decision.

Complete the following exchanges with the appropriate two-word verbs.

1. A: Harold is always _____ the telephone, so our bill is always high.

   B: He doesn't make a lot of long distance calls, does he?

A: No, but those message units[38] add up.

B: Well, instead of complaining to me, you should _____ it

with him.

2. A: Would you do me a favor?

B: What is it?

A: Will you _____ this lease when you have some time? I want to

make sure I know what I'm signing.

B: Okay. Let's do it right now. There's no time like the present.

3. A: Are you still _____ an apartment?

B: Yes. I've _____ a half dozen places already, but they were all too

expensive.

A: Have you tried going to an agency?

B: No. Can you recommend a good one?

A: Well, I think they are all more or less[39] the same. Why don't you just _____

_____ one _____ in the phone book?

4. A: It's awfully[40] hot in here. Let me open a window.

B: _____ ! That window is cracked.

A: Don't worry. I'll be careful with it.

5. A real estate agent has just showed an apartment to someone:

A: What do you think?

---

[38]message units: units charged per minute for local calls.
[39]more or less: about.
[40]awfully: very.

B: I like it; it's a lovely apartment.

A: Do you want it then?

B: Well, I have to _____ it _____ with my

husband first.

A: That's fine. Just give me a call if you decide to take it.

6 THE "INEXPENSIVE" MEAL

I. NARRATIVE

Shortly after Mr. Lin had finished moving into his new apartment on Saturday, he went grocery shopping. So many days of restaurant food had made him really **look forward to** cooking his favorite dishes, but he **was in for** a big disappointment. When he tried to turn on his stove, nothing happened. No one had told him that he was supposed to call the gas company first and open an account. He then went to the refrigerator in order to put away his groceries. He now discovered that the electricity was also disconnected.

In spite of this problem, Mr. Lin still had to eat that night. In fact, he was getting hungrier and hungrier, so he went out and walked around his neighborhood until he found a small cafeteria-style restaurant. The restaurant was not crowded and had a big sign above the entrance: "The Home of the Inexpensive Meal." Mr. Lin went in, walked over to the counter, and chose several dishes.

When he got to the cashier, she added everything up and said, "That'll be $15.75." Mr. Lin could not believe his ears;[1] he asked the woman to please add up the bill again. When the cash register once more showed $15.75, the cashier said, "Well, you do have all main dishes." Mr. Lin was too embarrassed to return any of the plates, so he forced a smile and paid $15.75 for the "inexpensive meal." After he had finished eating, he felt so down[2] that all he wanted to do[3] was go home and go to bed. When he got home, he set up some candles and began to read. After he had read for a while, he felt better and before long he fell sound asleep.

QUESTIONS

1. Why was Mr. Lin really looking forward to cooking at home?
2. Why was Mr. Lin disappointed?

---

[1]can't believe one's ears: difficult to believe.
[2]down: in a bad mood, sad, depressed.
[3]all (he wanted to do): the only thing (he wanted to do).

3. Why wasn't there any gas?
4. What did Mr. Lin decide to do about dinner?
5. How come the bill in the cafeteria was so high?
6. Why didn't Mr. Lin just return some of the dishes?
7. What did he set up candles for?

II. DIALOGUE

Mr. Lin enters a restaurant to have dinner. He sits at a table.

LIN: Excuse me, may I have a menu, please?

WAITRESS: Oh, this is a cafeteria-style restaurant. Just get in line over there and help yourself.

LIN: Okay. What kind of food do you have?

WAITRESS: We have quite a variety of dishes. The choice is yours.

LIN: Okay. Thanks.

   (Mr. Lin has selected his dishes and walks over to the beverage counter.)

CLERK: Anything to drink, sir?

LIN: I'd like tea with lemon, please. And could I possibly have an extra slice of lemon?

CLERK: Sure.

LIN: Thanks. Where do I pay?

CLERK: The cashier is straight ahead, at the end of the counter.

QUESTIONS

1. How come Mr. Lin can't get a menu?
2. What would Mr. Lin like to drink?
3. Where is the cashier located?

III. GRAMMAR

A. Past Perfect Tense

We use the Past Perfect to talk about the first of two actions that happened in the past.

FORM: | had + Verb (Past Participle)

Affirmative: She *had ordered* takeout food[4] before we arrived.

Negative: She *hadn't ordered* takeout food before we arrived.

Question: *Had* she *ordered* takeout food before we arrived?

Wh- Questions: What *had* she *ordered* before we arrived?

Who/What/Which as Subject: Who *had ordered* the takeout food before we arrived?

Note: We usually use the Past Perfect together with the Past Tense; therefore, there are two actions in the sentence. Both actions are in the past; use the Past Perfect for the action which happened first.

B. Past Perfect Continuous Tense

We use the Past Perfect Continuous Tense to talk about an action that continued up to a certain time in the past.

FORM: had + been + Verb-ing

Affirmative: Warren *had been working* as a waiter for two years when the restaurant closed.

Negative: Warren *hadn't been working* as a waiter long when the restaurant closed.

Question: *Had* Warren *been working* as a waiter long when the restaurant closed?

Wh- Question: How long *had* Warren *been working* as a waiter when the restaurant closed?

Who/What/Which as Subject: Who *had been working* as a waiter for two years when the restaurant closed?

Dialogues

Complete the following dialogues using *Past Perfect, Past Perfect Continuous,* or *Past Tense.*

1.   Laura and Nancy are talking about Nancy's date the night before.

LAURA: How _____ your date _____
(go)

with Rudolph last night? He _____ you to the movies, didn't he?
(take)

---

[4]takeout food: food that a person takes out of the restaurant (instead of eating it there).

NANCY: Well, he _____ to take me to the movies, but he
                          (promise)

_____ me to dinner instead. But, you know, I _____
      (take)   (care; negative)

for[5] the restaurant. The atmosphere _____ terrible and so
                                                      (be)

_____ the food.
              (be)

LAURA: Well, what restaurant _____ you _____ to?
                                                                          (go)

NANCY: An Italian seafood restaurant called Caro's.

LAURA: Oh, that place! Why _____ he _____
                                                                    (take)

you there?

NANCY: He _____ he _____ their shrimp dishes
                      (say)   (hear)

couldn't be beat.[6]

QUESTIONS

1. Where had Rudolph promised to take Nancy?
2. Where did he take Nancy instead?
3. What did Nancy think of the restaurant?
4. What kind of restaurant did they go to?
5. Why did Rudolph choose that restaurant?

2.   Sari has invited her friends, Anna and Tina, to dinner. She is waiting for them in the
restaurant. Tina enters the restaurant alone.

SARI: Hi, Tina. _____ you _____ Anna to
                                              (ask; negative question)

come, too?

TINA: Yes, but she _____ already _____
                                                                      (finish)

dinner when I _____ her to come.
                              (ask)

---

[5]care for: to like (used in negatives and questions).
[6]cannot be beat: the best; nothing is better than.

SARI: Oh, too bad. You know, I _____ her one night last week and
(call)

_____ her to dinner, but she _____
(invite)   (prepare; negative)

for her exams so she _____ any time.
(have; negative)

TINA: Yes, she was quite busy all last week.

QUESTIONS

1. How come Anna didn't go with her friends?
2. Why didn't Anna have time to go to dinner with Sari last week?

3. Jim and Tom are old friends. They haven't seen each other for a while; one day they run into each other on the street.

JIM: Tom! Wow, it's been a long time!

TOM: It sure has. How have you been?

JIM: Very well. How about you? Are you still a waiter at the Red Manor?

TOM: Oh, no. That place _____ out of business a few months ago.
(go)

JIM: Really? How long _____ you _____ there
(work)

when they _____ ?
(close)

TOM: About two years.

QUESTIONS

1. When did the Red Manor restaurant close?
2. How long had Tom been working there when it went out of business?

4. Sylvia is talking with her colleague, Linda.

SYLVIA: Why _____ you _____
(take; negative question)

Sheena to that Greek restaurant on South Street last night?

LINDA: She _____ there before and _____
(be)   (want)

to try someplace different.

SYLVIA: Oh, I _____ she _____
          (know; negative)

already _____ there. What _____ she
        (eat)

_____ the food?
          (think of)

LINDA: She _____ she _____ better Greek food
             (say)   (taste)

back home in New Orleans.

QUESTIONS

1.   Why didn't Sheena want to go to the Greek restaurant?
2.   What didn't Sylvia know?
3.   What was Sheena's opinion of the food?

5.   Peter is talking with his friend, Joe.

PETER: _____ you _____ from Frank yesterday?
                                  (hear)

JOE: Yes, he _____ me last night. Why?
                           (call)

PETER: Oh, I just know that he _____ to reach you for a few days.
                                        (try)

I'm glad he finally _____ hold of you.
                                  (get)

QUESTIONS

1.   What had Frank been trying to do?
2.   When did Frank get hold of Joe?

C. Sentence Patterns

Recall this sentence from the narrative:
So many days of restaurant cooking had *made him* really look forward to cooking his favorite dishes . . . .

PATTERN

> Subject + make + someone do something
> someone + Adjective

She *made the children wash* their hands.
The food *made him ill*.

Complete the following exchanges with an appropriate response using *make*.

> ***Example:*** A: Will you stop talking about food?
> B: Why? What's the matter?
> A: You're *making me hungry*!
> (me-hungry)

1. In a steak house:

A: Look at that steak! I ordered it well done, but it's rare. In fact, it's practically raw.

B: Well, _____ .
(them-take it back)

2. In a coffee shop:

A: The check adds up to $17.75. How is that possible?

B: The waitress probably made a mistake. You'd better _____ .
(her-check it again)

3. In a pizza shop:

A: Order me another soda, will you?

B: Another one? You just finished one.

A: I know, but the pizza _____ .
(me-thirsty)

4. A: Let me tell you, don't ever eat out in a restaurant with Irwin. I was out with him last

night. Never again!

B: Why not?

A: He ate like a pig! He really _____ .
(me-sick)[7]

5. In a sidewalk cafe:

A: Wow! Look at all the desserts they have here: chocolate layer cake, strawberry

shortcake, lemon meringue pie, chocolate mousse, apple pie . . . .

B: There's really enough to _____ isn't there?
(your mouth water)[8]

---

[7]make me sick: (a) to make one feel disgusted; (b) to cause one to become ill.
[8]make one's mouth water: to make one want to eat or drink something.

6.   In a restaurant:

A: Let me pay the check.

B: No, you always pay. I'm paying this time.

A: Let me handle it.

B: No. Now don't _____ . I'm paying and that's final.
$\qquad\qquad\qquad\qquad\qquad\qquad\qquad$ (me – angry)

A: Okay. Okay.

Recall this sentence from the narrative:
In fact, he *was getting hungrier and hungrier* . . . .

PATTERNS FOR ADJECTIVES

$$\text{get} + \begin{cases} \dfrac{\text{more and more}}{\text{less and less}} + \begin{array}{l}\text{two-or-more-syllable}\\\text{Adjective}\end{array} \\[2ex] \text{Adjective-er and Adjective-er} \end{cases}$$

This restaurant *is getting more and more expensive.*

PATTERNS FOR NOUNS

$$\dfrac{\text{more and more}}{\text{less and less}} + \text{Non-Count Noun}$$

$$\dfrac{\text{more and more}}{\text{fewer and fewer}} + \text{Count Noun}$$

More and more health food restaurants are opening all over.

Complete the following exchanges using one of the above patterns.

Example: In a restaurant:
   A: The check comes to $32. Can you believe it? Thirty-two dollars for lunch!
   B: What can you do? It's getting *more and more expensive*
   $\qquad\qquad\qquad\qquad\qquad\qquad\qquad\qquad$ (expensive)
   to eat out these days.

42ND ST. DINER

Fruits, Juices and Appetizers

ORANGE JUICE	.60
TOMATO JUICE	.50
GRAPEFRUIT JUICE	.50
PINEAPPLE JUICE	.50
V-8 JUICE	.60
APPLE JUICE	.50
HALF GRAPEFRUIT	.90
FRESH FRUIT CUP	.90

Eggs & Omelettes

TWO COUNTRY FRESH EGGS,	
Any Style	1 40
with Ham, Bacon or Sausage	2 10
TWO COUNTRY FRESH EGGS	
with Corned Beef Hash	2 10

Griddle Specialties

THREE GOLDEN PANCAKES	
with Butter and Syrup	1.50
with Bacon, Ham or Sausage	2.30
with Two Eggs	2.60
FRENCH TOAST	
with Butter and Syrup	1.50
with Bacon, Ham or Sausage	2.30
with Two Eggs	2.60

Entrees

BAKED CHICKEN	3.25
SALISBURY STEAK	3.25
BAKED MEATLOAF	2.90
BAKED VIRGINIA HAM	3.85
BREADED PORK CHOP	3.00
FRANKS and BEANS	2.75

ABOVE SERVED WITH POTATO AND VEGETABLE

Beefburger Corner

4 OZ. OF PURE BEEF

BEEFBURGER	1.60
CHEESEBURGER	1.80
when served with bacon	.60 extra
PIZZA BURGER	2.00
SWISS CHEESEBURGER	1.90
CHILI BURGER	2.10
TWIN HAMBURGER DELUXE	3.80
BEEFBURGER DELUXE	2.60
CHEESEBURGER DELUXE	2.80
SWISS BURGER DELUXE	2.90
PIZZA BURGER DELUXE	3.00
CHILI BURGER DELUXE	3.00

ALL ABOVE SERVED WITH COLE SLAW AND PICKLE
ALL DELUXES SERVED WITH LETTUCE TOMATO
FRENCH FRIES, COLE SLAW AND PICKLE

CALIFORNIA SALAD
Cottage Cheese
Jello
Fruit Salad
3.00

GREEK SALAD
Fresh Chopped Greens,
Anchovies, Olives
and Feta Cheese
Small 3.00
Large 4.00

Desserts

CHEESE CAKE	1 00
JELLO	80
LAYER CAKES	90
FRESH FRUIT SALAD	.90

Sandwich Board

EGG:

FRIED EGG	85
BACON or HAM and EGG	1 75
SALAMI and EGG	1 85
PASTRAMI and EGG	2 00
EGG SALAD and BACON	2 25
WESTERN EGG	1 75

CHEESE:

AMERICAN CHEESE	1 55
AMERICAN CHEESE and HAM	2 25
SWISS CHEESE	1 80
SWISS CHEESE and HAM	2 15
PROVOLONE CHEESE	1.50
MUENSTER CHEESE	1.65
CREAM CHEESE	1.10
CREAM CHEESE and JELLY	1 35
CREAM CHEESE and TOMATO	1 35
GRILLED AMERICAN CHEESE	1.65
GRILLED AMERICAN CHEESE	
with HAM or BACON	2.10
GRILLED AMERICAN CHEESE	
with TOMATO	1.90
GRILLED SWISS CHEESE	2 00
GRILLED SWISS CHEESE with HAM	
or BACON	2.25
GRILLED SWISS CHEESE	
with TOMATO	2.25

MEAT:

MEATLOAF	2.10
MEATBALL	2.00
BOILED HAM SANDWICH	1.90
BACON, LETTUCE and TOMATO	1.85
BEEF SALAMI	2.00
BOLOGNA	1.75
LIVERWURST	1.75

Side Orders

COLE SLAW	.80
POTATO SALAD	.80
ONION RINGS	1.25
HOT VEGETABLES	.80
LETTUCE and TOMATO	1.00
COTTAGE CHEESE	.95
BAKED BEANS	.90

Beverages

COFFEE	40
SANKA	50
TEA	40
ICED TEA	65
ICED COFFEE	65
HOT CHOCOLATE	55
ICED COLD MILK	.75

Diner menu

159

1. In a restaurant:

    A: I asked the waiter for a glass of water ten minutes ago.

    B: I know. The service _____ here.
                                (bad)

2. In a restaurant:

    A: Wow! This dish is delicious. How's yours?

    B: Great. In fact, I think the food is even better than the last time we were here.

    A: You're right. This place just keeps _____ .
                                                (good)

3. A: How was the restaurant where you ate last night?

    B: The food was quite good, but the prices were outrageous.[9]

    A: I know. It's _____ to find a restaurant that has both good food
                        (difficult)

    and reasonable prices.

4. In a fast-food restaurant:

    A: Business isn't very good tonight.

    B: It hasn't been good for a while.

    A: I guess _____ are eating at home nowadays.
                        (people)

5. A: Don't let that hot sauce stay on the meat too long.

    B: Why?

    A: Because it will _____ until it's impossible to eat.
                            (hot)

---

[9]outrageous: in excess, too much; too high (price).

IV. EXPRESSIONS AND IDIOMS

● *look forward to*: to expect with pleasure.

```
Subject + look forward to + Verb-ing
                             Noun
```

Note: We usually use *look forward to* with the Present (or Past) Continuous Tense.

Recall this sentence from the narrative:

So many days of restaurant food had made him really *look forward to* cooking his favorite dishes . . . .

Complete the following exchanges with an appropriate response using *look forward to.*

Example: A: Do you want to go out to dinner with us tonight?
B: *No, thank you. I'm looking forward to having an eve-*
  (have an evening at home)
ning at home for once.[10]

1. A: You didn't go to Georgia's dinner party last night. How come?

    B: I had already accepted another invitation before she told me about her party.

    A: She was really disappointed. She _____ .
      (see you)

2. A: Have you been to the new French restaurant that opened last week? You know, the

      one in the downtown shopping mall?

    B: I'm going there tonight.

    A: Oh, you'll love it. It's super!

    B: So I've heard. Everybody has been raving about[11] the place, so _____

      there.

---

[10]for once: as a change from the usual.
[11]rave about: to praise very highly.

3.   A: I understand Anton's restaurant has hired a new chef.

       B: Yes, that's what the newspaper said. I haven't been there in a long time, so I

       _____ .
                                       (go back)

4.   A: I _____ to Enrique's new restaurant tomorrow night, aren't you?
                     (go)

       B: Well, I was.

       A: What do you mean?

       B: He went out of business two days ago.

       A: What? So fast? He's only been in business for a month or so.

       B: I know, but when they opened that fast-food joint[12] right next door to him two

           weeks ago, his business went right down the drain.[13]

5.   A: Why don't you have dinner with us at that new seafood place tonight? The food is

           great: crab, shrimp, oysters . . . .

       B: Sounds good, but no thanks. I _____ tonight.
                                           (a home-cooked meal)

● *be in for*: unable to avoid, sure to get.

+---------------------------------------+
| Subject + be in for + a + Noun |
+---------------------------------------+

Recall this sentence from the narrative:
So many days of restaurant cooking had made him really look forward to cooking his favorite dishes, but *he was in for* a big disappointment.

> ***Example:***   A: Morris and Jill are going to the Sunrise Diner tonight.
>   B: Oh, the last time I went there I found that their prices
>   had almost doubled.
>   A: No kidding! I guess Morris and Jill *are in for quite a*
>   (surprise)
>
>   *surprise.*

---
[12]joint: a small, usually cheap, restaurant.
[13](go) down the drain: get lost; be spoiled.

1. A: What are you ordering?

    B: I'm having the fried chicken.

    A: Oh, I had that last time I was here.

    B: How was it?

    A: Fabulous! You _____ .

(treat)

2. A: Harry decided to have "Quality Catering" cater[14] his party next week.

    B: Oh, too bad he didn't talk with me first. They catered my party last weekend. The

        food was only so-so[15] and the service poor.

    A: Well, then I'm afraid Harry _____ .

(disappointment)

3. A: Look at that line in front of the restaurant!

    B: Oh, I don't know why we didn't call and make a reservation. Now it looks like we

        _____ .

(long wait)

4. A: Do you know I'm going into the restaurant business?

    B: Really? Well, I hate to tell you how many restaurant businesses fail each year.

    A: Why are you always so negative?

    B: I'm sorry. I didn't mean to be. It's just that you may _____

        _____ . The restaurant business isn't an easy one.

(more than you bargained for)[16]

    A: I know it's not, but I'm determined to make a go of it.[17]

---

[14]cater a party: to have a company supply all the food and drinks as well as serve the guests.
[15]so-so: not very good.
[16]bargain for: be ready for; expect. *More than one bargained for/on*: to have more trouble or problems than one expected.
[17]make a go of: to make something succeed.

● *in spite of*: despite, no matter.

> in spite of + $\frac{\text{the/a}}{\text{this/that}}$ + Noun

Recall this sentence from the narrative:
  In spite of this problem, Mr. Lin still had to eat.

Complete the following exchanges with an appropriate response using *in spite of.*

  Example: A: How was your luncheon at the country club[18] yesterday?
  B: *Well, I enjoyed the food in spite of the bad service.*
                (bad service)

1.   A: How about eating at the cafeteria today?

  B: How come you always want to eat there? It's always so crowded with students, and

  I hate crowds.

  A: I know, but it's the cheapest place around, so I always end up going there

  _____ .
                (crowd)

2.   A: I heard you went to a barbecue yesterday. Did you have fun?

  B: Well, it was a bit chilly outside, but we had a good time _____ .
                                (weather)

3.   A: We finally tried that new restaurant you had recommended a few months ago.

  B: What did you think?

  A: The food was excellent, but we didn't realize it was such an expensive place.

  B: What did the bill come to?

  A: $150 for four people.

  B: That's pretty steep![19] Are you sorry you went?

  A: No. _____ we're glad we went.
                (expense)

----

[18]country club: an elegant club which has recreation facilities.
[19]steep: expensive.

4. A: Let's go over to Water Street for lunch today. There are a lot of street vendors[20]

over there and it's always fun to watch all the people.

B: But I don't feel like eating a hot dog.

A: You don't have to. There are all kinds of food stands[21] and pushcarts[22] there. You

can get Chinese food, Greek food, Italian food, any kind of food. There are people

selling salads, yogurt, ice cream, health food, shish kabob . . . .

B: Yes, yes, but it's too noisy to eat out on the street.

A: Oh, c'mon. I'm sure you can have a good time _____ .
　　　　　　　　　　　　　　　　　　　　　　　　　　　　　　(noise)

V. SITUATIONAL DIALOGUES

1. Paul and Barbara enter a restaurant.

HOSTESS: How many, sir?
PAUL: Table for two, please.
HOSTESS: Do you have a reservation?
PAUL: Yes, Mr. and Mrs. Paul West. I called about half an hour ago.
HOSTESS: Oh, yes. Here is your name on the list.
PAUL: Is it possible to sit by the window?
HOSTESS: Certainly. Right this way.

QUESTIONS

　1. In whose name did Paul make the reservations?
　2. When did Paul West make the reservation?
　3. Where would they like to sit?

2. David and Sheila are sitting in a restaurant.

WAITER: May I take your order now?
DAVID: We're not ready to order yet. We need a couple of minutes more.
WAITER: Fine. Can I get you something to drink in the meantime?

---

[20]street vendors: people who sell food in the streets.
[21]food stands: small outdoor structures where people sell fruit, vegetables, and other foods.
[22]pushcarts: The carts which the street vendors use. The carts can have stoves to keep food hot or
　iceboxes to keep food cold.

DAVID: Sheila?

SHEILA: A glass of red wine would be fine.

DAVID: I'll have the same. Wait, why don't you bring us a carafe.[23]
(The waiter returns in a few minutes)

DAVID: Okay, we're ready now.

SHEILA: I'll have a sirloin steak please.

WAITER: How would you like that done, Ma'am?

SHEILA: Medium rare.

WAITER: This evening we have broccoli, peas in white sauce, string beans in wine sauce, or corn on the cob.

SHEILA: Broccoli, please. And I'll have a baked potato as well.

WAITER: Would you care for some soup? The soup of the day is onion soup.

SHEILA: No. No soup for me.

DAVID: I'd like the fried shrimp platter. And a bowl of clam chowder.

WAITER: Fine. What salad dressing would you like?

SHEILA: French.

DAVID: I'll have blue cheese.

WAITER: Okay. Thank you.

QUESTIONS

1.   What do David and Sheila want to drink?
2.   How would Sheila like her steak?
3.   What does David order?
4.   What kind of salad dressing does Sheila want?

3.   Jennifer and Carl have just finished eating in a restaurant.

CARL: Waiter! May we have the check please?

WAITER: Here you are, sir.

JENNIFER: Let me have the check. It's my treat.

CARL: Oh no. I'll tell you what. Let's go dutch.[24]

JENNIFER: No. I'm paying and that's that. (To the waiter) Do you take American Express?

WAITER: Yes, we do.
(He takes her card and returns with a charge slip)
Just sign here, Ma'am.

JENNIFER: Carl, how much tip should I leave?

CARL: It's up to[25] you, but I usually leave fifteen or twenty percent.

---

[23]carafe: a container used to serve wine.
[24]go dutch: each person pays for himself/herself.
[25]be up to (someone/something): to depend on.

·MENU·

APPETIZERS

JUMBO SHRIMP COCKTAIL	5.75
CRAB COCKTAIL Chunks of Snow Crab topped with our own House Cocktail Sauce	4.75

SALADS

HOUSE GARDEN SALAD Fresh Iceberg and Romaine Lettuce topped with Cucumbers, Tomatoes (Choice of Dressing)	3.50
CHEF'S SALAD Fresh Lettuce topped with Ham, Turkey, American and Swiss Cheeses, Slices (Choice of Dressing)	5.25

ENTREES

Available after 5:00 PM
All entrees served with Bread and Butter.
Choice of Dinner Salad or Soup of the Day.
Choice of one: Steak Fries, Rice Pilaf or Baked Potato.

RIB EYE STEAK, charboiled	10.50
T-BONE STEAK, charboiled	12.75
BROILED CENTER CUT PORK CHOPS	7.50
BROILED HALIBUT STEAK	8.75
TROUT w/ALMONDS, pan fried	7.50

SIDE ORDERS

Cheezy Garlic Bread	1.75
Dinner Salad	1.50
Steak Fries	1.50
Onion Rings	1.25

BEVERAGES

Coffee	.75
Tea	.75
Soft Drinks	.75
Milk	.75

DESSERTS

Chocolate Cheesecake	2.75
Blueberry Cheesecake	2.50

Restaurant menu

QUESTIONS

1. Who offered to pay the check first?
2. What does Carl suggest?
3. What does Jennifer insist on?

4. Don and Barbara are in a restaurant. They have just finished eating.

DON: Waiter, would you bring us the check, please?

WAITER: Yes. Here you are.

DON (looking at the check):   I don't think this is correct. Would you check it again, please?

WAITER: Certainly. (adds up the check again) The total is correct, sir.

BARBARA: Why do you think it's incorrect, Don?

DON: It seems too high.

BARBARA (to the waiter):   May I see the check for a moment?

WAITER: Of course.

BARBARA: Oh, yes, there is a mistake here. We didn't order dessert. Could you please take this off the check?

WAITER: Oh, I'm terribly sorry. I'll change it for you.

QUESTIONS

1. Why does Don think that the check is incorrect?
2. What was the mistake?

VI. VOCABULARY BUILDER

food   baked food/ethnic food/fast food/fried food/seafood/spicy food/ takeout food

bar   clam bar/dessert bar/juice bar/salad bar/snack bar

dish   cold dish/hot dish/low-calorie dish/spicy dish

VII. ROLE PLAY SUGGESTIONS

1. Call a restaurant and reserve a table.
2. You are in a restaurant. Order (a) breakfast, (b) lunch, (c) dinner.

VIII. PREPOSITION PRACTICE

A. Prepositions That Show Logical Relationships

USE **FOR** TO SHOW:

purpose (i.e., in order to get, have, etc.)	People go to McDonalds, Burger King, and Wendy's **FOR** fast-food meals.
comparison	**FOR** a Mid-Eastern restaurant, the food is very bland. [i.e., compared to other Mid-Eastern restaurants, the food at this one is bland.]

USE **ON** AND **ABOUT** TO SHOW:

a subject or topic

I just bought a book **ABOUT** Chinese cooking.
                         ON

She generally gives lectures **ABOUT** proper
                              ON

nutrition.

USE **EXCEPT** TO SHOW:

omission

No one can eat those spicy meals **EXCEPT** Cathy.

Everyone is ordering chef's salad **EXCEPT** Roger.

Complete the following exchanges with the appropriate preposition.

1. A: Oh, Janet, don't keep lecturing us _____ nutrition.

    B: Don't worry. No one here _____ me will be around[26] in a few

        years, if you keep on eating the way you do.

2. A: I prefer going to the local bakery _____ my pastries.

    B: I don't know. The supermarket has the same things at a cheaper price.

    A: They're not the same. This book _____ additives says that local

        bakeries don't use chemicals or preservatives.

    B: Nobody _____ you believes that.

---

[26]be around: be here, be alive.

3.   A: Marjorie, do me a favor, okay?

     B: Sure. What is it?

     A: Well, when you go to the butcher's _____ veal, pick up a few

          lamb chops for me.

     B: You got it.

4.   A: I'm taking Roger out _____ a vegetarian meal tonight.

     B: Whose idea was that?

     A: Mine. I wanted to try something different.

5.   A: Is that all you're eating?

     B: Yeah, I'm full.

     A: _____ such a big guy, you have a small appetite.

B. Additional Preposition Combinations

think about (IS):
to consider

think about your sensitive stomach.

Before you eat greasy foods again, you should

to have an opinion about a
situation/event

What do you *think about* that food poisoning
incident at Maxim's restaurant?

think of (IS):
to have an opinion of a person,
place, or thing

What do you *think of* that new French cafe on
Fourth Street?

to bring to mind

I can't *think of* the name of the place where
we ate last Saturday.

to consider

I'm *thinking of* going into the restaurant business. (In this case, *think of* has the same
meaning as *think about*.)

think up (S):
to invent, create by thinking

I wonder what you'll *think up* next.

eat up (S):
to eat all of something

He *ate up* the appetizers.

eat out (IS):
to eat at a restaurant

We haven't *eaten out* in months.

Complete the following exchanges with the appropriate preposition combinations.

1.   A: What a day! I didn't even have time to _____ what we are

going to eat tonight.

B: I'd like to _____ tonight; perhaps we can go to a Spanish

restaurant.

2.   A: Melvin, can't you see your ice cream is melting?

B: I know, that's why I'm _____ it _____ as

fast as I can.

3.   Two people are eating in a fancy restaurant:

A: What do you _____ their entree[27] selection?

B: Incredible! Who _____ all these exotic[28] dishes?

A: They have a great new chef. He's created a lot of new dishes. I'm sure you won't be

disappointed in the food.

4.   A: Mom, I'm full. I can't eat anymore.

B: But you haven't touched your vegetables. Before you can leave the table, you must

_____ your vegetables.

5.   A: The aroma of this Mid-Eastern restaurant reminds me of my grandmother's home.

B: Well, it makes me _____ a spice shop that I used to go to when

I was a kid.[29]

_____

[27]entree: main course.
[28]exotic: uncommon, strange.
[29]kid: small child.

7 HOW WILL MR. LIN FURNISH HIS APARTMENT?

I. NARRATIVE

After Mr. Lin paid his deposit fees to the electric and gas companies, he was practically broke. He had only a few dollars left to spend on furniture. A fellow student, Mr. Gupti, told him that most students furnish their apartments with odds and ends[1] that they find on the streets. At first, Mr. Lin didn't believe his classmate, but then one afternoon, as he was walking home from class, he saw a couple of students with lamps, chairs, and tables. On the corner in front of a large apartment building there was a pile of old, beat-up[2] furniture and students were simply taking what they wanted before the sanitation truck hauled everything to the city dump.

Mr. Lin walked over to the pile and picked up two slightly damaged chairs and a small table. As the weeks went by,[3] Mr. Lin found other "street furniture" and took home a lamp, a bookcase, two more chairs and a small dresser. "Soon this place will be completely furnished," he thought. "The only things I'll need to buy are a new bed and a desk."

One morning Mr. Lin opened the local newspaper and saw a large advertisement for Crazy Jack's: "CRAZY JACK'S FURNITURE STORE WILL BEGIN ITS ANNUAL BED SALE TOMORROW AND WE WILL NOT BE UNDERSOLD. IF YOU FIND A CHEAPER BED, WE'LL GIVE YOU DOUBLE YOUR MONEY BACK!" The next day he decided to go there to look over the selection and check out the prices.

As soon as[4] he entered Crazy Jack's, which was packed with customers, a smiling, high-pressure salesman approached him. The salesman said, "Hi, my name is Sam, and I'll be glad to show you around. Now, what'll it be[5] today?" Mr. Lin told Sam that he wanted to see the single beds that were on sale. Sam took Mr. Lin to the second floor, and as they walked up the stairs, Sam kept on repeating, "Now, I'm sure

---

[1]odds and ends: thrown-out or leftover items.
[2]beat up: old, worn; in poor condition.
[3]go by: pass.
[4]as soon as: immediately after.
[5]What will it be: What do you want to buy?

you'll love this bed. It'll last ten years. It'll give you the sleep of your life.[6] It'll make you a happy man. Yes sir, it will. You really should **take advantage of** this special price of $79.95. It's really **worth** it!"

Mr. Lin sat on the bed. The mattress was very firm, just the way he liked it, and it was a very good buy. Mr. Lin told Sam, "I'll take it." After Sam wrote out the sales slip, he said, "Well, you know, we won't deliver, so you'll have to arrange to get the bed to your apartment yourself. And you must remove it by next Friday; otherwise, we'll have to charge you a storage fee. And, by the way, there is no warranty on your bed because it's a floor sample. These are company rules."

Now Mr. Lin realized why the price was so cheap.

QUESTIONS

1. How come Mr. Lin was almost broke?
2. How do many students get free furniture?
3. In what shape[7] were the table and chairs which Mr. Lin found?
4. What caught Mr. Lin's eye while he was reading the paper?
5. What kind of bed was Mr. Lin interested in seeing?
6. Why do you think the bed was so cheap?

II. DIALOGUE

Mr. Lin enters a furniture store to look for a bed.

SALESMAN: Hello, my name is Sam. I'll be glad to show you around. Now, what'll it be today?

LIN: I'm interested in buying a single bed.

SALESMAN: Beds are on the second floor. I'll take you up.
(On the second floor)
Here's a nice one. It's very well built and the mattress is very firm.

LIN: How much is it?

SALESMAN: $119 plus tax.

LIN: Do you have anything cheaper?

SALESMAN: Yes. This one is only $79. Why don't you lie down on it and see how it feels?

LIN: Okay. (He lies on the bed) I guess I'll take it. How long will it take to deliver it? I'd like it as soon as possible.

---

[6]the (sleep) of your life: the best. Also note the following expressions: the time of your life; the surprise of your life.
[7]shape: condition.

SALESMAN: I'm sorry, we don't deliver on special sale items. And you must remove the bed by Friday.

LIN: All right, I'll make arrangements. Do you accept personal checks?

SALESMAN: Sorry, sir, during this sale we're accepting cash only. No checks or credit cards. No refunds or exchanges.

LIN: Oh, I wanted to pay by check. Okay, I'll pay cash then. Is there a warranty on the bed?

SALESMAN: No, there isn't. This is a floor sample. That's why the price is so low.

QUESTIONS

1. Where are the beds located in this store?
2. What's the price of the first bed?
3. Why won't the store deliver the bed?
4. What is the store's policy on personal checks?
5. How was Mr. Lin planning to pay?
6. How did he finally pay?
7. How come there isn't a warranty on the bed?

III. GRAMMAR

A. Future Tense

We use the Future Tense to talk about what is going to happen in the future. There are three forms used to show future tense:

BE GOING TO

FORM: be going to + Verb (base form)

Affirmative: He *is going to buy* a new car.

Negative: He *is not going to buy* a new car.

Question: *Is* he *going to buy* a new car?

Wh- Question: When *is* he *going to buy* a new car?

Who/What/Which as Subject: Who *is going to buy* a new car?

Use *be going to* to talk about what you intend or plan to do.

Example: A: Are you *going to* pay cash for that?
B: No, I'm *going to* use my credit card.

WILL

FORM: | will + Verb (base form) |

Affirmative: I *will* return the jacket.
                  I'll

Negative: I *will not* return the jacket.
               won't

Question: *Will* you *return* the jacket?

Wh– Question: When *will* you *return* the jacket?

Who/What/Which as Subject: Who *will return* the jacket?

Use *will* mainly to talk about
(1)   a promise or a sense of determination:

Example: A: Please don't forget to go to the hardware store. It's the
                    last day of the sale.
              B: Don't worry. I'*ll go* for you. I promise.

(2)   a request or an offer of help:

Example: A: *Will* you take the children shopping?
              B: I can't. But I'm sure David *will*.

(3)   a prediction:

Example: A: Should I buy this bed?
              B: Yes. You'*ll love* it. It *will last* for ten years.

Use the *negative* of *will* to talk about
(1)   a promise not to do something:

Example: A: Please don't tell anyone I sold it.
              B: Don't worry. I *won't tell* a soul.

(2)   a refusal:

Example: A: I don't have enough money to buy that stereo.
              B: Why don't you ask your parents to lend you some?
              A: It's no use. They *won't lend* me any more money.

(3)   something that doesn't work or is broken:

Example: A: Lend me your pen for a minute.
              B: You have one right there on your desk.
              A: I know, but it *won't write*.

THE OTHER CAR
FROM METROPOLIS MOTORS

OLDS CUTLASS
LS, 4 Dr., Blue, Auto, A/C, PS, PB, PW, PL, V. Roof. 8 cyl, plush Velour Int. 44,000 mi. **$6,790**

BUICK CENTURY
2 Dr. Tan, Auto. A/C PS, PB, PW, P. Seat, Power Output Radio, P. Antenna, Velour Bucket Seats 32,000 mi. **$8,700**

FIREBIRD ESPIRIT
Auto, A/C, AM/FM & Cassette, PS, PB, T-Tops, etc. 44,000 mi. **$7,990**

PLYMOUTH RELIANT
4 Dr. Brown, Auto, A/C, PS, PB, AM/FM & 8 Track, etc. 11,000 mi. **$6,790**

OLDS DELTA 88 HOLIDAY
Blue, Auto. A/C PS, PB, PW, PL, Elec Sun Roof, Loaded, Loaded, etc. etc. **$6,495**

TRANS AM
T-Tops, Auto, PS, PB, PW, AM/FM & Cassette, T-Top Locks, Bra Loaded 19,000 mi. **$12,990**

CHEVROLET CITATION
5 spd., Sun Roof, Radio, AC 50,000 mi. **$3,490**

PLYMOUTH HORIZON
2 Dr., TC3, 5 spd., AC, PS, PB, 4 cyl., AM/FM & Tape Deck, Red/White **$3,990**

T-BIRD
Bucket Seats & Console. WSW, Auto, AM/FM & Tape Deck, Red/White 38,000 mi. **$4,695**

FIREBIRD FORMULA
Auto, A/C, PS, PB, PW, Mags, AM/FM & Cassette, etc. **$6,295**

DATSUN 210 4 DR.
Red, AC, AM/FM & Cassette, WSW, BSM, etc. 36,000 mi. **$6,295**

DODGE RAM CHARGER
Auto, Front-Wheel Drive, AM/FM & Cassette, Tilt Wheel, Lug, Rack, etc. 44,000 mi. **$6,895**

GRAND PRIX
Auto, AC, PS, PB, AM/FM, WSW, WC, Medeco Lock, ½ Roof, Red 35,000 mi. **$7,290**

OLDS OMEGA 2 DR.
Blue, Auto, AC, AM/FM & Cassette, Wheel Locks, etc. Velour Int. 13,000 mi. **$8,250**

PORSCHE 924
Auto, PW, etc. Loaded 37,000 mi. **$12,800**

MONTE CARLO
LOADED, A/C, PS, PB, PW, 31,000 mi. Tu-Tone, etc., etc. MUST SEE! **$7,990**

One Year Warranty guaranteed by the number **1** and only Pontiac dealer for New York

METROPOLIS MOTORS
555-5050

OVER 50 OTHERS TO CHOOSE FROM!!

Car sales advertisements

PRESENT CONTINUOUS TENSE

FORM: | be + Verb-ing |

Affirmative: I'm *taking* him to a wholesale warehouse this afternoon.

Negative: I'm *not taking* him to a wholesale warehouse this afternoon.

Question: Are you *taking* him to a wholesale warehouse this afternoon?

Wh- Question: When *are* you *taking* him to a wholesale warehouse?

Who/What/Which as Subject: Who *is taking* him to a wholesale warehouse this afternoon?

Use the *Present Continuous Tense* to talk about what you are definitely doing in the future.

Example: A: I'm *going to* the department store after lunch.
B: You were there this morning. How come you're *going* again?
A: I'm *returning* the tapes I bought. They're defective.

Dialogues

Complete the following dialogues using either *Future Tense* or *Present Tense*.

1. Suzi and her friend, Janice, are shopping in a large department store. They are in the women's department. Suzi is trying on a coat.

JANICE: _____ you _____ that coat, Suzi?
(buy)

SUZI: I'm not sure. I _____ usually _____ such
(buy; negative)

expensive clothes. Do you like it?

JANICE: Yes, I do. It looks good on you.

SUZI: It costs $499 though. I _____ never _____
(be able to)

pay for it.

JANICE: Well, I always _____ the prices in some of the other
(check out)

stores before I buy. You may find a similar coat someplace else for a lower price.

SUZI: Well, I usually _____ that, too. In fact, I
(do)

_____ to Sim's later this afternoon. _____
(go)

you _____ with me?
(go)

JANICE: Sure. I _____ with you.
(go)

QUESTIONS

1. Why is Suzi hesitant to buy the coat?
2. What does Janice think of the coat?
3. What does Janice usually do before she decides to buy something?
4. Why is Suzi going to Sim's later in the afternoon?

2. Jeff and his colleague, Weldon, are at the office. Jeff is planning to buy a new suit.

JEFF: I _____ a custom-made suit.
(get)

WELDON: Really? _____ you usually _____
(buy; negative question)

ready-made suits?

JEFF: Yes, I usually _____ . But this time I
(do)

_____ a little.
(splurge[8])

WELDON: Where _____ you _____ it made?
(have)

JEFF: I _____ to Lord's Men's Store this evening after work.
(go)

WELDON: They _____ open that late. They _____
(be; negative)   (close)

at 5:00 P.M. every day except Friday.

JEFF: I _____ not _____ until
(wait; negative)

Friday. I _____ just _____ the boss to let me
(ask)

off early today.

---

[8]splurge: to spend a lot on something that is not a necessity.

WELDON: Fat chance![9] You know he _____ you. He
                                                              (let; negative)

never _____ us leave early.
                    (let)

JEFF: You _____ ! I _____ him.
                      (see)   (persuade)

QUESTIONS

1.   What kind of suit does Jeff usually buy?
2.   What kind is he going to buy this time?
3.   How is Jeff going to get to the store before 5 P.M.?
4.   What does Weldon think the boss will say?
5.   Is Jeff discouraged by what Weldon says?

3.   Howard is trying to vacuum his apartment, but the vacuum cleaner won't work properly.
His roommate, Tom, comes in.

HOWARD: That does it![10] I _____ this vacuum cleaner
                                              (return)

to the store right now. It just _____
                                                  (pick up; negative)

this dirt. _____ you _____
                                                              (go)

with me?

TOM: Sure, but _____ they _____ it back?
                                                          (take)

You've had it for a month already.

HOWARD: I'm sure they _____ .

TOM: But what if they _____ ? Please don't make a big scene[11] like

you always do.

HOWARD: Don't worry. I _____ you again.
                                          (embarrass; negative)

QUESTIONS

1.   Why is Howard returning the vacuum cleaner?
2.   Why does Tom think the store won't take the vacuum back?

---

[9]fat chance: no way; impossible.
[10]that does it: Use this phrase to show that you have no more patience or will not endure something
  any longer.
[11]make a scene: to cause a big disturbance.
  create

3. What is Tom afraid Howard will do?
4. What does Howard promise?

4.   Stephanie is talking with her roommate, Jennifer.

JENNIFER: _____ you _____ me over to the
                                                         (take)

shopping mall tomorrow?

STEPHANIE: No, I _____ .

JENNIFER: C'mon, Stephanie. Don't be that way! They _____
                                                                                         (have)

a big sale this weekend.

STEPHANIE: They _____ a big sale every weekend.
                                         (have)

JENNIFER: But there _____ any more appliance sales
                                            (be; negative)

until the next major holiday.

STEPHANIE: Okay. Okay. I _____ you.
                                                              (take)

QUESTIONS

1.   What does Jennifer want Stephanie to do?
2.   When will the next appliance sale probably be?

B. Sentence Patterns

Recall this sentence from the narrative:
. . . most students furnish their apartments with odds and ends *that they find on the streets.*

Restrictive Adjective Clauses: These clauses provide information describing a noun which is necessary to the meaning of the sentence.

Relative pronoun is the object of the clause.

Main clause + that/which/who(m) + Subject of clause + Verb of clause

They used furniture (which) they found on the street.
I bought the books (that) you recommended.

Note: We can omit the relative pronoun when it is in the object position:

   Example: I bought the books you recommended.

Relative pronoun is the subject of the clause.

Main clause + that/which/who + Verb of clause

These are the appliances which are on sale.
He found two chairs that are on sale.

Note: We cannot omit the relative pronoun when it is in the subject position.

Complete the following exchanges with an appropriate response using a restrictive adjective clause.

> *Example:*   A: What store are you going to for your stereo?
>   B: We're going to the store *(that) you recommended.*
>   (you recommended)

1.   A: How will you get enough cash to make a down payment on the car?

     B: I'll use _____ .
                        (my friend lent me)

2.   A: Is he buying all the textbooks _____ today?
                                          (need)

     B: No, today he's just buying _____ .
                                      (ones-be on sale)

3.   A: Where are they going to get the money for all the new furniture?

     B: They're going to use _____ .
                                (have in the bank)

4.   A: I can't find the style of dress _____ .
                                           (want)

     B: Well, let's go to another store. Why don't we try Lord's? They may have the style

          _____ .
                        (look for)

5.   A: Do you have this jacket in a size 38?

     B: Yes, right over here.

     A: These jackets are on sale, aren't they?

     B: No, not these. Only the ones _____ are on sale. It's
                                          (have a red tag)

          a "red tag" sale.[12]

---

[12]"red tag" sale: a sale in which the items on sale have a red tag attached to them.

6. A: Oh, there are so many shirts here to choose from! You have such good taste; how

about helping me pick one out?

B: Well, first of all, I prefer shirts _____ . I think they always fit better
(tapered)

and look nicer.

A: Okay, but just keep in mind[13] that I can't afford anything _____ .
(costs more than $25)

Recall this sentence from the narrative:
As soon as he entered Crazy Jack's, *which was packed with customers*, a smiling, high-pressure salesman approached him.

Nonrestrictive Adjective Clauses: These clauses provide additional, though not essential, information describing a noun.

Relative pronoun is the subject of the clause.

Noun + which/who(m) + Verb of clause

The salesman, *who was wearing a bow tie*, talked loud and fast.

Relative pronoun is the object of the clause.

Noun + which/who(m) + Subject of clause + Verb of clause

That bed, *which they bought for $20*, has lasted for ten years.

Notes: We mark off the nonrestrictive clause with commas.
Use *who(m)* or *which* in nonrestrictive clauses. Do *not* use *that*.
Nonrestrictive clauses are more common in writing than speaking.

Combine the following pairs of sentences into a single sentence using a nonrestrictive adjective clause.

Example: The new department store just opened last Monday. It is having a sale today.

The new department store, which just opened last Monday, is having a sale today.

1. Bob Martin started working last year. He is now the company's best salesperson.

_____

_____

---

[13]keep in mind: remember.

2. Tropical fruits are imported. They are not always available in local supermarkets.

_____

_____

3. Jaguars are quite expensive. They are among the most popular luxury cars.

_____

_____

4. The hardware store was jammed with people. It was having a "going-out-of-business" sale.

_____

_____

5. These ties are made of genuine leather. They are in fashion now.

_____

_____

6. Tapes are becoming more popular these days. They are just as expensive as records.

_____

_____

7. I bought this television on sale. It has never given me a problem.

_____

_____

8. Victor bought this cassette recorder from a man on the street. It has lasted for ten years!

_____

_____

9. You should know the price. It's $19.99.

_____

_____

10. This video tape recorder is selling at half price. It is the best one on the market.[14]

_____

_____

IV. EXPRESSIONS AND IDIOMS

● _be worth_: equal in value to.

Subject + be worth + Noun
Verb-ing

Recall this sentence from the narrative:

You really should take advantage of this special price of $79.99. It's really _worth_ it!

Complete the following exchanges with an appropriate response with _be worth_.

Example: A: Why didn't you buy that blouse? You liked it, didn't you?
   B: Yes, but I didn't think it _was worth the money_.
                                    (money)

1.   A: Let's drive over to the mall on Veteran's Highway. I need to buy some shaving

   cream.

   B: Why don't you just go to the drugstore around the corner?

   A: Because it's cheaper at the mall.

   B: Listen, it _____ all the way over there just to save ten cents!
              (drive; negative)

2.   A: Why aren't Alex and Irene talking to each other?

   B: They had a big argument this morning.

---

[14]on the market: for sale, available to buy.

A: Over what?

B: Oh, Irene forgot to pick something up for Alex when she went shopping.

A: I don't think that _____ over.
                         (argue)

B: Well, you know Alex and Irene; they're always arguing about something.

3.   A: Look at these two statues. What do you think? Should I buy them?

B: Sure, if you like them.

A: Do you think _____ ?
                     (the money)

B: How much are they?

A: Twenty dollars each.

B: Oh, I'm sure _____ .
                    (twice that)

● *take advantage of*: to make good use of; to make unfair use of a person.

Recall this sentence from the narrative:
   You really should *take advantage of* this special price of $79.99.

Complete the following exchanges with an appropriate response using *take advantage of*.

   Example: A: Didn't you say you needed to buy some new pants?
                     B: Yes, but I'm going to wait.
                     A: Why wait? *You should take advantage of this sale and buy now.*

1.   A: I'm going to a car dealer with my brother tonight. He's looking for a used car.

B: Why are you going with him?

A: Well, he doesn't know much about cars, so he's afraid the salesman might

_____ .
                (him)

2.   A: How come you bought all these vitamins? Were they on sale or something?

B: Yes, I decided to _____ . If you buy one large bottle, the
                         (their special offer)

second one is half price.

3. A: I checked out Phil's car yesterday. It's in great condition.

B: Are you going to buy it?

A: Well, he'll give me a good deal[15] on it, but I'm still not sure. What do you think?

B: I think it's a good opportunity. You should _____ .
   (it)

V. SITUATIONAL DIALOGUES

1. Mr. Lin is in an audio/video shop.

LIN: Excuse me, do you carry Mitachi portable recorders?

CLERK: Video or audio?

LIN: Audio.

CLERK: No, they're not in stock right now.

LIN: Okay. Oh, where is the discount tape section?

CLERK: Down the next aisle, on your left.

LIN: How much is this package of tapes?

2D CLERK: Let's see. Those are $8.50 for a pack of five. We have a special on these imported tapes though. There's a twenty percent discount on them this week. They're normally $1.49 each. With the discount, they're only $1.19 each.

LIN: Hino tapes? I've never heard of this brand. Are they any good or do they break easily?

2D CLERK: Frankly speaking, they won't hold up[16] that long. You'll probably be happier with the more expensive ones.

LIN: All right. I'll take this $8.50 package.

QUESTIONS

1. Why isn't Mr. Lin able to buy a Mitachi tape recorder?
2. How much is the package of tapes?
3. Which tapes are on sale this week?
4. How much is the discount on Hino tapes?
5. What does the salesperson say about Hino tapes?
6. Which tapes does Mr. Lin end up buying?

2. Mr. Lin is shopping in a department store.

LIN: Where is the men's department?

CLERK: On the second floor. You can take the escalator; it's right down this aisle.

---

[15] a good deal: a bargain; a good buy; a good price.
[16] hold up: to last.

(in the men's department)

LIN: (holding a pair of pants) Do you have these pants in a size twenty-nine waist?

2D CLERK: If it's not on the rack, then we don't have it. What size are those you have there?

LIN: These are a thirty.

2D CLERK: Well, you can always have them taken in[17] a bit. There is no charge for alterations.

LIN: Okay. I'll try them on then. Where is the fitting room?

2D CLERK: Right over there.

LIN: Oh, yes. I see it.

QUESTIONS

1.   Where is the men's department located?
2.   How can Mr. Lin get up to the second floor?
3.   What size pants does Mr. Lin wear?
4.   How much does the store charge for alterations?

3.   Mr. Lin is shopping in a department store.

LIN: Excuse me, where can I pay for this?

CLERK: There's a cashier right over there, against the wall.

(at the cashier)

2D CLERK: How are you paying, sir?

LIN: Will you accept a personal check?

2D CLERK: We need two forms of identification.

LIN: I have my passport and international driver's license.

2D CLERK: Those'll do.

LIN: I'm buying this as a gift. If it doesn't fit, can I exchange it?

2D CLERK: Yes, but all refunds and exchanges require a receipt. So make sure you save it.

LIN: Okay. Thank you.

QUESTIONS

1.   How does Mr. Lin want to pay for his purchase?
2.   What does the store require if you want to pay by check?
3.   What forms of I.D. does Mr. Lin have with him?
4.   What must you have in order to make an exchange or get a refund?

---

[17]take in: to make smaller. Also note, *let out*: to make bigger.

Clothing store ad

4. In a department store. Anthony would like to exchange a pair of pants and get a refund on a jacket.

ANTHONY: I'd like to exchange these pants. They don't fit.

SALESPERSON: Okay. What size do you need?

ANTHONY: Well, these are a thirty-one waist. I need a size thirty-two.

SALESPERSON: Fine. Let me get a pair for you. Oh, do you have your receipt?

ANTHONY: Yes, here it is. I also want to return this jacket. The person I bought it for doesn't like it, so I'd like a refund.

SALESPERSON: Okay. You have to take that to the return desk. It's straight ahead, on your right.

QUESTIONS

1. Why does Anthony want to exchange the pants?
2. Why does he want a refund on the jacket?
3. Where does he have to go to get a refund?

VI. VOCABULARY BUILDER

store	bookstore/candy store/department store/drugstore/grocery store/jewelry store/record store/stationery store/storehouse/storekeeper/storeroom
sale	back-to-school sale/Christmas sale/closeout sale/Fourth of July sale/fire sale/garage sale/holiday sale/Labor Day sale/rummage sale/summer clearance sale/warehouse sale/white sale
shop	camera shop/card shop/clothing shop/florist shop/gift shop/tobacco shop/thrift shop

VII. ROLE PLAY SUGGESTIONS

1. Purchase an item of clothing at a department store. Ask for your size. Inquire about alterations.
2. Bring something you bought back to the store for (a) a refund, (b) an exchange.

VIII. PREPOSITION PRACTICE

A. Prepositions That Show Logical Relationships

USE **BY** AND **WITH** TO SHOW:

how something is done.

They go to the discount stores in the suburbs **BY** train.
The little girl tried on the shoes **WITH** the help of her mother.

USE **WITHOUT** TO SHOW:

    lack of something.

The little girl tried on the shoes **WITHOUT** the help of her mother.

USE **ON ACCOUNT OF, BECAUSE OF, DUE TO,** AND **OWING TO** TO SHOW:

    cause [use a noun after these phrases].

OWING TO his lack of money, he couldn't buy a thing.

USE **BESIDES, IN ADDITION TO** TO SHOW:

    additional ideas or information.

He bought three jackets **IN ADDITION TO** four suits.

Complete the following exchanges with the appropriate preposition.

1.   A: Have you bought a desk yet?

       B: No, not yet.

       A: _____ one, it's going to be mighty[18] hard to work.

       B: You're right. Tomorrow I'll go _____ bus to that big unpainted

          furniture store[19] right off the expressway.

       A: _____ the desk, you should look for some bookcases.

2.   A: Why didn't you go to a thrift shop[20] for these things?

       B: I was going to do that, but _____ a fast-talking salesman,

          I bought everything at the department store.

3.   A: John, where can I buy a used typewriter?

       B: Did you look on the bulletin boards around campus?

---

[18]mighty: very.

[19]unpainted furniture store: a store that sells unfinished furniture for less than painted or finished furniture.

[20]thrift shop: a store that buys and sells used items.

A: You know I never thought of that. I don't know what I would do _____

your advice.

4. A: What's wrong with the radio you just bought?

B: I don't know, I can't get any stations, and _____ that problem,

I can't adjust the volume.

A: Well, you have a complete warranty, don't you?

B: Yes, but I've got to send it back _____ parcel post and that's a

hassle[21] because I lost the original box it came in.

B. Additional Preposition Combinations

take on (S):
to challenge (in a contest, fight)	Our prices are unbeatable. We'll *take on* any store.
to assume	I just can't *take on* more responsibility.

take off (S):
to remove	*Take off* the price tag.
to reduce, deduct	You can *take off* ten percent because everything is on sale.
to leave	I'll *take off* tomorrow for Florida.
to begin flight	Their plane will *take off* at 6:30 P.M.
not to go (to school or work)	I'm *taking off* from work tomorrow.

take over (S):
to assume control; substitute for	Jamesway Stores has just bought Royal Drugs and will *take over* its management next month.
	I'm going out for awhile. Will you *take over* for me?

Complete the following exchanges with the appropriate preposition combination.

1. Two employees in a store:

A: Can you _____ the counter for a minute?

B: Sure, but don't _____ for too long. I have to go soon.

_____
[21]hassle: a lot of trouble.

2. In a thrift shop:

  A: I'm going to shorten these pants and let out the jacket a few inches so that the suit

  will fit me.

  B: It looks like a lot of work to me. You sure do like _____

  big projects.

3. A: Right after we buy Morty a present, we're _____ for Cape Cod.

  B: Great! But before you give it to him, don't forget _____ the

  price tag!

4. A: That French designer's clothing is very chic.[22]

  B: Yes, I think his designs will _____ the market this summer.

5. In a thrift shop:

  A: Do you have sales in this store?

  B: No, but you can _____ fifteen percent on all items with red tags.

6. A: I just got a hundred-dollar gift certificate[23] from Christopher's for my birthday.

  B: Well, I just got paid, so let's _____ for a few hours and go on a

  shopping spree.[24]

---

[22]chic: very stylish.
[23]gift certificate: a certificate bought at a store for a specific amount of money. The certificate can only
 be applied toward purchases at that store.
[24]shopping spree: to go shopping and buy many things.

8 IF I WERE YOU, I'D DROP ONE COURSE

I. NARRATIVE

Mr. Lin brought his bed home with the help of Mr. and Mrs. Fasteau, his neighbors. Another neighbor, Mr. Sharon, sold Mr. Lin a desk. Now he was **all set** to begin his studies. Mr. Lin had been so busy getting settled that he almost forgot that today he had to register for his classes. He read the registration instructions and went immediately to see the foreign student advisor. He then went to the chairperson of the Department of Chemical Engineering who suggested some courses to take.

He was now ready to go to the registration area in the auditorium. It was filled with anxious students who were all trying to get the courses they wanted. As Mr. Lin walked by the different departmental tables, he kept hearing the same comments: "I wish Professor 'so and so'[1] were teaching that course," or "I wish I had known about that course; I would have taken it." Mr. Lin stood in lines, filled out cards and then handed his choice of sections to the professor at the Chemical Engineering table. The professor checked a tally sheet[2] and said, "Oh, I'm sorry, those sections are closed. If you had just come a little earlier, I would have had a course card for you."

Mr. Lin revised his program several times until he finally put together[3] a 9 A.M. to 4 P.M. schedule. He then went to the bursar's office[4] to pay his tuition. The assistant bursar added up his courses and asked, "Is this your first semester?" Mr. Lin nodded, and she continued, "Well, you have too many credits. If you were a special visiting scholar, you could take eighteen credits, but first semester students can not take more than sixteen credits."

Mr. Lin asked what he could do. The assistant bursar said, "You can try to see the dean to get permission to take 18 credits, or you can drop one course. If you come back tomorrow, you'll probably be able to see

---

[1]so and so: used when either you do not know the name of the person or do not want to mention it.
[2]tally sheet: a sheet which lists the course sections and the number of students in each section.
[3]put together: to construct; arrange.
[4]bursar: the person in charge of collecting tuition and fees.

him, but there will be a long wait. You'd **be better off** dropping one course. Of course, if **you'd rather** wait to see the dean, you can." Mr. Lin was exhausted and didn't want to come back the next day, so he **ended up** dropping one course. After he stood in two more lines, he finally received his ID card. He now understood the full meaning of the expression, "registration hassle."

QUESTIONS

1. How did Mr. Lin manage to get his bed home?
2. Where did he get his desk?
3. How come he almost forgot about registering?
4. Who did Mr. Lin see first?
5. Who did he see about planning his program?
6. What did the professor at the Chemical Engineering table tell Mr. Lin?
7. Under what circumstances could he take eighteen credits without permission from the dean?
8. What did the assistant bursar say he'd be better off doing?

II. DIALOGUE

Mr. Lin is registering for classes.

ASST. BURSAR: It looks like you've got too many classes here.

MR. LIN: What's the maximum number of credits I can take?

ASST. BURSAR: It depends. You're a full-time student?

MR. LIN: Yes, I am.

ASST. BURSAR: You can take up to sixteen credits then.

MR. LIN: Is there any way I can take eighteen?

ASST. BURSAR: If you're a visiting scholar you can. Otherwise, you need to get the dean's permission.

MR. LIN: I'm not a visiting scholar. Can I see the dean now or do I need to make an appointment?

ASST. BURSAR: He's not in now. If you come tomorrow, you'll probably be able to see him. But I can tell you now that there will be a long wait. You'd be better off dropping one course. Eighteen credits will be a lot of work, anyway.

MR. LIN: Do you think so?

ASST. BURSAR: Definitely. If I were you, I'd drop one course. This is only your first semester. No need to overdo[5] it.

MR. LIN: Maybe you're right.

---

[5]overdo: to do too much; to try to do more than one can.

QUESTIONS

1. What's the maximum number of credits Mr. Lin can take?
2. If Mr. Lin were a visiting scholar, how many credits could he take?
3. If Mr. Lin wants to take eighteen credits, what will he have to do?
4. What does the assistant bursar advise him to do? Why?

III. GRAMMAR

Conditional Sentences

A. Future Possible

We use the *Future Possible* to talk about actions that *may* occur in the future.

Recall this sentence from the narrative:
    If you *come* back tomorrow, you'*ll* probably *be able to* see him . . . .

PATTERNS

"if" Clause	Main Clause
if + Present Tense	Future Tense
	Modal

If I *get* out of class on time tomorrow, I *can go* to the movies with you.
If you *don't register* soon, most of the classes *will be* closed.

"unless" Clause	Main Clause
unless + Present Tense	Future Tense
	Modal

Unless you *register* soon, most of the classes *will be* closed.
I *can go* to the movies with you tomorrow unless I *get* out of class late.

Complete the following exchanges using the conditional.

> *Example:* A: Are you going to register for Professor Ledesma's economics class?
> B: I will *if it's still open.*
>   (still open)

1. A: I think I'm going to withdraw from my geology class. I'm not doing very well. Do

    you know if I need permission?

B: It's too late to withdraw officially. _____ now you
                                                                (withdraw)

_____ the course.
                                      (fail)

2.   A: How is Dr. Liberti's biology class?

B: It's great. She's really a good teacher. _____ something
                                                                    (understand; negative)

she _____ it again for you.
                          (explain)

3.   A: Are you planning to take Chemistry II next semester?

B: I'd like to, but I'm not even passing Chemistry I right now. _____ ,
                                                                                              (pass)

I can't go on to Chemistry II.

4.   A: I'm only going to take eight credits this term.

B: Really? I think you'd be better off registering for twelve credits. If you can't handle

all the work, _____ .
                                      (drop one course)

5.   A: I'm taking Math 14 this term. Why don't you take it with me? We can help each

other study.

B: No. I don't like math.

A: So what! You _____ graduate
                                      (be able to; negative)

_____ . Do it now and get it over with.[6]
                (fulfill the math requirement)

6.   A: Does Professor Winant want our next paper to be typed?

B: Yes, she does. She _____ unless it's typed.
                                      (accept; negative)

7.   A: I heard you've been accepted at Harvard. Congratulations!

B: Thanks, but I _____ go _____
                          (be able to; negative)   (get a scholarship)

---

[6]get (something) over with: to complete an unpleasant task.

THE CITY UNIVERSITY OF NEW YORK

The University Application Processing Center
Box 136, Bay Station
Brooklyn, New York 11235

APPLICATION FOR ADMISSION

INCLUDING
SPECIAL PROGRAMS (SEEK OR COLLEGE DISCOVERY)
TO THE LOWER FRESHMAN CLASS AS A
MATRICULATED STUDENT

_____
H.S. Home Room
or Official Class

TO BE FILLED OUT BY APPLICANT. PRINT IN INK.

1. Since graduating from high school or receiving GED diploma, have you attended a college or university? yes ☐ no ☐

IF YOUR ANSWER IS YES, DO _NOT_ USE THIS FORM. CONTACT THE OFFICE OF ADMISSION SERVICES (947-4800) FOR THE APPLICATION FOR ADVANCED STANDING.

Students who hold temporary visas, U.S. citizens and permanent residents who have completed part or all of their education abroad, must fill out the International Student Application. Please call 868-6200 for information.

2. Expected date of entrance _____
   Month (Feb. or Sept.)   Year

3. Name of Applicant Mr. _____
   Ms.
   Last   First   Middle   (Any prior last name used)

3a. Male ☐ Female ☐

4. Address (home) _____
   House No.   Street   Apt. #   Borough or Town   City   State   Zip Code

5. How long have you lived at this address? _____ years and _____ months.

6. Social Security Number ☐☐☐ - ☐☐ - ☐☐☐☐   Telephone No. _____
                                                        Area Code

7. Date of Birth _____ Date of H.S. Graduation (or _Expected Graduation_) _____
   Month   Day   Year   Month   Year

8. Name of High School _____

9. Address of High School _____
   City   State

10. Choices of College and Curriculum:

   Before entering your college choices, read the Guide to Admissions carefully. Then indicate your choices in the boxes printed below, following the directions given. Remember that your choices will be honored on the basis of your standing among other applicants and the available room within the programs and/or colleges.

   CHOICES   1st   2nd   3rd   4th   5th   6th

Applicants may indicate up to six choices. You should only choose colleges and programs that you are willing to attend. You will be admitted to one college ONLY-the first choice for which you are eligible.

10a. Intended major _____
     (if undecided, please indicate)

11. How long have you lived in New York City? (within the boroughs of the Bronx, Brooklyn, Manhattan, Queens or Staten Island) _____ years and _____ months.

12. How long have you lived in New York State? _____ years and _____ months.

13. Are you a citizen of the United States? ☐ Yes ☐ No Birthplace _____

   If _no_, which of the following indicates your status as a non-citizen? (Check one)   Date of entry

   ☐ Immigrant (permanent resident) Alien Registration Number _____
   ☐ Other (be specific) _____   month/year
                          Expiration Date   Country of Citizenship

   DO NOT WRITE IN THIS SPACE

   S _____   _____   _____

   R _____   _____   _____

   V _____   _____   _____

   _____   _____   _____

   NEW YORK STATE HIGH SCHOOLS ONLY
   SCHOOL AUTHORITIES MUST COMPLETE THIS SECTION
   FOR ALL CURRENT CANDIDATES FOR GRADUATION.

   Number of Students in Graduating Class _____ Student's Rank _____

College admission application

A: Why not? If they _____ you a scholarship,
                         (give; negative)

_____ .
                    (take out a loan)

B. Present Unreal

We use the *Present Unreal* to talk about a present situation that is not true (contrary to fact).

Recall these sentences from the narrative:
   If you *were* a special visiting scholar, you *could* take eighteen credits . . . .
   I wish Professor "so and so" *were teaching* that course.
   If I *were* you, I *would drop* one course.

PATTERNS

"if" Clause	*Main Clause*
if + Past Tense Past Continuous Tense	would + Verb (base form) might could

If I *had* enough money, I *would go* to school full time.
If I *were* you, I *wouldn't worry* about it.

Note: With the verb "be" use *were* with both singular and plural subjects in the "if" clause.

Present Unreal Conditional ("wish" Clauses):

wish + (that) + Subject of clause + Verb (Past Tense) (Past Continuous Tense)

I wish I *were* a full-time student.
She wishes that she *didn't have to* study so hard.
I wish I *were studying* French instead of Italian.

Complete the following exchanges.

   Example: A: I can't make up my mind[7] whether to take computer
                       science or accounting.
                  B: If I *were* you, *I'd take computer science*.
                       (be)   (take computer science)

1.   A: I'm really swamped[8] with work! I don't know why I ever decided to take twenty

         credits this semester. I just can't handle it.

---

[7]make up (one's) mind: to decide.
[8]swamped with: overcome, have too much to do.

The City University of New York
International Students Admissions Office
Office of Admission Services
101 West 31st Street
New York, New York 10001

APPLICATION FOR ADMISSION
FOR STUDENTS EDUCATED ABROAD
(Please Print or Type all Information)

This form should be used by all applicants to undergraduate programs who hold (or expect to obtain) temporary (non-immigrant) visas and by U.S. citizens and permanent residents who have completed part or all of their education outside of the United States.

Part I

Date you expect to enter the University (choose **one** only)

. . . . . . February, 19 . . . . (Applications must be returned BEFORE October 15 for freshman applicants and November 1 for transfer applicants)

. . . . . . September, 19 . . . . . . (Applications must be returned BEFORE January 15 for freshman applicants and March 1 for transfer applicants)

Only **one** application form is necessary. Any additional information or documents will be added to this original application.

Note: Completed applications, including all educational credentials and $25 application fee must be received on or before the deadline date. For further instructions see the information booklet for international undergraduate applicants.

Name of applicant: Mr. /Ms. _____

Last   *First*   *Middle/Maiden*   Sex: Male . . . . . . Female . . . . . .

(All last names used must be reported)

Mailing address (while in New York City): _____

Care of   *Number and Street*   *Apt. #*

Telephone No. _____

Borough   *City*   *State*   *Zip code*   *area code*

Permanent home address: _____

Number and Street   *City*   *State*   *Country*   *zip code*

If you change your address please notify us immediately.

Date of birth _____   Social Security No. ☐☐☐-☐☐-☐☐☐☐

Month   *Day*   *Year*

CHOICE OF COLLEGE AND CURRICULUM. Write your choices in the boxes below using the code numbers listed on the enclosed curriculum code sheet. Your application will not be considered if your choices are not written clearly and **in code.**

1st	2nd	3rd	4th	5th	6th
☐☐☐☐	☐☐☐☐	☐☐☐☐	☐☐☐☐	☐☐☐☐	☐☐☐☐

Are you a veteran of the United States Armed Forces?   yes . . . . . . no . . . . . .

Of what country are you a citizen? . . . . Country of birth: . . . .

What type of visa do you now hold? . . . . Alien registration number . . . .

If you are not in the U.S.A., what type of visa do you expect to obtain? . . . .

If you are in the U.S.A., on what date did you arrive? . . . .

If you are a N.Y.S. resident, how long have you lived in the state? . . . .

If you now hold a student (F) visa, write the name of the school which issued the I-20 form and the date on which it expires: . . . .

What is your native language? . . . .

What other languages do you speak (in order of fluency)? . . . .

What is your anticipated major? . . . .

Have you taken the Test of English as a Foreign Language (TOEFL)? ☐ **YES**   ☐ **NO**

If Yes, when? . . . .

If No, when are you scheduled to take it? . . . .

This examination is required of all non-immigrants whose native language is not English. For further information, see the information booklet.

NOTES ON DOCUMENTS

1. All transcripts of higher education must be sent to C.U.N.Y. **directly from the school you attended.**

2. All other documents (high school transcripts, diplomas, etc.) **must be included in this application** before you submit it to this office.

1

Foreign student application

B: Well, if I _____ you, _____ while you can
               (be)   (drop a course now)

still withdraw officially; otherwise, all your grades will suffer.

2.   A: I've been trying to figure out that calculus problem the teacher assigned last week,

but I can't seem to get it. Do you think you could help me out a little?

B: Well, if I _____ it myself, I _____
              (understand)   (be willing)

to help you, but I can't figure it out either.

3.   A: How is your philosophy course going?

B: It's not bad, but I wish Professor Wittgenstern _____ it.
                                            (teach)

A: Why's that?

B: Well, I've had her before and I just feel that if she _____
                                          (teach)

the course, we _____ .
                  (learn a lot more)

4.   A: A few of us are going over to the student lounge. How about coming along?

B: I _____ to join you if I _____
      (love)   (have)

time, but I've got to study for an exam tomorrow.

5.   A: Can I register for eighteen credits?

B: Are you a matriculated[9] student?

A: No, I'm not.

B: Then the maximum is fifteen credits.

A: What if I _____ matriculated?
                           (be)

B: In that case, you _____ up to eighteen credits.
                         (take)

---

[9]matriculated student: a college student who is studying for a degree. A nonmatriculated student is a student who is attending college but not working for a degree.

6. A: I see you're taking English composition this semester.

 B: Yeah, but I really dislike writing. Believe me, if it _____ ,
 (not required)

 I _____ .
 (not take)

 A: Well, there's an opportunity in everything, so since you're taking the course any-

 way, make sure you get something out of it.[10]

7. A: Have you been working on your term paper? It's due in three weeks.

 B: I haven't worked on it that much yet. I wish we _____
 (have)

 more time. If we _____ , I'm sure I _____ a
 (do) (get)

 good grade on it.

 A: Well, we don't, so you'd better get cracking.[11]

C. Past Unreal

We use the *Past Unreal* to talk about something in the past that is contrary to what did actually happen.

Recall these sentences from the narrative:
 If you *had* just *come* a little earlier, I *would have had* a course card for you.
 I wish I *had known* about that course; I *would have taken* it.

PATTERNS

"if" Clause	*Main Clause*
if + Past Perfect	would have + Past Participle
	could have
	might have

If I *had known* about it, I *would have told* you.
If he *hadn't picked* me up, I *would have been* late for class last night.

---

[10]get something out of (something): to get or obtain some value.
[11]get cracking: to get started; begin working.

Past Unreal Conditional ("wish" Clauses):

> wish + (that) + Subject of clause + Verb (Past Perfect)

He *wishes* he *had known* about it earlier.
I *wish* they *hadn't cancelled* that course.

Complete the following exchanges:

> *Example:* A: Can you tell me what data processing courses are still open?
>
> B: I'm afraid they're all closed. If you *had come* yesterday,
> (come)
>
> you *could have registered* for Data Processing 211. It
> (register)
> was still open last night.

1. A: I'm taking Journalism II. It's a great course.

    B: You're kidding! They're offering it this term?

    A: Sure. Didn't you know?

    B: No. If _____ , I certainly _____ it.
        (know)   (take)

2. A: How did you do on yesterday's test?

    B: I got a C. I suppose I _____ if I _____ ,
        (do better)   (study more)
        but I also had to work on a history term paper.

3. A: My physics text cost me a fortune![12]

    B: Are you in Physics III?

    A: Yes, with Dr. Namis.

    B: I wish you _____ . I took it last term and I _____
        (tell me)   (sell)
        you my used textbook.

4. A: I heard you're living off campus now. How is it?

---
[12]cost a fortune: very expensive.

B: To tell you the truth, I wish I _____ . I don't like the
                                              (stay in the dorm)

people I share the apartment with.

5.   A: Thanks again for reminding me about the assignment that was due yesterday.

B: Did you manage to get it in?

A: Yes, but I don't know what _____ if you
                                              (happen)

_____ me.
                 (not remind)

B: Well, you _____ late with the paper, that's all. I don't think the
                       (be)

professor _____ your grade.
                              (lower)

6.   A: I wish I _____ you had an 8 A.M. class yesterday.
                         (know)

B: Why?

A: I _____ ; I drove to school yesterday at 7:00 A.M.
                 (give you a ride)

B: Oh, well, it doesn't matter. But thanks anyway.

7.   A: I wish they _____ the Introduction to Psychology course
                              (cancel; negative)

last term.

B: Did you need to take it?

A: Sure. If I _____ it, I _____ the
                      (be able to take)   (complete)

requirements for my major.

IV. EXPRESSIONS AND IDIOMS

● *be all set*: ready; prepared.

be all set + to + Verb (base form)

Recall this sentence from the narrative:
    Now he was *all set to* begin his studies.

Complete the following exchanges with an appropriate response using *all set*.

    Example: A: C'mon! If you don't hurry, we'll be late for class!

                      B: All right! *I'm all set. Let's go!*

1.   A: Are you ready to go home?

        B: Well, as soon as I go to the bursar's office and pay my registration fee, _____

                _____ .
                                      (go)

2.   A: You'd better take statistics this semester instead of putting it off.[13]

        B: Why? Is it a required course?

        A: Yes, and you can only take it this fall. It's not being offered in the spring. So if you

             take it now you _____ ; otherwise, you'll have to wait
                               (graduate next June)

             another semester.

3.   A: Have you completed registering yet?

        B: Not quite. I still have to see the chairperson of the Math Department.

        A: What for?

        B: I need her to waive a prerequisite[14] and then I _____ .
                                                 (register)

4.   A: Can't I take a nursing course this semester? After all, my curriculum is prenursing.

        B: Not yet. You still have to take remedial mathematics and remedial English. Once[15]

             you pass those, you _____ .
                           (take some nursing courses)

5.   At college registration:

        A: I've gotten all my course cards. What about you?

---

[13]putting it off: to delay doing something.

[14]prerequisite: a course which a student must take before taking another course. *Waive a prerequisite*: to not require the student to take the prerequisite course.

[15]once: as soon as; only after.

B: I have, too. What do we do next?

A: Well, we just pay our tuition and fees, get a bursar's receipt, and then we ＿＿＿＿

＿＿＿＿＿＿＿＿＿＿＿＿＿＿＿＿＿＿＿＿＿＿＿＿ .
(leave)

- *be better off*: to be better (i.e., to do one thing is better than doing the other)

be better off + Verb-ing

be better off + "if" Clause

Recall this sentence from the narrative:
You'd *be better off* dropping one course.

Complete the following exchanges with an appropriate response using *be better off.*

Example: A: Aren't you going to look for off-campus housing this semester?
B: No, I think I'm *better off living on campus.*
(live on campus)

Example: A: I can't believe how long the line is!
B: Well, maybe we'd be better off *if we came back* to-
(come)
morrow.

1. A: You're taking too many electives.[16]

    B: Do you think so?

    A: Yes. You ＿＿＿＿＿＿＿＿＿＿＿＿＿＿＿＿＿＿＿＿＿ first.
    (if-complete some requirements)

2. A: I'm really having trouble deciding on a curriculum. All my friends keep giving me

    different suggestions.

    B: Well, I think you ＿＿＿＿＿＿＿＿＿＿＿＿＿＿＿ instead of just asking
    (talk with an academic advisor)

    your friends.

---
[16]elective: a course which is not required.

3.   A: It's really hard to be a full-time student and work full time, too. I'm really falling

behind.[17]

B: Well, maybe you _____ and only working part-time.
                                    (get a loan)

4.   A: I thought you said you were going to take Spanish I with me this term.

B: I was, but since I had some Spanish in high school my advisor said I _____

_____ . I may be able to go right into Spanish II.
              (take a placement test first)

5.   A: I have a conflict in my schedule. I don't know what to do.

B: Can't you rearrange your schedule?

A: No, the other sections of the courses I need are closed.

B: Then you'll have to drop a course. What's the conflict?

A: Math 010 conflicts with History 301. I don't know which one to drop.

B: Well, since you want to major in computer science, you _____

_____ . Math 010 is a prerequisite for several computer
        (drop the history course)

courses, so it's important to take it right away.

● *would rather:* prefer

| would rather + (not) + Verb (base form) |

Recall this sentence from the narrative:
Of course, if *you'd rather* wait to see the dean, you can.

Complete the following exchanges with an appropriate response using *would rather*.

Example: A: I'm here to see a counselor.
                 B: Well, there are quite a few people ahead of you. You
                      can wait, but it'll be a while.
                 A: No, *I'd rather come back tomorrow morning. Thanks.*

---
[17]fall behind: to fail to keep even with; lag.

1. A: How about going over to the registrar[18] with me now?

   B: I think I _____ . I'm sure it's jammed[19] over there now.
   (wait until later this afternoon)

2. A: Let's go over to the student lounge for a while.

   B: _____ . I need to get some work done.
   (not)

3. A: Since Carl is so short of money, why doesn't he take out a student loan?

   B: He _____ .
   (try to get financial aid first)

4. A: Is your sister planning to go away to college?

   B: I don't think so. She says _____ .
   (at home and commute)

5. A: Do you think I should take Spanish or Russian?

   B: Which _____ you _____ ?
   (take)

   A: Well, _____ Russian, but I've heard that it's very difficult.
   (study)

- *end up:* in the end (as in a final result, decision, or situation)

```
end up + Verb-ing
```

Recall this sentence from the narrative:
. . . he *ended up* dropping one course.

Complete the following exchanges with an appropriate response using *end up*.

   Example: A: Were you able to get into a computer technology course?
   B: *No. They were all closed, so I ended up registering for a data processing course instead.*

1. A: Did Ben transfer to the State University as he wanted to?

   B: No. They wouldn't accept a lot of his credits, so he _____ .
   (stay where he was)

---

[18]registrar: person in charge of academic records.
[19]jammed: crowded.

2.   A: You really missed out[20] by not coming to the campus mixer[21] with us last night; we

         had a great time. What happened to you?

    B: Oh, I had an experiment to complete, so _____ .
                                                            (stay-biology lab-midnight)

3.   A: I'm thinking about taking twenty credits this semester. You did it last term; how did

         it go?

    B: I _____ . It was too much for me.
                          (drop a course)

4.   A: Is Henry still living off campus with you?

    B: No. He didn't like sharing a house with us.

    A: Really? How come?

    B: I don't know. I went out of my way[22] to make him feel welcome, but he _____

       _____ .
                               (leave anyway)

5.   A: How many credits are you taking this semester?

    B: Eighteen.

    A: Eighteen! And you're working part-time, too? What does your advisor think about

         that?

    B: She thinks I'll _____ , but I'm sure I can handle it.
                         (have to drop one course)

    A: Well, it is a heavy course load.

    B: Listen, if I put my mind to it,[23] I can do it.

---

[20]miss out: to miss something good.
[21]campus mixer: an on-campus party, often sponsored by a student club or organization.
[22]go out of one's way: to make an extra effort; to do more than usual.
[23]put one's mind to it: to concentrate; put all of one's energy and attention on one thing.

academic calendar

Spring Semester	**January 15 to May 18**
Residence halls open	Sat., Jan. 12
Registration	Tues.-Wed., Jan. 15-16
First classes meet, 8:00 a.m.	Thur., Jan. 17
Last day for late registration, changing or adding courses	Tues., Jan. 22
Last day to withdraw from class and receive a 100% tuition refund	Fri., Jan. 25
Last day to withdraw from class and receive a 75% tuition refund	Fri., Feb. 1
Last day to withdraw from class and receive a 50% tuition refund	Fri., Feb. 8
Last day to withdraw from class and receive a 25% tuition refund. (No refunds made after this date.)	Fri., Feb. 15
Last day for electing Pass/No Credit grading system	Fri., Feb. 15
Mid-semester reports of unsatisfactory work to Registrar, 9:00 a.m.	Mon., Mar. 4
Spring recess:	
Classes recess, 10:00 p.m.	Fri., Mar. 15
Classes resume, 8:00 a.m.	Mon., Mar. 25
Last day students may withdraw from a class	Fri., Apr. 5
Academic advising for Summer Session and for Fall Semester	Mon.-Fri., Apr. 22-26
Advance registration for Fall Semester	Mon.-Fri., Apr. 29-May 3
Good Friday holiday	Fri., Apr. 5
University offices closed	Fri., Apr. 5
Last day of classes	Wed., May 8
Study days	Thur.-Fri., May 9-10
Final examinations	Mon.-Fri., May 13-17
Baccalaureate and Commencement	Sat., May 18
Residence halls close	Sat., May 18
Summer Session	**May 21 to August 16**
Residence halls open	Sun., May 19
Registration for Three Weeks Term (Term I)	Tues., May 21
Classes begin; late registration ends	Wed., May 22
Last day to withdraw from class and receive a 100% tuition refund	Wed., May 22
Last day to withdraw from class and receive a 75% tuition refund	Thur., May 23
Last day to withdraw from class and receive a 50% tuition refund	Fri., May 24

Drop/add form

V. SITUATIONAL DIALOGUES

1. A student is talking with the chairperson of the History Department.

    STUDENT: Can I receive credit for a history course which I took at another college?

    CHAIRPERSON: Do we offer a comparable course here? I mean, do we have a course with a similar title and catalogue description?

    STUDENT: No. I just looked in the catalogue.

    CHAIRPERSON: Well, perhaps, we can give you elective credit for the course.

    STUDENT: As a liberal arts elective?

    CHAIRPERSON: Yes, but I'll have to discuss it with the registrar. I'll let you know.

    QUESTIONS

    1. What does the student want to know?
    2. What must the chairperson do before he can allow the student to receive elective credit for the course?

2. A student is talking with a counselor.

    STUDENT: I'd like to drop a course. What do I do?

    COUNSELOR: Take this program change form to your instructor and ask him or her to initial it after the course title.

    STUDENT: Is there a deadline for withdrawal without penalty?

    COUNSELOR: Yes, there is. You must have your instructor sign this form before the fourth week of class.

    QUESTIONS

    1. What would the student like to do?
    2. What must the student have her instructor do?
    3. When is the deadline for withdrawing without penalty?

3. A student is talking with a counselor.

    STUDENT: Is it possible to take this course on a pass or fail basis?

    COUNSELOR: Yes, but you have to get the permission of the chairperson of the department first. Then you have to pay an additional fee, and finally you need to tell the instructor during the first week of class.

    QUESTIONS

    1. What does the student want to do?
    2. Whose permission does he need to obtain in order take the course on a pass or fail basis?

4. A student with an F-1[24] visa is talking with a foreign student advisor.

STUDENT: I'm now enrolled in the American English Language Institute, and I'd like to attend your university next semester. Can you tell me what I should do?

FOREIGN STUDENT ADVISOR: Sure. First you have to fill out the matriculation forms. You can get them at the admissions office. Then you have to bring me the financial support documents. I'll look them over and if everything is in order, then I'll issue you an I-20.[25]

STUDENT: Will you notify the American English Language Institute?

ADVISOR: No, after I give you the I-20, take it to the Institute so that they can finish filling it out. The Institute will also need to complete an I-538.[26]

STUDENT: Is that all?

ADVISOR: Well, no. You then have to take the completed I-20 and I-538 forms as well as proof of financial support to the Immigration Office.

STUDENT: Oh, yeah. Then I have to wait for approval of transfer.

ADVISOR: Right, and remember go to Immigration as soon as possible because you need to get your approval sixty days before you begin attending the college.

STUDENT: Oh. I think I've got it. Now how do I get to the admissions office?

ADVISOR: No problem. It's just on the other side of the student union. You know the big modern building you passed to come to the office.

STUDENT: Oh, I know where it is!

QUESTIONS

1. What does the student want to do?
2. Where can the student get matriculation forms?
3. Who has to fill out the I-538 form?
4. By when must the student obtain approval to transfer?

VI. VOCABULARY BUILDER

college
agricultural college/coed college/college bursar/college campus/college credit/college curriculum/college entrance exam/college exchange program/college faculty/college financial aid/college loans/college placement/college registrar/college registration/college student/college tuition/college transcript/collegiate sports/private college/teachers college

---

[24]F-1 visa: student visa.
[25]I-20: form used to maintain a foreign student's status as a student.
[26]I-538: form used to transfer from one school to another.

university	university alumnus/university campus/university chair/university fellow/university fellowship/university fraternity/university graduate/university honors/university research center/university scholar/university scholarship/university sorority/university undergraduate/private university/state university
degree	associate's degree/bachelor's degree/college degree/doctoral degree/four-year degree/master's degree/two-year degree

ABBREVIATIONS FOR SOME SCHOLASTIC DEGREES

A.A.	Associate of Arts	2-year, undergraduate
A.S.	Associate of Science	2-year, undergraduate
B.A.	Bachelor of Arts	4-year, undergraduate
B.S.	Bachelor of Science	4-year, undergraduate
M.A.	Master of Arts	graduate
M.S.	Master of Science	graduate
M.B.A.	Master of Business Administration	graduate
Ph.D.	Doctor of Philosophy	graduate
Ed.D.	Doctor of Education	graduate
J.D.	Juris Doctor	law
M.D.	Medical Doctor	medicine

VII. ROLE PLAY SUGGESTIONS

1. Find out if you can receive transfer credit for a course you took at a different college.
2. Find out the maximum number of credits you can take in one semester.
3. Find out how to drop a course.

VIII. PREPOSITION PRACTICE

A. Prepositions That Show Logical Relationships

USE **LIKE** TO SHOW:

similarities.   Professor Smith has two Ph.D. students. They look **LIKE** Smith, talk **LIKE** Smith, and even think **LIKE** Smith.

USE **AS** FOR:

in the role of.   I'm now speaking **AS** a foreign student advisor.

USE **BEHIND** TO SHOW:

support.   Don't give up. We're all **BEHIND** you.

reason for.   There are probably a lot of good reasons **BEHIND** her decision.

Complete the following exchanges with the appropriate preposition.

1.   A: I've seen crazy registrations before, but this one takes the cake.[27]

      B: I know, it's _____ a madhouse in here.

2.   A student and a professor:

      A: Thank you for your advice, professor.

      B: Anytime.

      A: I want you to know I appreciate the fact that you always speak to me _____

         _____ a friend, not _____ a teacher.

3.   A: I'd like to apply for a tuition waiver.[28] Are those the application forms?

      B: No. They look _____ them though. Wait a minute and I'll get

         them for you.

4.   A: Our lab reports were due yesterday, and I see you haven't handed them in yet.

      B: I know, but I'm not _____ you; I can't hand anything in until

         I feel it is perfect.

5.   A: Jim Davis is running for[29] student body president, and I think he'll win.

      B: Why's that?

      A: Jim has all of the fraternities[30] and sororities[31] _____ him.

---

[27]take the cake: to exceed all others (when talking about people or situations, usually in a bad way).
[28]tuition waiver: permission to attend classes and receive credit without paying tuition.
[29]run for: to seek office.
[30]fraternity: a social club for male students.
[31]sorority: a social club for female students.

B. Additional Preposition Combinations

drop out (IS):
to quit, to withdraw

Francis *dropped out* of school last year. So now they call him a "drop out."

drop in/over/by (IS):
to visit

My classmates always *drop in* for a beer.

drop off (S):
to deliver

I *dropped off* my laundry before I went to class.

hang around (IS):
to be somewhere, doing nothing definite

I can't *hang around* the fraternity house[32] all day, so please call me as soon as you finish your exam.

hang on (IS):
to persevere; not to give up

Don't drop the course. *Hang on* until you see your first test grade.

to wait

A: Is Joanne there?
B: *Hang on* a second. I'll get her.

hang up (S)/***hang up on*** (IS):
to place on a hook

He always *hangs* his coat *up* before he goes to his seat.

to replace the receiver on the telephone

He *hangs up on* her all the time.

Complete the following exchanges with the appropriate preposition combination.

1.   On the phone:

A: Registrar's office.

B: The assistant registrar, please.

A: Okay. _____ , please. She'll be right there.

(She now comes to the telephone)

C: Ms. Morse speaking. May I help you?

B: Yes, I'd like to know when I can come to get a copy of my transcript.[33] I'm in a

hurry.

---

[32]fraternity house (frat house): residence of members of a fraternity.
[33]transcript: a student's academic record.

C: Well, why don't you _____ this afternoon? It won't be busy, so

I'm sure we can do it for you in a few minutes.

2.   Student and a counselor:

A: I'm doing poorly in all my classes, and I'd like to _____ of school

for a year and work.

B: Well, I advise you to _____ until the end of the semester. If you

_____ now, you'll get all F's.

A: Maybe you're right. I'll get cracking. I think I can pass every course if I put my mind

to it.

3.   Two students in the cafeteria:

A: Edward, do me a favor, okay?

B: Sure. What is it?

A: On your way to the Science Building, _____ these two books at

the library.

B: No problem.

4.   Two students:

A: Peggy, I need a ride home today. Can you take me?

B: When is your last class?

A: It's over at four o'clock. How about you?

B: My last class is at one o'clock, but I can _____ until four o'clock.

I don't mind.

Student Aid Application

School Year 1984-85

Warning: If you use this form to establish eligibility for federal student aid and you purposely give false or misleading information on this form, you may get a $10,000 fine, a prison sentence, or both.

Section A—Student's Information

1. Student's name

Last | First | M.I.

2. Student's permanent mailing address (See instructions for question 5 for state abbreviation.) Mail will be sent to this address.

Number, street, and apartment number

City | State | Zip code

3. Student's social security number

4. Student's date of birth

Month | Day | Year

5. Student's state of legal residence

State

6. The student is
1 ☐ a U.S. citizen
2 ☐ an eligible noncitizen (See instructions.)
3 ☐ neither of the above (See instructions.)

7. Student's expected year in **college** during 1984-85. (Check only one box.)
1 ☐ 1st (freshman)
2 ☐ 2nd (sophomore)
3 ☐ 3rd (junior)
4 ☐ 4th (senior)
5 ☐ 5th (undergraduate)
6 ☐ first year graduate or professional (beyond a bachelor's degree)
7 ☐ continuing graduate or professional

8. Will the student have a bachelor's degree by July 1, 1984?
Yes ☐ 1 No ☐ 2

9. The student is
1 ☐ unmarried (single, divorced, or widowed)
2 ☐ married   3 ☐ separated

10. How many dependent children does the student have? (If none, write in "0.")

11. Is the student a veteran of the U.S. armed forces? (See instructions.)
1 ☐ Yes
2 ☐ No

Section B—Student's Status

Read the instructions to find out who counts as the student's parent before you answer 12, 13, and 14. If you leave an answer blank it will be counted as a "Yes."

		Yes No		Yes No		Yes No		Yes No
12. Did or will the student live with the parents for more than six weeks (42 days) in	1981?	1☐ 2☐	1982?	1☐ 2☐	1983?	1☐ 2☐	1984?	1☐ 2☐
13. Did or will the parents claim the student as a U.S. income tax exemption in	1981?	1☐ 2☐	1982?	1☐ 2☐	1983?	1☐ 2☐	1984?	1☐ 2☐
14. Did or will the student get more than $750 worth of support from the parents in	1981?	1☐ 2☐	1982?	1☐ 2☐	1983?	1☐ 2☐	1984?	1☐ 2☐

For federal aid: If you answered "Yes" to any of the questions for 1983 or 1984 in Section B, you must fill in the green shaded areas.
• **Exception:** If you are married, fill in both the green and the gray shaded areas.
• If your parents are separated or divorced, if your parent is widowed or single, or if you have a stepparent, you must read the instructions before going on.
For state aid: If you answered "Yes" to any of the questions for 1981 through 1984 in Section B, and you do not meet the state criteria for veterans cited in the instructions (page 7), you must fill in the green shaded areas.

For federal and state aid: If you answered "No" to all 6 questions for 1983 and 1984 in Section B, you must fill in the gray shaded areas; some colleges or programs may also ask you to fill in the green shaded areas. If you answered "Yes" to any of the six questions for 1981 and 1982, the green shaded areas must be completed for state aid as well.

Section C—Household Information

Parents

15. The parents' current marital status is:
1 ☐ single   3 ☐ separated   5 ☐ widowed
2 ☐ married   4 ☐ divorced

16. The parents' state of legal residence is

17. The age of the older parent is

18. The total size of the parents' household during 1984-85 will be (Include the student even if he/she does not live at home. Also include parents and parents' other dependent children. Include other people only if they meet the definition in the instructions.)

19. a. Of the number in 18, how many will be in college during 1984-85? (Include the student who is applying for aid and others who will be in college at least half-time.)

b. Of the number in 19a, how many of the student's parents will be in college at least half-time during 1984-85?

Student (and spouse)

20. The total size of the student's household during 1984-85 will be (Include the student, student's spouse and dependent children. Include other people only if they meet the definition in the instructions.)

21. Of the number in 20, how many will be in college during 1984-85? (Include the student who is applying for aid and others who will be in college at least half-time.)

Section D—Income and Expense Information

		Parents	**Student (and spouse)**

22. The following 1983 U.S. income tax return figures are (See instructions.)

22. (Parents)
1 ☐ from a completed return. Go to **23**.
2 ☐ estimated. Go to **23**.
3 ☐ a tax return will not be filed. Skip to **28**.

22. (Student and spouse)
1 ☐ from a completed return. Go to **23**.
2 ☐ estimated. Go to **23**.
3 ☐ a tax return will not be filed. Skip to **28**.

Tax Filers Only

23. 1983 total number of exemptions (IRS Form 1040–line 6e, 1040A–line 5e, or 1040EZ–write in "01.")

23. (Parents) __ __
23. (Student) __ __

24. 1983 income from IRS Form 1040–line 32, 1040A–line 14, or 1040EZ–line 3 (Use the worksheet in the instructions.)

24. $_____.00   **24.** $_____.00

25. a. 1983 U.S. income tax paid (IRS Form 1040–line 49, 1040A–line 23, or 1040EZ–line 9)

25a. $_____.00   **25a.** $_____.00

b. 1983 state and local income taxes paid

25b. $_____.00   **25b.** $_____.00

26. 1983 payments to an IRA and/or Keogh (IRS Form 1040–total of lines 25a and 26 or 1040A–line 11a)

26. $_____.00   **26.** XXXXXXXXXXXX

27. 1983 itemized deductions (IRS Form 1040, Schedule A–line 26. Write in "0" if deductions were not itemized.)

27. $_____.00   **27.** $_____.00

28. 1983 income earned from work (See instructions.)

28a. Father $_____.00   **28a.** Student $_____.00
28b. Mother $_____.00   **28b.** Spouse $_____.00

Student aid application

5.   Two students:

A: Do you have a date for the dance Saturday night?

B: No, I don't.

A: Why don't you ask that girl in your history class?

B: Oh, you mean Kathy?

A: Yeah.

B: Forget it. She hasn't spoken to me in a week. In fact, the last time I called her she

_____   me.

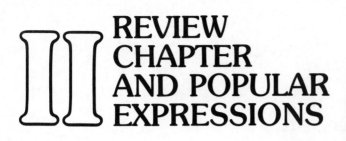

II REVIEW CHAPTER AND POPULAR EXPRESSIONS

I. CREATE A DIALOGUE

Create a dialogue using the words and expressions listed.

1. Two roommates talking about the phone bill:
   A: cut down on
      long distance calls
   B: take into account
      my family
      out of state
   A: call
      weekends
      cheaper

   _____

   _____

   _____

   _____

2. A super and a new tenant:
   TENANT: come on in
           would like you
           hook up
           stove
   SUPER: you have got to
          gas company
          first

_____

_____

_____

_____

_____

3. Two roommates:
   A: look forward to
         home to Canada
         holidays
         come along
         spare room
   B: take advantage of
         opportunity to see Canada

_____

_____

_____

_____

4. A professor and a student:
   PROFESSOR: fail
                 the last two tests
                 be better off
                 drop
                 otherwise
                 end up
                 fail the course
   STUDENT: would rather
               not drop
   PROFESSOR: had better
                 get cracking

_____

_____

_____

_____

_____

5. Two students are talking about tomorrow's exam:
   A: be all set
      exam
      tomorrow?
   B: have yet to
      open a book
   A: put things off

_____

_____

_____

_____

_____

6. Two friends are talking about apartments:
   A: was planning to
      buy a condominium
      have second thoughts
   B: how come?
   A: too expensive for
      in the long run
      be better off
      rent

_____

_____

_____

_____

7. A woman is shopping in a thrift shop:
   A: what will it be?
   B: dress
   A: on sale
   price
   can't be beat
   B: can
   take off
   a few dollars
   A: no
   keep in mind
   quality

   _____

   _____

   _____

   _____

   _____

8. A husband and wife are discussing dinner:
   A: eat out
   tonight
   for once
   B: can go
   French restaurant
   brother
   rave about
   A: don't care for
   French food
   how about
   Italian

   _____

   _____

   _____

   _____

9. Two people are talking about going shopping:
   A: go shopping
   B: weather
      bad
   A: in spite of
      Savemark's
      red tag sale

   _____

   _____

   _____

   _____

   _____

10. A couple are going to prepare a midnight snack:
    A: run out of
       mayonnaise
    B: no problem
       takeout restaurant
       instead
       buy sandwiches
       open until midnight
    A: takeout food
       makes one sick
    B: then
       deli
       pick up
       mayo

    _____

    _____

    _____

    _____

    _____

11. Two friends. One is reading the newspaper when the other enters:
    A: what
       read?

B: look at
      apartment ads
      look for
      studio apartment
A: how much
      afford to
B: look for
      under two hundred dollars a month
A: be in for
      disappointment
      anything that cheap
B: keep on
      until

_____

_____

_____

_____

_____

12. Two college students:
A: why
      not drop by
      last night
B: swamped with
      work
A: miss out
      good time
B: term paper
      get over with

_____

_____

_____

_____

_____

13. Two college students:
   A: make up one's mind
   which elective
   B: computer course
   I'm sure
   get something out of
   A: too difficult for
   B: if
   put one's mind to
   do well

_____

_____

_____

_____

_____

II. POPULAR EXPRESSIONS FROM ENTERTAINMENT, MEDIA, AND THE ARTS

Origin	Expression	Definition	Example
Theatre	(be) a star	to be famous; to be the best in one's field	He's had some success, but he is not *a star*.
Theatre	(be) a ham ham it up	to be an actor; to act too much; to overact	When you accept the award, don't *be such a ham/ham it up*.
Theatre/ Movies	(be) a production make a production out of (something)	to make/do more than necessary	She can never simply prepare a meal. She's got to *make a production* out of it.
Dance	(be) on one's toes (keep)	to be/to keep alert	His method of teaching keeps you *on your toes*.

Complete the following exchanges with the appropriate expression from the above list.

1.   On the phone:

   A: How was Larry's birthday party?

B: It was extraordinary! He had over one hundred guests, a full orchestra, and enough food for an army.

A: I'm not surprised. Larry always loves to _____ everything.

2.   A: Congratulations, Rita, on scoring number one in the nation on the math achievement test. That's great! I saw your picture in the newspaper, too.

B: Thanks, Leon. I'm really happy, but I don't like all the attention I'm getting.

A: Well, you'll have to live with it,[1] because now you're really _____ .

3.   A: Boy, I've got to buy special food for our guests; I've got to spend days preparing the meal; then I've got to get the right music.

B: Wait a minute. We don't have to _____ a small dinner party.

4.   A: Do you have Professor Johnson for Speech 16?

B: Yes, and I really like her classes. The material she presents is challenging, and she always keeps us _____ .

A: Well, I have Professor Williams and he's good, too.

B: Really? I heard he's a big _____ and not a very good instructor.

A: It's true that he does _____ it _____ a bit, but that makes the class more interesting.

5.   Two sisters are talking:

A: Where can we take mother for her birthday?

---

[1]live with (something): to have to endure, bear (something).

B: Can't we go to a quiet little restaurant and just have a good meal?

A: Are you kidding? You know mom. She will be very upset if we don't _____

_____ her birthday.

III. GRAMMAR REVIEW

A. Tenses

Simple Past; Past Continuous; Past Perfect; Future.
Complete the following exchanges using the appropriate tense.

1. A: _____ you _____ the Academy Awards[2] last
                                          (watch)

    night?

    B: No, I _____ busy.
                              (be)

    A: What _____ you _____ ?
                                              (do)

    B: I _____ my history paper.
                            (write)

2. A: _____ you _____ us to the movies tonight?
                                          (take)

    B: I can't. I _____ the opera. I _____ you to a
                          (go)   (treat)

    movie on the weekend. That's a promise.

3. A: Where _____ you at ten o'clock last night?
                              (be)

    B: Home. Why?

    A: No one answered your phone.

    B: Oh, I _____ a movie from the television.
                        (video tape)[3]

    I _____ the phone.
                  (hear; negative)

4. A: _____ you _____ to the Apollo Art Gallery[4]
                                          (go)

    with Allison yesterday?

---

[2]Academy Awards: yearly movie awards.
[3]video tape: to record the picture and the sound on tape.
[4]art gallery: a place which exhibits works of art.

B: No, we _____ .

A: What happened?

B: When I _____ her the name of the artist, she said she
            (tell)

_____ his works before.
            (see)

5. A: Anna is upset because you _____ her to the opening[5]
                                    (invite; negative)

   of the show.

   B: Oh, no. I thought you already _____ her to come.
                                        (ask)

   I _____ her up right now and apologize.
        (call)

6. A: Where's the latest issue of *Newsweek*?

   B: I _____ it out. You told me you _____
        (throw)

   already _____ it.
              (read)

   A: Oh, that's right. I _____ at it last night.
                            (look)

7. A: I _____ Erika to the ballet for her birthday next week.
        (take)

   B: Oh, she _____ thrilled.
                (be)

   A: Now, don't tell her. I want it to be a surprise.

   B: Don't worry. I _____ anything. I promise!
                        (say; negative)

8. A: I called your sister last night, but she didn't seem too happy to hear from me.

   B: No, it's not that. She _____ her favorite T.V. program when
                                (watch)

   you _____ .
          (telephone)

9. A: Where _____ you yesterday? I _____ to reach
               (be)   (try)

   you all afternoon.

---

[5]opening: the first performance of a show, movie, etc. *Also* open: to begin performances.

B: I _____ research in the library all day yesterday.
        (do)

   Why _____ you _____ to reach me?
                      (try)

A: I _____ an extra ticket for last night's concert and
        (have)

   I _____ to invite you.
        (want)

B: Oh, that's too bad. I guess I _____ out.
                         (miss)

10. A: I want to use the tape deck[6] this afternoon, but something's wrong with it. It

    _____ .
         (record; negative)

    B: Let me have a look. No wonder it _____ . You have to
                          (record; negative)

    press the record button first.

    A: Oh, thanks. I _____ the piano concert that starts at three o'clock
              (tape)[7]

    this afternoon. Do you want to listen with me? I'm sure you _____
                        (love)

    it. Horowitz _____ .
                      (play)

B. Conditional

Complete the following exchanges using the appropriate form of the conditional.

1. A: Are you going to subscribe[8] to that new weekly magazine? It's coming out[9] next

   month.

   B: How much is it per issue?

   A: I don't know yet.

   B: I _____ if it _____ too expensive.
        (subscribe)   (be; negative)

2. A: Do you think I should get cable T.V.?[10]

---

[6]tape deck: tape recorder.
[7]tape: to record with a tape recorder.
[8]subscribe: to agree to receive (a newspaper, magazine, etc.) regularly for a period of time.
[9]come out: to appear; be published.
[10]cable T.V.: television which is connected to your house by a cable. You usually have to pay for it.

B: If I _____ (be) you, I _____ (negative) . I don't think it's worth it.

A: Well, maybe if they _____ (lower) the rates, someday

I _____ (get) it.

3. A: Why didn't you go to see that new play? It was very good.

B: I _____ (go) to see it if it _____ (close; negative)[11] so soon. It closed a week after it opened!

4. A: You must go and see "The Red Room." It's outstanding.[12]

B: I _____ (go) this week if I _____ (have) time. Where is it playing?

A: It's at the Bijou. If I _____ (be) you, I _____ (go) to an early show. At night the lines are quite long.

5. A: Why didn't you attend the party last night? We had a ball.[13]

B: I _____ (come) if I _____ (have) time, but I had to study.

A: So you were burning the midnight oil[14] again! I think you work too hard. You have to have some free time once in a while,[15] too.

---

[11]close: (refers to a play, show, etc.) to stop performing.
[12]outstanding: excellent.
[13]have a ball: to have a very good time.
[14]burn the midnight oil: to study late at night.
[15]once in a while: sometimes; occasionally.

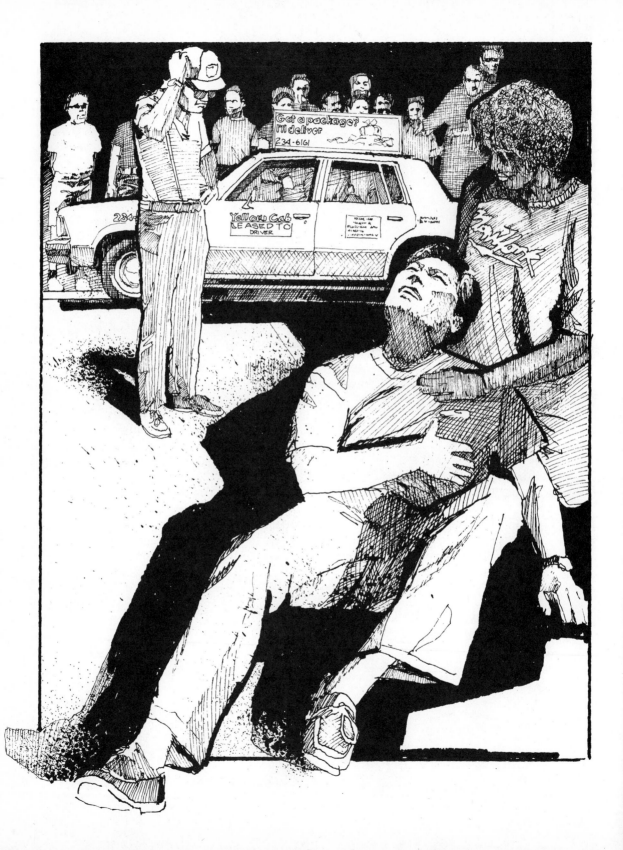

9 THE ACCIDENT

I. NARRATIVE

By the time[1] Mr. Lin paid for his courses at the bursar's office, it was already 7:15 in the evening. He was exhausted. All he wanted to do now was to go home and sleep. Unfortunately, his mind was on[2] the day's events, and as he crossed the street, he didn't realize that he was stepping in front of a taxicab. The cab driver, who **was** just **about to** stop to let out a passenger, slammed[3] on his brakes, but it was too late. The taxi struck Mr. Lin and threw him several feet onto the sidewalk. Mr. Lin felt a sharp pain in his left side as his books flew out of his hands.

Within seconds a crowd of pedestrians surrounded him. There must have been ten people trying to help him. A woman placed her coat under his head; a young man put Mr. Lin's books in a neat pile by his side. Just as a third pedestrian was telling Mr. Lin that an ambulance was on its way, a police car pulled up. "Don't worry," the officer began, "an ambulance is on the way. You know, you're the luckiest pedestrian I have ever seen because the impact could easily have killed you." The other police officer began to ask both Mr. Lin and Mr. Sveros, the taxi driver, a lot of questions. Mr. Sveros kept repeating, "He should have seen me. I was right there. He should have seen me." The ambulance pulled up before the police officer could finish filling out the accident forms. Two emergency medical technicians[4] jumped out of the ambulance and quickly checked Mr. Lin's condition. They then decided to take him to the emergency room for x-rays.

On the x-ray table Mr. Lin kept worrying about how this accident might interfere with his studies. His mind was going a mile a minute.[5] "**If only** I had been more careful crossing the street! Now what? Will I have to stay in bed for a long period? Will medical appointments make me miss classes? Will I have to withdraw?" Mr. Lin felt a great sense of relief when

---

[1]by the time: after the time needed to do something.
[2]one's mind is on (something): to be thinking about something other than what one is doing at the present.
[3]slam: to hit hard.
[4]emergency medical technicians: medically trained ambulance drivers.
[5]one's mind is going a mile a minute: to be thinking very quickly, usually when worried about something, or considering various possibilities.

the emergency room doctor told him, "You have a few bad bruises and two broken ribs. You can go to classes, but take it easy. Rest is the only thing that will cure you." He was also pleased to find out that he didn't have to pay the $215 medical bill. His student fee included a medical insurance plan which covered this type of emergency room treatment. He thought to himself, "If this accident had happened before I finished registering, I would have been out of luck."

When he left the emergency room, he met the cab driver. Mr. Sveros had come to the hospital to make sure that Mr. Lin was not badly hurt. They talked for a few minutes and Mr. Sveros offered him a ride to his apartment "on the house."[6] Mr. Lin gladly accepted the offer. Later, as he entered his small apartment, Mr. Lin **couldn't help** thinking that this had been one of the most fortunate days of his life. It was good to be still alive!

QUESTIONS

1. What did Mr. Lin want to do after he had paid for his courses?
2. Why didn't Mr. Lin realize he was stepping in front of a moving taxi?
3. What did the taxi driver do when he saw Mr. Lin?
4. What did the pedestrians do?
5. Why did one of the policemen tell Mr. Lin he was lucky?
6. What did the taxi driver keep saying?
7. What did the medical technicians decide to do?
8. What was Mr. Lin worried about?
9. Why didn't Mr. Lin have to pay the medical bill himself?
10. How did Mr. Lin get home from the hospital?
11. How come Mr. Lin couldn't help thinking he had been very fortunate?

II. DIALOGUE

A police officer is speaking with Mr. Lin shortly after his accident.

OFFICER: Tell me what happened.

MR. LIN: Well, I wasn't paying attention when I started to cross the street, and I stepped in front of a taxi. I didn't realize it was still moving.

OFFICER: Can you walk?

MR. LIN: Not very well.

OFFICER: Where does it hurt?

MR. LIN: My side hurts with each step I take.

---

[6]on the house: free; no charge.

OFFICER: Okay, don't try to walk anymore. Don't worry. An ambulance is on the way. You know, you're actually one of the luckiest pedestrians I've ever seen; the impact could have easily killed you.

MR. LIN: Yes, I guess it could have.

OFFICER: You'll have to fill out a form. Do you have any identification with you?

MR. LIN: I have my passport. By the way, how did you get here so fast?

OFFICER: Someone dialed 911[7] and reported the accident. We were in the area and got a radio call. It only took a minute or so to get here.

QUESTIONS

1. How come Mr. Lin didn't realize that the taxi was still moving?
2. What hurt when Mr. Lin tried to walk?
3. How did the police get there so quickly?

III. GRAMMAR

A. Past Modals: should have, must have, might have, could have

Recall these sentences from the narrative:

. . . you're the luckiest pedestrian I have ever seen because the impact *could* easily *have killed* you.

He *should have* seen me.

FORM:

| should + (not) + have + Past Participle |
| must |
| might |
| could |

These forms are all used to talk about the *PAST*.

SHOULD HAVE

We use this to talk about something that was a good idea or advisable to do, but was not done:

John *should have called* the police at 911. (It was advisable to call, but John didn't call.)

---

[7]911: the number to dial for emergencies throughout the United States.

MUST HAVE

We use this to talk about one possibility which we think probably happened:
John *must have called* the police. (Someone called the police. It wasn't us, so it probably was John.)

MIGHT HAVE

We use this when we have more than one possibility in mind, and we are not sure which possibility actually happened:
John *might have called* the police. (Someone called the police. One possibility was that John called, but maybe Jane or someone else called.)

COULD HAVE

We use this to talk about something that was possible but did not happen, or to say that someone had the ability to do something, but didn't do it. When we use *could not have*, we think it was impossible for something to have happened.
John *could have called* the police. (John was near a phone and thus had the ability to call.)
John *couldn't have called* the police. (John was out of town, so it was impossible for him to call.)

Could have is also used with the same meaning as *might have*.

Complete the following exchanges with *should have, could have, must have,* or *might have*. In some cases, more than one answer is possible.

Example: A: She's not in the outpatient ward[8] and she's not at the Rooston Clinic.[9]
B: Then she *must have gone* to Dr. Cox around the corner. She usually goes to him.

1.   A: Where did you take her after she spilled boiling water on herself?

B: I drove her to Linden General Hospital first, but they sent us to another hospital because they didn't have a burn expert.

A: You _____ a special-burn-unit hospital in the Yellow Pages.[10]
(look up)

That way you _____ some time.
(save)

---

[8]outpatient ward: the place where people wait to see doctors who work for the hospital or clinic.
[9]clinic: a center for health-care services.
[10]Yellow Pages: a phone directory that lists business numbers. It also lists hospitals with specialty units after the name of the hospital.

2. A: I understand that Mrs. Sanchez's daughter got food poisoning.

B: Yes, she _____ something bad at school. I don't know
                    (eat)

how else[11] she _____ food poisoning.
                                    (get)

3. A: I just paid a thousand dollars for my hospital bill.

B: Wow! And you were only there for a week! Don't you have insurance?

A: Of course.

B: Well, ask your hospital to recheck your bill. Who knows? They _____

_____ a mistake.
                                    (make)

4. In a police station:

A: I was mugged.[12] They took everything. Watch, wallet, rings, and even my tiepin.

B: What time did it happen?

A: Around 2 A.M.

B: Well, you're lucky that you weren't hurt. What were you doing walking around out-

side at that hour?

A: I know. _____ better than to walk in that neighborhood
                              (know)

so late at night.

5. A: Gloria, someone broke into my apartment yesterday.

B: Do you know when?

A: Sometime after 11 A.M. and before 6 P.M.

B: Well, about four in the afternoon, I saw a guy[13] on the fire escape.

---

[11]how else: by what other means; in what other way.
[12]mug: to rob (on the street).
[13]guy: a man.

A: Didn't you call the cops?[14]

B: No, I didn't.

A: You _____ them! The guy you saw _____ the
    (call)   (be)

burglar and they _____ him.
                        (catch)

6. In a pharmacy:

A: Hi, I'm Mr. Hyde. Is my prescription ready?

B: I'm sorry. I don't see anything here for you. Are you sure your doctor called it in?

What's the doctor's name?

A: Dr. Jeckyl. I was in his office when he called it in.

B: Oh, I know. My assistant _____ it in the back. One second
                                    (put)

and I'll check.

7. A: I just got my dental bill.

B: How much was it?

A: Sixty dollars, just for a checkup and having my teeth cleaned.

B: What did I tell you? You _____ to my dentist.
                                        (go)

8. A: I had to have surgery on my mouth.

B: Because of the accident?

A: Yes. My head hit the dashboard and I lost a few teeth.

B: You _____ your seat belt.
        (be wearing; negative)

A: No, I wasn't.

9. A: Where did Deb go?

---
[14]cops: police.

B: She went to her doctor.

A: She _____ . Doctor Lemens is out of town this week.
(negative)

B: Well, she _____ another doctor.
(go)

10. A: I got a get-well card[15] from Jeanne today.

B: Oh, Andy _____ her about your operation.
(tell)

A: No, he _____ . He still doesn't know about it.
(negative)
I wonder how Jeanne found out.

B: Beats me![16] Karen _____ it to her, or maybe Larry did.
(mention)

IV. EXPRESSIONS AND IDIOMS

● *be (just) about to:* ready to, close to doing something

be (just) about to + Verb (base form)

Recall this sentence from the narrative:
    The cab driver, who *was* just *about to* stop to let out a passenger, slammed on his brakes . . . .

Complete the following exchanges with an appropriate response using *be (just) about to:*

Example: A: Where are you going?
B: Out shopping.
A: You really shouldn't wear all that jewelry just to go shopping! You could get mugged!
B: I know. *I was just about to take it off.*
(take off)

1. On the phone:

A: I can't talk to you long, Morgan. We _____ .
(go out for a walk)

---

[15]get-well card: a card sent to a sick person to wish him/her a speedy recovery.
[16]beats me: I don't know; I have no idea.

B: Now? Isn't it a little late?

A: Why? Don't you think it's safe to go out at night around here?

B: Well, just remember that there are fewer people out on the streets at this hour, so you should keep alert, just in case.[17]

2.   A: You look terrible! Are you sick?

B: Yes. In fact, I _____ when you came in. I think I'm
(call the doctor)
coming down with[18] the flu.

3.   On the phone:

A: Hello. I'd like to speak to Dr. Bruson, please.

B: I'm sorry. The doctor can't speak with you now. He _____ .
(leave for the hospital)
If you leave your name and number, he'll get back to you later.

4.   A: I'm going out to the store. Do you want me to pick up your prescription on my way back?

B: Oh, yes. I'm glad you asked. I _____ and have them
(call the drugstore)
deliver it. Are you sure it's no trouble for you to pick it up?

A: Of course not.

5.   A: Our downstairs neighbor locked himself out of his apartment. I just saw him as I was coming in. He was so angry I thought he was going to break the door down.[19]

B: Oh, is that what that racket[20] was? I'm glad you told me. I _____
(call the police)
because I thought someone was trying to break into[21] his apartment.

---

[17]just in case: as a precaution; in order to be prepared (for trouble).
[18]come down with: get, catch (a disease, sickness).
[19]break down: to knock (a door, wall) down by hitting it.
[20]racket: a lot of noise.
[21]break into: to force one's way into (a house, etc.).

PATIENT INFORMATION (Please print.)

_____

Date: ....

Mr.
Mrs.
Miss ....
     Last Name   First Name   Middle Name

Address: ....
      Street   City   State   Zip
                                                    Code

Telephone: ....

....
Social Security Number   Date of Birth   Age

Occupation: ....

Driver's License Number: ....

Place of Employment: ....

Marital Status: .... Spouse's Name: ....

In case of emergency call: ....

Telephone: ....

Insurance Company: ....

Policy Number: ....

Signature: ....

Patient in-take form

A: I don't know why he just doesn't call a locksmith.

6. In a car:

A: We're not going anywhere until you put on your seat belt!

B: All right! Take it easy! I _____ .
(buckle it up)

A: Sorry. I didn't mean to jump on[22] you. It's just that I get nervous when people don't

wear seat belts.

● *if only:* it would be good if something happened; I wish.

Recall the following sentence from the narrative:
If only I had been more careful crossing the street!

Notes:

a. Use *Present Unreal* and *Past Unreal Conditional* forms (Chapter 8) with *if only* for present and past situations:

Present-Unreal Situations:

if only + Subject + Verb (Past Tense)

If only this *were* a safe neighborhood!

Past-Unreal Situations:

if only + Subject + Verb (Past Perfect)

If only I *had called* the police sooner, they would have caught the thief.

b. Use *would* with *if only* for future situations:

Future:

if only + Subject + would + Verb (base form)

If only the police *would catch* the man who mugged her!

Complete the following exchanges with an appropriate response using *if only*.

> **Example:** A: <u>*If only I had known*</u> Billy was walking home last night.
> (know)
> B: Why? What happened?

---

[22]jump on (someone): become angry at; yell at (someone).

A: Someone robbed him on his way home. If I had known he was planning to walk home by himself, I would have told him to stay at his friend's house for the night.

1. In a dentist's office:

A: Dr. DeGregoria, are you going to have to pull the tooth?

B: Yes, I'm afraid so. _____ in when it first started bothering
(come)

you, we might have saved it, but it's too late now.

2. A: I'm sorry to hear that Jane was in an accident. Was she hurt badly?

B: No, she wasn't injured as seriously as we thought at first. _____
(be wearing)

her seat belt, she wouldn't have been hurt at all.

3. In a hospital:

A: How are you feeling today?

B: Better. But now I'm sick over the hospital bill. _____ major
(have)

medical coverage!

A: You don't?

B: No, so the insurance is only covering part of the bill.

A: Is it paying for the round-the-clock[23] private nurses you had last week?

B: Not completely. It only pays twenty percent of the bill, up to five thousand dollars.

4. A: Jeff was hurt last night when someone tried to mug him.

B: Oh, I'm sorry to hear that. Was he hurt badly?

A: His arm was broken when he tried to fight off[24] the guy.

B: Oh! _____ him the money! The police say you shouldn't resist.
(just give)

[23]round-the-clock: for a twenty-four hour period.
[24]fight off: to defend oneself against an attacker.

● *can't help:* to be unable to avoid or stop.

can't help + Verb-ing

Recall this sentence from the narrative:
 Mr. Lin *couldn't help thinking* that this had been one of the most fortunate days of his life.

Complete the following exchanges with an appropriate response using *can't help.*

Example: A: How's the bad back?
 B: It's better now, but I <u>*can't help thinking*</u> about how care-
          (think)
 less I was when I lifted those heavy boxes.

1. A: Did Barbara burn herself badly on her new electric stove?

 B: Yes, she did, but she's fine now.

 A: Well, you know, I _____ responsible for that because I was the
             (feel)

 one who told her to buy an electric stove.

2. A: How much is your auto insurance?

 B: Three hundred and twenty-five dollars a year.

 A: Really? Do you know how much Warren pays?

 B: I think about the same.

 A: I _____ why I pay so much more than you two do.
          (wonder)

 B: The answer is obvious, isn't it? You've had more accidents than the two of us put

 together.[25]

3. A: I wish you wouldn't walk home alone from work late at night.

 B: Why not?

 A: Well, it's hardly the safest way to get home.

[25]put together: combined; in total.

B: Oh, it's not a problem. I always walk along well-lit streets and besides, there are always lots of people on the streets. Stop worrying so much!

A: I _____ .
                          (it)

4. A: I just found out that I have to have an operation.

B: What's the matter?

A: I have a hernia.

B: Well, that's not too serious.

A: I know, but I _____ about it. I've never been in the
                          (be upset)

hospital before.

B: Relax! There's nothing to worry about.

5. A: Are you going to do the driving on tomorrow's trip?

B: No, Steve's driving.

A: Could you drive instead?

B: Why? Steve's not a bad driver.

A: Well, every time I get in a car with him, I _____ the accident he
                                              (remember)

had. I was with him and we both ended up in the hospital.

B: I didn't know that. Were you seriously hurt?

A: Steve fractured two ribs, and I got a broken nose.

6. A: I hate riding the subway.

B: Oh, it's not that bad.

A: But I _____ afraid, especially at night.
                          (feel)

B: Well, if you have to ride the subway late at night, at least be sure to wait for a train in the center of the platform or near the token booth.

A: Why?

B: There aren't as many passengers on the trains at night as there are during the rush hour.

V. SITUATIONAL DIALOGUES

1. A patient enters the emergency room of a hospital.

NURSE: Please be seated. Are you well enough to answer a few questions?

PATIENT: I think so, but I might have to vomit.

NURSE: OK. Here's a special bag in case you have to throw up. Now, do you have any medical insurance?

PATIENT: I am a student and have university medical insurance. Here is my card with all the coverage information on it.

NURSE: That's fine. You've got emergency room coverage.

(A doctor walks out of an examination room)

DOCTOR: Please come into this room.

PATIENT: OK.

DOCTOR: Now, what's the problem?

PATIENT: I just can't stop vomiting. I feel dizzy and have chills and fever. I've been this way since yesterday morning.

DOCTOR: Do your bones ache?

PATIENT: Well, yes. My legs hurt and I have a dull pain in my back and chest.

DOCTOR: Do you have a sore throat?

PATIENT: Well, it's a little hard for me to swallow.

DOCTOR: OK. Let me check your heart, blood pressure, and reflexes.
(He checks them)
I think you have a virus or flu bug that's been going around, but just to be on the safe side I'm checking for more serious conditions. If the vomiting does not stop after you take the medication I'm prescribing, then please call me.

QUESTIONS

1. What kind of insurance does the student have?
2. How long has the student been sick?
3. What symptoms does the student have?

Fire box

SOS dial 911 for Emergency help
SOS marque 911 para Emergencia
This location is:
Este local:

911 emergency information on public telephone

4. What's the doctor's diagnosis?
5. What should the student do if the vomiting doesn't stop?

2. Three students enter the emergency room. One has blood on her face.

NURSE: (to the injured student) OK. Just sit down in this wheelchair and let's get a look at the wound. OK. It looks like a broken nose.
(She goes into another room and returns with an ice pack)
Hold this ice pack over your nose and the doctor will see you as soon as possible.

NURSE (to second student): Now, does she have insurance?

STUDENT: No.

NURSE: Who's going to pay the bill, then?

STUDENT: I will. You see, we had a car accident and I was driving.

NURSE: Well, you have car insurance, so I'm sure you're covered for bodily injury. I'll send you the bill and then you can submit it to your car insurance company.

STUDENT: About how much do you think it'll be?

NURSE: Well, we'll have to take x-rays and set the broken nose. I'd say about two hundred and fifty dollars.

QUESTIONS

1. What injuries does the student have?
2. Who's going to pay the hospital bill?
3. How was the student injured?
4. What will the doctors have to do?
5. How much does the nurse think the bill will come to?

3. Debbie is at the doctor's office for a checkup.

NURSE: Before the doctor sees you, I'd like to ask you a few questions about your medical history.

DEBBIE: Fine.

NURSE: Have you had any childhood diseases? Measles, mumps, chicken pox?

DEBBIE: No, I haven't.

NURSE: What vaccinations[26] did you have when you were a child? Polio, smallpox, measles?

DEBBIE: Oh, I had all of those.

NURSE: Have you ever had an operation?

DEBBIE: I had my tonsils removed when I was eleven.

NURSE: Are you allergic[27] to anything?

---

[26]vaccination: an injection used to protect a person from a disease.
[27]allergic: to be extremely sensitive to particular foods, insect stings, etc.

DEBBIE: Not that I know of.

NURSE: Well, are you allergic to any medications? Penicillin?

DEBBIE: No, I'm not.

NURSE: When was the last time you had a complete checkup?

DEBBIE: About a year and a half ago.

NURSE: Do you have medical insurance?

DEBBIE: Yes, I have Blue Cross.

NURSE: Well, that's it. Just wait right here. The doctor will be in to see you in a minute.

QUESTIONS

1. What childhood diseases has Debbie had?
2. What vaccinations has she had?
3. What kind of operation did she have?
4. What allergies does she have?
5. When was the last time she had a physical?[28]
6. What kind of medical insurance does she have?

4.   In a police station.

WOMAN: I'd like to report a robbery.

DESK SERGEANT: Just a moment. Officer O'Malloy will be right with you to fill out a report.

O'MALLOY: OK, what happened?

WOMAN: I was walking to my car on East Fifteenth Street when two young men and a young woman approached me. As they walked by, one young man grabbed my purse and one reached for my gold necklace. I struggled, so they threw me to the ground, kicked me, and then ran off. They only got my purse.

O'MALLOY: You took quite a chance with your life. Sometimes these muggers have knives or guns. You could have been killed. You should be happy you're able to walk in here to report it. You know, it's usually better not to resist.

WOMAN: I know, but I was so mad.

O'MALLOY: Give me their description, and I'll notify the patrol cars in the area. Maybe we can get them. In the future, make sure that you don't have any gold chains or jewelry showing and that you don't keep valuables in your purse.

QUESTIONS

1. What happened to the woman?
2. Where did the incident occur?
3. What did the muggers try to steal?
4. Why shouldn't she have resisted?
5. What should the woman do in the future?

---

[28]physical: a medical examination.

VI. VOCABULARY BUILDER

emergency   emergency entrance/emergency equipment/emergency number/emergency room/emergency treatment

hospital   hospital attendant/hospital bed/hospital care/hospital gown/hospital insurance/hospital room/hospital ward

clinic   dental clinic/mental health clinic/outpatient clinic/pediatric clinic

ache   backache/earache/headache/stomachache/toothache

LIST OF COMMON MEDICAL SPECIALISTS

Name	Specialized Area
allergist	allergies
cardiologist	heart
dermatologist	skin
gynecologist	women
internist	internal organs
psychiatrist	mental illness
ophthalmologist	eyes
G.P.	general practitioner [not a specialist]

VII. ROLE PLAY SUGGESTIONS

1. You're not feeling well. Call a doctor to make an appointment. Describe your symptoms.
2. Your apartment has been robbed! Call the police and report the robbery.
3. Your house is on fire! Call the fire department.
4. Someone in your family is very sick! Call for an ambulance.

VIII. PREPOSITION PRACTICE

A. Prepositions with Opposite Meanings: INTO-OUT OF

USE **INTO** TO SHOW:

motion to the inside of	The firemen walked **INTO** the smoke-filled room.
change of condition	He got **INTO** serious trouble with the police.
insertion	He plugged the light cord **INTO** the socket.
against	Someone just bumped **INTO** her car.

USE **OUT OF** TO SHOW:

motion to the outside of	The firemen walked **OUT OF** the smoke-filled room.
change of condition	His car went **OUT OF** control. The patient is **OUT OF** danger now.
removal	He pulled the light cord **OUT OF** the socket.

Complete the following exchanges with the appropriate prepositions:

1. A: Hello, 911.

    B: Yes, I need an ambulance. Someone just smashed[29] _____ my

    car and my friend is unconscious.[30] I think he went _____ shock

    after we were hit.

    A: Where was the accident?

    B: On Interstate 16 between exits 14 and 15. Please hurry.

    A: Don't move the injured person. We're on our way.

2. A: Hello, 911.

    B: Yes, someone just walked _____ my store with all my jewelry.

    A: Where is your store located?

    B: Forty-sixth and Ninth Avenue. Gail's Jewelers.

    A: We have a patrol car one block away. It'll be right over.

3. A: Hello, 911.

    B: Help! My apartment is on fire! I just had time to pull my baby _____

    bed and run to the phone.

    A: Don't go _____ your apartment again! Do you hear me? Now,

    where do you live?

---

[29]smash: to strike, to hit.
[30]unconscious: not awake, not alert.

B: 1644 West Hampsted Avenue, two blocks east of Wilshire. Hurry, please hurry.

A: We're on our way!

4.   A: What happened to you?

B: I was stepping _____ the bathtub when I tripped and hit my head

on the washbowl.

A: C'mon, get _____ the car. Let's go to the emergency room and

have someone look at it.

5.   A: Gee, you have a bad burn on your right hand. How did it happen?

B: Well, I was pouring hot oil _____ the frying pan when some of it

splattered.[31] I couldn't get my hand _____ the way fast enough.

A: Have you gone _____ town to see a doctor?

B: Not yet. I'll go today.

B. Additional Preposition Combinations

care for (IS):
to like

I don't *care for* those vitamins.

care to (IS):
to wish, want [questions and
negative sentences]

She doesn't *care to* have additional insurance.

care about (IS):
to be concerned

He *cares about* the health of his friends.

Complete the following exchanges with the appropriate preposition combination.

1.   A: What do you think about our new medical insurance plan? Isn't it great?

B: I don't _____ it because it doesn't cover large hospital expenses.

---

[31]splatter: to spill.

A: I'm happy with it. It covers the normal doctor bills, and frankly I _____

(negative)

large hospital expenses.

B: Are you crazy? At over a hundred dollars a day you'll be broke in no time.[32]

A: No problem. Don't forget we have Blue Cross/Blue Shield hospital coverage, which will cover major expenses.

B: Oh, you're right.

2. A: I've had bad headaches for two weeks now. Do you have a good doctor? I don't _____ the price. I just want someone who can help me.

B: Well, then go to Dr. Papier. She's very good and she will take good care of[33] you.

3. Two friends are talking:

A: Did you see Dr. Ramos yet?

B: I sure did and I really like him. He's thorough and he _____

his patients.

4. A: James, I heard that you were hurt at work. What happened?

B: I fell down some stairs.

A: How'd that happen?

B: Les, I don't _____ discuss the details right now.

[32]in no time: very soon; very quickly.
[33]take care of: to attend to; to provide for the needs of (someone).

10 THE REGISTERED LETTER

I. NARRATIVE

Mr. Lin **was used to** carrying only cash in his country and did the same here. When he had to pay a utility bill, he went to the post office and bought a money order. On his way over to the post office one day, he bumped into[1] his neighbor, Mr. Sharon, who asked him, "Why the rush?" Mr. Lin answered that he had to get to the post office before it closed so that he could buy a money order to pay his telephone bill. Mr. Sharon said, "Listen, to pay by money order is a waste of time and energy; just open a checking account. Writing a check is the easiest way to pay your bills. And if you open a checking account at your savings bank, it won't even cost you a penny!"

The next day, Mr. Lin went to his savings bank and opened a special checking account. This account allowed him to write checks free **as long as** he kept a five-hundred-dollar minimum balance in his savings account. For the next two months everything went smoothly. Then one day, Mr. Lin found a notice in his mailbox saying that the postman had tried to deliver a registered letter from his bank. Since Mr. Lin hadn't been home to sign for[2] the letter, he now had to go to the post office to pick it up.

The following day, when he went to the post office, he asked the postal employee why he had to sign for the letter. The woman he asked was not only very happy to answer Mr. Lin's question, but also to explain the difference between certified and registered mail. She went on[3] to tell him about airmail, air express, and regular or surface mail. "Well," she concluded, "I think you now know all about the postal system. I don't think I left anything out."[4] Mr. Lin thanked her, signed for his letter, and opened it.

---

[1]bump into: to meet unexpectedly.
[2]sign for: to sign a receipt stating that you received a letter or package.
[3]go on: to continue.
[4]leave out: to omit.

By this time, he was quite curious to find out what the letter was about. It was a form letter[5] telling him that his account was overdrawn[6] and he now had to pay a penalty because his check had bounced.[7] Mr. Lin couldn't understand how he could have overdrawn his account. He knew he had written only three checks during the last month; he was sure that he had more than enough in his account to cover the total amount of those checks. "Well," he thought, "*as long as* I'm downtown, I *might as well* go right over to the bank and straighten this out."[8]

After he had stood in line a half hour to see the service officer, Mr. Lin found out that the bank had listed a $22.50 check as $225.00. Mr. Lin had forgotten to write out the amount on the center line, and the upper right-hand corner of the check was blurred. The service officer was pleasant but very businesslike and said, "Well, these things happen sometimes. Just write a check for the correct amount and we'll cancel the other check, but you still have to pay a service charge for the overdrawn check." Mr. Lin now wondered whether or not opening a checking account had in fact been a wise decision after all.

QUESTIONS

1. What was Mr. Lin used to doing in his native country?
2. How did Mr. Lin pay his bills?
3. Why was Mr. Lin in such a hurry to get to the post office?
4. How did Mr. Sharon feel about[9] paying bills by money order?
5. According to Mr. Sharon, what's the easiest way to pay bills?
6. What kind of account did Mr. Lin open at his savings bank the next day?
7. Under what condition could Mr. Lin write checks at no charge?
8. Why did Mr. Lin have to go to the post office?
9. What was the letter from the bank about?[10]
10. Why had Mr. Lin's check bounced?

II. DIALOGUES

1.   Mr. Lin goes to the post office to pick up his registered letter. He enters the building and speaks to a clerk.

MR. LIN: Excuse me, I got this notice to pick up a registered letter. Where do I go?

CLERK: Window 12. It's over there on your right.

---

[5]form letter: a printed letter sent out in great numbers.
[6]overdraw: to write a check for more money than is available in the account.
[7]bounce: to have a check return because there is not enough money in the account to cover the amount of the check.
[8]straighten out: to correct.
[9]how does (one) feel about: what is (one's) opinion of something.
[10]what is (something) about?: What is the content of (something)? What does (something) concern?

Registered mail form

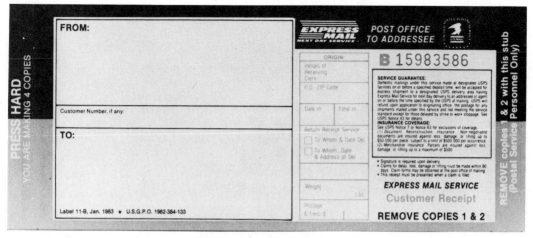

Express mail form

MR. LIN: Thanks.

(to the clerk at Window 12) I'd like to pick up a registered letter.

CLERK: Do you have your notification slip?

MR. LIN: Oh yes, of course. Sorry. . . . Here you are. By the way, I'd like to send some important papers back home to China. What's the safest way to send them?

CLERK: Well, normally you can send important mail either registered or certified and ask for a return receipt. However, there's no certified mail to China, only registered. Also, you can insure registered mail for up to four hundred dollars.

MR. LIN: I see. And what if[11] I want to send a package overseas?

CLERK: Well, you can send it either airmail or surface mail. Surface mail is cheaper; but, of course, it takes a lot longer. Probably a month or more.

MR. LIN: How big can the package be? I mean, is there a size limit?

CLERK: Yes. The length and girth[12] combined cannot exceed seventy-nine inches. The maximum weight is forty-four lbs.

MR. LIN: OK. Well, thanks for all the information. I appreciate your taking the time to tell me all this.

CLERK: That's what I'm here for. Here's your registered letter. Have a good day.

QUESTIONS

1.   Where can Mr. Lin pick up his registered letter?
2.   What's the safest way to send important papers?
3.   How much can a registered letter be insured for?
4.   What is the advantage of using surface mail to send a package overseas?
5.   What is the drawback in using surface mail?
6.   What's the size limit for packages being sent overseas?
7.   What's the weight limit?

III. GRAMMAR

A. Gerunds

A Gerund is a *Verb* + *ing*. We use a Gerund the same ways that we use a Noun:

SUBJECT

Recall this sentence from the narrative:

Writing a check is the easiest way to pay your bills.

The Gerund *writing* is the Subject of the sentence.

---

[11]what if: supposing.
[12]girth: the distance around an object.

DIRECT OBJECT

No one enjoys *waiting* in line at the bank.

The Gerund *waiting* is the Direct Object of *enjoys*.

A verb which follows these verbs takes the gerund form:

admit	delay	finish	practice	regret
appreciate	deny	mind	quit	risk
consider	enjoy	miss	recall	resume

OBJECT OF PREPOSITION

He gave *up trying* to get a credit card at that bank.

The Gerund *trying* is the Object of the Preposition *up*.

In general, a verb which follows a preposition (any preposition except "to") takes the gerund form. There are a few expressions, however, that use a gerund after "to":

be accustomed to	look forward to
be used to	

PREDICATE NOMINATIVE

The post office's top priority is *delivering* mail on time.

A Predicate Nominative follows the Verb *be* and is equivalent to the Subject. In the example sentence, the Gerund *delivering* is the Predicate Nominative and tells us exactly what the Subject *priority* is.

B. Infinitives

An Infinitive is *to* + *Verb* (base form). We use an Infinitive in the following ways:

SUBJECT

Recall this sentence from the narrative:
       . . . *to pay* by money order is a waste of time and energy. . . .

The Infinitive *to pay* is the Subject of the sentence.

DIRECT OBJECT

I need *to buy* some air mail stamps.

The Infinitive *to buy* is the Direct Object of the sentence.

A Verb which follows these Verbs takes the Infinitive form:

agree	fail	learn	pretend	try
decide	hesitate	need	promise	want
demand	hope	plan	refuse	wish
desire	intend	prepare	seem	

A verb which follows these verbs can take the infinitive or gerund form with no change in meaning:

begin	hate	love	start
continue	like	prefer	

A verb following these verbs can take the gerund or infinitive form, but note the change in meaning:

forget	remember	stop

He *stopped to buy* a money order. [He stopped at the bank, post office, etc., in order to buy a money order.]
He *stopped buying* money orders. [He doesn't buy money orders any more.]

BE + ADJECTIVE CONSTRUCTIONS

it + is + (not) + Adjective + Infinitive

It *is* not safe *to mail* cash.

Complete the following exchanges with an appropriate response using either a Gerund or an Infinitive.

> **Example:**   A: Can we leave now?
> B: What's the rush?
> A: I need *to get* to the bank before it closes.
>   (get)

1.   A: What kind of account did you *decide* _____ ?
                                                              (open)

   B: Well, I *intended* _____ a checking account.
                                      (open)

A: What happened?

B: You have to maintain a very large balance in your account in order to get free

checking. Now I'm *considering* _____ to another bank to see if
(go)

I can get a better deal.

2. A: I just invested five thousand dollars in C.D.s.[13]

B: Why don't you invest some of your money in the stock market? That's what I *plan*

_____ .
(do)

A: No, I don't *want* _____ _____ money. I *prefer*
(risk)   (lose)

_____ my money into[14] something safer.
(put)

3. A: Did you *stop* _____ my check on your way home?
(deposit)

B: Oh, no! I *forgot* _____ at the bank.
(stop)

A: Listen, that check has to be deposited today, and you *agreed* _____
(handle)

it for me.

B: You're right. I apologize. I'll go back out right now and do it.

4. A: Did you mail the package?

B: No, I couldn't. The post office *refused* _____ it.
(accept)

A: How come?

B: It was overweight. The limit is forty-four pounds. This package is fifty-two pounds.

A: A forty-four-pound limit? I don't *recall* _____ that in the post
(see)

office's mailing guide.

B: Well, you'd better check the guide again. I doubt that they *failed* _____
(put)

it in there.

_____
[13]C.D. (certificate of deposit): a high-interest savings account.
[14]put (money, time, effort) into: to invest.

5. A: Those papers *need* _____ on the West Coast by Monday, and
        (be)

        today is Friday. Why haven't you sent them out yet?

    B: Sorry. I didn't *finish* _____ them out until last night.
        (fill)

    A: Why do you always *delay* _____ things until the last minute?
        (do)

    B: Don't worry. I'll send them by overnight Express Mail. They'll get there tomorrow.

    A: All right. But you'd better *quit* _____ .
        (put things off)

    B: You're right. I *promise* _____ things on time from now on.[15]
        (do)

6. A: Where are you off to?[16]

    B: The post office. I have to get a money order.

    A: When are you going to open a checking account? _____ a check
        (write)

        is the most convenient way to pay bills.

    B: It's just as easy _____ to the post office. Have you seen how
        (go)

        crowded the banks around here are during lunch time? I *hate* _____
        (spend)

        my whole lunch hour in the bank!

7. A: I really *regret* _____ so much money for school.
        (borrow)

    B: Why? You got a student loan, right? The interest isn't that high and you don't *begin*

        _____ it back until after you finish school.
        (pay)

    A: Well, I *plan* _____ on to graduate school.
        (go)

    B: Fine. If you *continue* _____ at grad school, you don't have to
        (study)

        pay until you finish.

8. A: I *regret* not _____ an I.R.A.[17] last year.
        (open)

---

[15]from now on: starting now.
[16]be off to: to leave for; to be on the way.
[17]I.R.A. (Individual Retirement Account): a special savings plan for one's retirement.

B: Well, I *hate* _____ "I told you so."
    (say)

A: Then don't say it!

B: All right. I'm only kidding! But to tell you the truth, most of the time you do *hesitate*

    _____ when it comes to money.
    (act)

A: Well, I don't *deny* _____ worried about money.
    (be)

B: _____ worried is one thing, but letting that stop you from
    (be)

    _____ is another.[18] Listen, I don't *pretend* _____
    (invest)   (be)

    a financial expert, but it's not that difficult _____ a little reading
                                                      (do)

    and find out the best places to invest your money.

A: You're right. In fact, I'll *start* _____ the *Wall Street Journal*[19]
                                        (buy)

    tomorrow. I must start _____ _____ my money!
                            (learn)   (manage)

9. A: Did you *remember* _____ how much it costs to send a certified
                              (find out)

    letter overseas?

B: Oh, I *forgot* _____ . I'm sorry.
                   (ask)

A: That's all right.

B: No, it's not. I *promised* _____ for you. I'll just jump in the car and
                              (find out)

    go back over there. It's only five minutes away.

A: Oh, no. That's too much trouble.

B: No, it's not. I don't *mind* _____ back. I always *like*
                               (go)

    _____ my promises. Besides, I *need* _____ my
    (keep)   (check)

    post office box anyway.

---

[18]be . . . one thing . . . be another: doing the first thing is okay, but doing the second is not.
[19]*Wall Street Journal*: an important financial newspaper.

C. Participles

Participles are Verb forms. They are used in the following ways:

ADJECTIVES

Some Participles used as adjectives may be placed before a Noun. They may also serve as objective complements.

As an adjective:
>   This is an *interesting* article on finance.

As an objective complement:
>   This article is *interesting*.

Note that the Present Participle (Verb + ing) and the Past Participle (Verb + ed) have different meanings:

(1)   The *Verb + ing* Participle refers to the thing or person which is causing a feeling, emotion or state.
>   That book isn't interesting to her.

(2)   The *Verb + ed* Participle describes a feeling, emotion, or state.
>   She's not *interested* in that book.

Participles that can be placed before a Noun and that can also be used as Objective Complements include:

amazed	annoyed	bored	confused	damaged
amazing	annoying	boring	confusing	damaging
disappointed	embarrassed	excited	exhausted	
disappointing	embarrassing	exciting	exhausting	
interested	pleased	satisfied	surprised	tired
interesting	pleasing	satisfying	surprising	tiring

PARTICIPLES WITH VERBS OF PERCEPTION

Recall this sentence from the narrative:
>   . . . Mr. Lin *found* a notice in his mailbox *saying* that. . . .

PATTERN

Verb of Perception + Object Noun/Pronoun + Verb-ing

>   I *saw him cashing* the checks when I was in the bank.

We use this pattern with the following verbs of perception:

feel	notice	smell
find	see	watch

Complete the following exchanges with an appropriate response using a Participle.

    Example: A: Do you know anything about all these C.D.'s that banks now offer?

                B: Not really. It's all very *confusing*.
                                   (confuse)

                A: Well, at least I'm not the only one who's *confused* then.
                                            (confuse)

1.   A: Don't you do your banking at Mid-state Federal anymore?

       B: No, I don't. I wasn't _____ with their service. I was also fed up
                                 (satisfy)

          with[20] the errors they kept making on my statements.

       A: Oh? That's _____ . I've always found their service to be excellent.
                         (surprise)

2.   A: I noticed you _____ in line at the bank this afternoon.
                         (stand)

       B: I was cashing my paycheck. Standing in that line was really _____ .
                                                   (tire)

          I'm _____ .
                             (exhaust)

       A: Well, I have a suggestion. Why don't you have your check deposited directly?[21]

          Then you won't have to stand in line every week.

3.   A: I lost my bank passbook again. I can't believe it!

       B: Well, you'd better get over to the bank and tell them.

       A: I know, but they just gave me a new passbook last week. This is the second time I've

          lost it in the last three weeks. I'm _____ to go back there!
                                          (embarrass)

       B: I realize that it's _____ , but you still have to let them know
                         (embarrass)

          right away.

4.   A: The post office just issued a new commemorative stamp in honor of The Metro-

          politan Opera.

---

[20]be fed up (with): to be dissatisfied with; to have had too much of.
[21]direct deposit: The employer sends the bank the paycheck so that it is deposited directly in the person's account on payday.

B: Oh?

A: You don't sound very _____ about it.
(excite)

B: Well, I'm not _____ in stamp collecting.
(interest)

A: Oh, I thought you were a stamp collector.

B: No. I think collecting stamps is a rather _____ hobby. At least
(bore)

   for me it is.

5.   A: Did you receive the package I sent you?

   B: Yes, I did. Unfortunately, it was _____ .
(damage)

   A: What! I'm really _____ because I wrapped it very carefully.
(surprise)

   B: These things happen sometimes.

   A: Well, at least it was insured. I'll go to the post office tomorrow and file a claim.

6.   A: I used that new overnight delivery service last week, but my letter still arrived late.

   On top of that,[22] they didn't even inform me that they had delivered it a day late.

   I'm very _____ in their service.
(disappoint)

   B: Well, sometimes that happens. Most of the time they do deliver the next day

   though.

   A: I know, but I'm _____ because the letter needed to be there
(annoy)

   the next day.

IV. EXPRESSIONS AND IDIOMS

● *be/get used to:* to be/become accustomed to.

be/get used to +	$\dfrac{\text{Verb-ing}}{\text{Noun}}$

---

[22]on top of: in addition to.

Bank deposit and withdrawal slips

Recall this sentence from the narrative:

Mr. Lin *was used to* carrying only cash in his country. . . .

Complete the following exchanges with an appropriate response using *be/get used to.*

> ***Example:***   A: Has she ever thought about getting a credit card?
> They're very convenient.
> B: No, she says she *is used to paying* with cash.
> (pay)

1.   A: You still keep most of your money in a savings account! Why? There are so many

other ways to get more for your money nowadays.

B: I suppose I _____ just _____ a bank account at
(have)

the neighborhood savings bank.

A: Well, you can still maintain a savings account, but you don't have to put all of your

money into it.

2.   A: Would you mind showing me how to use this automatic cash machine?[23]

B: To tell you the truth, I just got my banking card last week, so I _____
(use; negative)

these machines either. Let's just read the instructions that are printed here.

3.   A: I opened my first checking account a few months ago.

B: It makes paying your bills a lot easier, doesn't it?

A: Oh, sure. The only thing I don't like is balancing my checkbook every month.

B: Oh, you'll _____ that.
(do)

4.   A: Well, today's payday. Get set[24] for another long wait at the bank!

B: I don't mind waiting in line. I _____ .
(it)

A: I don't think I'll ever _____ in line for an hour! But I guess I have
(stand)

[23]automatic cash machine: machines which give a depositor cash from his checking account.
[24]get set: to get ready; prepare.

to put up with it.[25]

5. A: What are you looking over?

    B: Oh, this bank statement that came today.

    A: You look confused.

    B: I can't _____ . They're very confusing.
        (these new bank statements)

    A: Let me have a look. You're right. There's a lot of information here. Well, let's just

        go over[26] it carefully and I'm sure we'll figure it out.[27]

● *as long as:* (a) if; providing that; (b) since this is so.

as long as + Subject + Verb

Recall these sentences from the narrative:
This account allowed him to write checks free *as long as* he kept a five-hundred-dollar minimum balance in his savings account. [if]
. . . *as long as* I'm downtown, I might as well go right over to the bank . . . . [since this is so]

Complete the following exchanges with an appropriate response using *as long as*.

Example: A: Do you think it's safe to mail these glasses to him?
            B: Sure, *as long as* you pack them carefully.

1. A: If I mail this letter tomorrow, do you think it will arrive by Saturday?

    B: Let's see. Tomorrow is Friday. Well, it should arrive the next day _____

    _____ early Friday morning.
                        (put it in the mail)

2. At a teller's[28] window in a bank:

    A: I'd like to cash this check.

    B: Fine. How would you like it?

---

[25]put up with: to bear; endure.
[26]go over: to examine; review.
[27]figure out: to find the answer; solve.
[28]teller: the bank employee who takes deposits, cashes checks, and handles day-to-day transactions.

A: Tens and twenties, please. And _____ , let me give you my next
                                          (here)

Christmas Club[29] payment.

3.   A: Will you accept a personal check?

     B: _____ .
                    (some identification)

     A: Will my driver's license do?[30]

     B: That will be fine. Also, please write your phone number on the check.

4.   A: _____ now, could you mail these letters for me?
                    (go out)

     B: Sure. I'll just drop them in the mailbox on the corner.

5.   A: Do you think this package is wrapped well enough? I want to send it overseas.

     B: _____ , I'm sure it's fine. The post office doesn't want
              (use Scotch tape; negative)

          you to use Scotch tape on packages.

● *might as well:* probably should.

Subject + might as well + Verb (base form)

Note: We often use *as long as* in the same sentence with *might as well*.

Recall this sentence from the narrative:
    . . . *as long as* I'm downtown, I *might as well* go right over to the bank . . . .

Complete the following exchanges with an appropriate response using *might as well* or *as long as . . . might as well*.

    Example: A: Remind me to buy some stamps tomorrow, will you?
              B: *Well, as long as we're out, you might as well stop and*
                  buy them today.

1.   A: Didn't you pick up your paycheck yet? Today's payday.

---

[29]Christmas/Chanukah Club: a special savings account. The depositor makes payments every
  month until December so that he/she will have money for the holidays.
[30]do: to be acceptable.

B: I've been so busy that I haven't had a chance to go upstairs and get it yet. What time is it now?

A: 3:05.

B: Oh, the bank is already closed. Well, I _____ tomorrow then.
(pick up)
It's too late to cash it today anyway.

2. In a post office:

A: I'd like to send this letter to Japan by surface mail.

B: All right. Let me weigh it for you. It's only two ounces. You _____
(airmail)
it won't cost you very much. It'll take a long time to get there by surface mail.

A: How long do you think it will take?

B: About a month.

A: Okay. I guess you're right. _____ , I _____ .
(not expensive)   (by air)

3. A: How about going out together for lunch?

B: I'd love to, but I'm short of cash.

A: Oh, come to think of it,[31] I don't have much cash with me either.

B: Well, we _____ it then.
(forget about)

A: No, I'll just stop at the bank's cash machine and get some cash.

4. A: I'd like to open a regular checking account. I've filled out all the forms.

B: Fine. How much would you like to open the account with?

A: One thousand dollars.

[31]come to think of it: We use this phrase when we suddenly realize or remember something.

B: _____ , you _____ .
(put that much money in)   (open a special checking account)

We give you interest on your money and you can write checks free.

A: Do I have to maintain a minimum balance?

B: Yes, five hundred dollars.

V. SITUATIONAL DIALOGUES

1. Mr. Walker is in a post office.

   CLERK: May I help you?

   MR. WALKER: Yes, please. Can I have a change-of-address form?

   CLERK: Okay. Here's a change-of-address kit.[32] It contains a change-of-address form that you fill out and give to me. We use that to forward your mail. It also has some change-of-address cards.[33]

   MR. WALKER: Thanks. I'd also like to send this package by Express Mail. It goes to Fargo, North Dakota.

   CLERK: Let me check the next-day-service directory to make sure we deliver there. (He checks it.) No problem. OK, it weighs less than two pounds so the price is $9.35. Just fill out this address label.

   MR. WALKER: OK. By the way, how much is insurance?

   CLERK: No charge. Every package is insured for loss or damage up to five hundred dollars.

   MR. WALKER: That's great.

   QUESTIONS

   1. What kind of form does Mr. Walker need?
   2. What is in the change-of-address kit?
   3. How does Mr. Walker want to send his package?
   4. How much is the package insured for?

2. Ms. Sills is opening a savings account.

   MS. SILLS: I'd like to open a savings account.

   BANK OFFICER: Fine. I'll need some information to fill out an application for you. Name?

   MS. SILLS: Sills, S-I-L-L-S. My first name is Belle.

---

[32]kit: a package of materials or equipment.
[33]change-of-address card: a card showing your new address which you can send to stores where you have accounts, to magazine publishers, or to friends.

PLEASE PRINT

Street Address	City		State	Zip

Telephone		Mother's Maiden Name or My Password
Home	Business	

Birthplace	Birthdate

Employer	Bank Card Account No.

Checking Account No.	Savings Account No.

SOLE PROPRIETOR ONLY

Type of Business	DUNS No.

TRUSTEE ACCOUNT ONLY (Beneficiary Identification)

Birthplace	Birthdate	Father's Name	Mother's Maiden Name

TAXPAYER INFORMATION

Taxpayer Identification Number To Be Used
For Tax Reporting Purposes:

☐ I am neither a citizen, resident, nor doing business in the United States.

☐ I am subject to backup withholding under the provisions of Internal Revenue Code Section 3406(a)(1)(C) as notified by the Internal Revenue Service.

FOR BANK USE ONLY

Identification	Exp. Date		Exp. Date
Driver's License_____ _____ Other_____ _____			

Sole Proprietor only
Fictitious Name Certificate

Received_____ Waived by_____

Date Opened	Opened By	Opening Deposit	MISC-307 Given By

First Year_____ SVC Chg _____ Courtesy Card Code _____

Mail/Hold Stmt _____ Country_____ Owner Code _____

0 Close_____ Status _____ Source_____

CHECKING		SAVINGS/TIME DEPOSIT	
TSSS _____	Daily Bl _____	SS Link_____	Min Int Waived_____
SIC _____	Multpl _____	Type Code_____	Legal Code_____
Stmt EOM _____		Rate_____	Term_____
Freq_____		Int. to be paid each calendar ☐ Mo. ☐ Qtr.	
Day 1 _____	Day 2 _____	☐ Yr. end ☐ at maturity ☐ reinvest at maturity	
Day 3 _____	Day 4 _____	Credit Interest To:	
Max. Check Amt._____		DDA:_____ SDA:_____	
		By Cashiers Check To: _____	

Entered by_____ Audited by_____ Reviewed by_____

Date Closed	Closed By	Closing Balance	Zero Close Code

Reason Closed	Closing Reason Code

Entered By_____ Audited By_____ Reviewed By_____

Savings and checking account applications

BANK OFFICER: Social Security Number?

MS. SILLS: 081-60-1234.

BANK OFFICER: OK. What's your address?

MS. SILLS: 4750 Peachtree Boulevard, apartment 7C.

BANK OFFICER: Home and work phone numbers?

MS. SILLS: My home number is 555-6211. My office number is 555-1700, extension 320.

BANK OFFICER: OK. Do you want to open a regular or joint account?

MS. SILLS: A regular account.

BANK OFFICER: How much would you like to deposit to open the account?

MS. SILLS: Twenty-five hundred dollars.

BANK OFFICER: All right. Let's go over to the teller and we'll get you a passbook.

QUESTIONS

1. What kind of account does Ms. Sills want to open?
2. What information does the bank officer need?
3. How much would Ms. Sills like to open her account with?

3. Ms. Comeaux is in a bank.

MS. COMEAUX: I'd like to see someone about getting a student loan.

OFFICER: I'm the loan officer so you've come to the right place. Now will you please fill out this loan application?

MS. COMEAUX: (fills out the application) OK, here it is.

OFFICER: It'll take about three weeks to process. We have to contact your employer and references as well as the college to make sure that you're a student in good standing. We have to make sure that the money will go for education.

MS. COMEAUX: I really have to know before that because registration is next week.

OFFICER: I'll put a rush on it. Call me at this number next Tuesday. Maybe I can give you a verbal approval then.

MS. COMEAUX: Great. Thanks for your help.

QUESTIONS

1. What kind of loan does Ms. Comeaux want?
2. How long will it take to process the application?
3. Why does it take that long to process it?
4. What does the bank want to make sure of?
5. Why is Ms. Comeaux in a hurry to get the loan?

4. Mr. Chin is in a savings bank.

MR. CHIN: I've got a savings account, but it is earning me only five percent interest. Do you have money market accounts which will give me a higher interest?

CLERK: We do have a special money market account, but you need twenty-five hundred dollars to open it.

MR. CHIN: Well, I don't have that much, but isn't there any other high-interest account I can open?

CLERK: Yes, there are C.D.'s. You need only five hundred dollars to open one, but you cannot make a withdrawal until its maturity date. We have three month, six-month, one-, two-, and three-year C.D.'s. The interest for each varies, but the interest will always be quite a bit higher than the standard savings account interest.

MR. CHIN: OK, I'd like to open a C.D. for three months. I'll give you my check for five hundred dollars.

CLERK: Today our three-month C.D. yields[34] eight and nine-tenths percent. Just fill these out and we're all set.

QUESTIONS

1. Why is Mr. Chin dissatisfied with his savings account?
2. How much do you need to open a special money market account?
3. What other high-interest accounts are available?
4. What kind of C.D. does Mr. Chin choose?
5. How much interest will he get on his money?

5. Laila and Joseph are discussing checking accounts.

LAILA: Why the worried look?

JOSEPH: Well, I'm just not good at keeping my checkbook balanced. I never know how much I have in my account and it costs me money.

LAILA: Why? What kind of a checking account do you have?

JOSEPH: A N.O.W. account. You know, the kind that earns interest if you keep a minimum balance; I keep dropping below the minimum, and each time I do that the bank charges me. All the money I make in interest goes to pay the penalty charges!

LAILA: Why not get a regular checking account? You don't get interest, but you don't have to worry about keeping a minimum balance.

JOSEPH: Well, I can overdraw my N.O.W. account up to five hundred dollars. So I actually have a five-hundred-dollar line of credit.[35]

LAILA: Well, that's not so great. I have a Master Card and I can borrow up to five hundred dollars as well. You should get a regular checking account and use Master Card when you need a quick loan.

JOSEPH: You know, you're right.

QUESTIONS

1. What is Joseph worried about?
2. What kind of checking account does he have?

---

[34]yield: to give; produce.
[35]line of credit: the amount of credit available to you.

3. What happens when his balance drops below the minimum?
4. How much credit does Joseph have with his N.O.W. account?
5. What does Laila think he should do?

VI. VOCABULARY BUILDER

check   bank check/certified check/check balance/checkbook/check deposit slip/checking account/check stop/check stub/monthly checking statement/paycheck/personal check

bank   bank branch/bank deposit box/bank loan officer/bank interest/bank manager/bank teller/bank vault/commercial bank/savings and loan bank

VII. ROLE PLAY SUGGESTIONS

1. Cash a check at the bank.
2. Ask the best way to mail a package overseas.
3. Open a savings or checking account.

VIII. PREPOSITION PRACTICE

A. More Opposites

AWAY FROM - TOWARD	Walk **TOWARD** the counter, not **AWAY FROM** it.
IN FRONT OF - IN BACK OF	The box is **IN BACK OF** the desk, not **IN FRONT OF** it.
INSIDE - OUTSIDE	The mail chute is **INSIDE** the post office, not **OUTSIDE** it.

Complete the following exchanges with the appropriate prepositions.

1. In the safe-deposit section of the bank:

A: I'm sorry, I can't let you _____ without seeing your safe-deposit

box[36] key.

B: OK. Here's my key, now can I go _____ the vault?[37]

---

[36]safe-deposit box: secure boxes stored in the safe-deposit vault.
[37]safe-deposit vault: a protected room where customers store valuables in metal safe-deposit boxes.

A: Yes, but please wait a second, until that woman moves _____

the door. I don't want the door to hit her as you open it.

2.   At the bank teller's window:

A: I'd like to open a savings account. Can I do it with this check for five hundred

dollars?

B: You sure can, but you'll have to see one of the assistant managers first.

A: Where are they?

B: There are two right over there. Mr. Sands, the man who is standing _____

_____ his desk, and Ms. Draper, the woman who is walking

_____ the quick-deposit box.[38] Or you can see Ms. Stevens. She is

the woman who is coming _____ us right now.

3.   A man asking a security guard for information:

A: Is there a mail chute in this building?

B: No, but there's a mailbox just _____ the building.

4.   At the bank:

A: Where is the chief loan officer?

B: Walk past those three offices, then turn right and go _____ the

windows. You'll see a red partition.[39] Her office is _____

that partition.

---

[38]quick-deposit box: a box for people to put deposit envelopes containing checks or cash for deposit.
A record of the deposit is returned to the depositor by mail.
[39]partition: an interior wall which often does not extend to the ceiling.

5.   In a bank:

   A: I'd like to cash this check please.

   B: Certainly, but you'll have to sign your name on the back of the check.

   A: Oh, I'm sorry. I thought I had already endorsed it. By the way, is there a public

   phone in here?

   B: No, but there's a phone booth just _____ the front door.

B. Additional Preposition Combinations

count on (IS):
to rely on

You can *count on* my support.

clear up (S):
to resolve

The Loan Department wants to *clear up* this problem by tomorrow.

clear away (S):
to remove

The mailman had to *clear away* the snow before he could deliver the mail.

make out (S):
to read/understand

The mailman cannot *make out* the address.

make out (IS):
to progress; result

After they took out another loan, they *made out* very well.

make up (S):
to invent

If you don't know the zip code, please don't *make one up!*

to recover

I hope this investment will help me *make up* the money I've lost.

to put together

Ask your banker to *make up* a new loan package for you.

make up (IS):
to become friends again after an argument

After he returned the money he had borrowed from me, we *made up.*

Complete the following exchanges with the appropriate preposition combination.

1.   A bank teller and a customer:

   A: Sir, could you please write out another withdrawal slip?

B: Why? I printed all the numbers.

A: Well, you used a felt-tipped pen and I can't _____ all the

numbers because the ink ran[40] in several places.

2. At a U.P.S.[41] office:

A: Will these packages arrive before March 15?

B: Oh, yes. You can _____ it. In fact, they'll be there by the tenth.

3. On the telephone:

A: Federal Express.[42] May I help you?

B: Yes, I sent a package to Dallas two days ago and it still hasn't arrived. My number is

1641-24.

A: OK, Mr. Nakayama. We attempted to deliver it, but our delivery person said that

there was no such address.

B: What! Do you think I'd spend eighty-four dollars to send a package to an address

which I _____ ?

A: No sir, but I can only go by the note from our deliveryman. Please hold for a

moment. I'm sure I can _____ this problem by calling directly to

our Dallas office.

B: Well, you may be able to _____ the problem, but how can I

_____ the money I've lost because the package was not delivered.

---

[40]run: to flow and spread (referring to ink, dye, paint).
[41]U.P.S. (United Parcel Service): a private company which delivers packages anywhere in the
United States.
[42]Federal Express: one of many overnight delivery services. These companies will deliver packages
anywhere in the United States, usually in one day.

KENNETH W PADGETT
3395 HOPI PL
SAN DIEGO   CA 92117

1/0/19   7

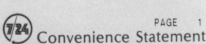
Convenience Statement

CHECKING ACCOUNT NUMBER 1903 72758 – PERIOD 03/25/81 TO 04/24/81

CHECKS

NUMBER	AMOUNT	DATE	NUMBER	AMOUNT	DATE	NUMBER	AMOUNT	DATE	NUMBER	AMOUNT	DATE
346	51.45	04 01	348	12.71	04 01	350	275.00	04 13			
347	22.21	04 02	349	33.55	04 03	351	23.20	04 22			

OTHER DEBITS

DATE	AMOUNT	DESCRIPTION
03 30	20.00	7/24 CASH WITHDRAWAL 0040 POINT LOMA OFFICE, S.D.
03 30	40.00	7/24 CASH WITHDRAWAL 0090 UNIVERSITY CITY OFFICE, S.D.
04 24	1.80	BELOW MINIMUM CHARGE

DEPOSITS

DATE	AMOUNT	DATE	AMOUNT	DATE	AMOUNT	DATE	AMOUNT	DATE	AMOUNT
04 06	342.00								

DAILY BALANCES

BALANCE	DATE	BALANCE	DATE	BALANCE	DATE	BALANCE	DATE	BALANCE	DATE
166.56	03 30	80.19	04 02	388.64	04 06	90.44	04 22		
102.40	04 01	46.64	04 03	113.64	04 13	88.64	04 24		

SUMMARY

BEGINNING BAL	CHECKS		OTHER DEBITS		DEPOSITS		OTHER CREDITS		ENDING BALANCE
226.56	6	418.12	3	61.80	1	342.00	0	.00	88.64

INTRODUCING YOUR 7/24 CONVENIENCE STATEMENT. NOW YOU CAN
INCLUDE ALL YOUR SAVINGS ACCOUNTS AND INSTALLMENT LOANS ON
YOUR MONTHLY STATEMENT. THE ENCLOSED BROCHURE TELLS YOU HOW.

Where money matters, but *people count*

FOR IMPORTANT INFORMATION - SEE REVERSE SIDE

Bank statement

4. In the post office:

A: I've come to pick up a registered letter. Here's the delivery slip.

B: OK. Please wait just a moment until I _____ these packages.

Your letter is at the bottom of the stack.

5. In a Federal Express office:

A: I'd like to send these two packages to this address.

B: OK. That'll be $9.95. They'll arrive tomorrow. Since both are going to the same

place, we can _____ one package for you.

A: That's a good idea. I would have done that myself, but I didn't have a large enough

box.

6. A: Could you lend me a few dollars? I couldn't get to the bank today.

B: I would, but I don't have much cash with me. Ask Artie.

A: Oh, no. We're not speaking to each other.

B: You two haven't _____ yet? You've been on the outs[43] for

a week.

A: I know. I'm waiting for him to apologize first.

7. Two friends are talking:

A: Did you know Sue got a bank loan yesterday?

B: She did! That's great. Now she can finally open her restaurant. I just hope she

_____ well.

A: She's a talented woman. I'm sure she'll succeed.

---

[43]on the outs: not friendly; angry with.

11 HE'S GOT A PART-TIME JOB

I. NARRATIVE

Life in the United States is expensive, especially for a graduate student who does not have a full scholarship. Mr. Lin knew **all along** that sooner or later[1] he would have to work part-time in order to make ends meet. Shortly after his mid-term exams, he decided to go to the university job placement office. The placement officer gave Mr. Lin a list of part-time positions which had been phoned in recently. Unfortunately, the jobs on the list either required a driver's license or were very far from the city, so they were of no use to[2] Mr. Lin.

Every day for almost a month, he looked on bulletin boards around the campus and checked the help-wanted ads in the local newspapers. No matter which company he called, however, the answer was always the same, "I'm sorry, but that position has already been taken." One day he spotted a big ad which had been placed by the Apex Employment Agency. The agency was looking for college grads interested in full- and part-time jobs. Mr. Lin called and was told to come in the next morning.

Even though he arrived on time for his appointment, he still had to wait an hour to see a counselor. Before he could say anything, the counselor said, "First of all, we need your resume.[3] When we have that, we'll contact your previous employers and check your references.[4] Then after we get you a job, you'll have to pay us twenty-five percent of your first month's salary. Now, what are you interested in?" Mr. Lin explained that he wanted a part-time job with flexible hours close to the university. The counselor checked some listings and made a few phone calls. He then turned to Mr. Lin and said, "I'm sorry, but we don't have anything at this time. Come back in about a month and don't forget to bring a resume. We may have something for you then."

---

[1] sooner or later: at some time in the future.
[2] be of no use (to someone): to be useless.
[3] resume: a summary of one's education and working experience.
[4] reference: 1. a statement about a person's ability or character. 2. a person who gives a statement about another's ability or character.

Mr. Lin left the office quite depressed. As he walked down the street, he began thinking, "I need a lift.[5] I think I'll splurge tonight in spite of my financial situation. I'll prepare some fancy Chinese dishes and invite Mr. Sharon and Mr. Gupti to dinner." Mr. Lin went to his local supermarket to pick up what he needed. As he was entering the store, a large sign in the window caught his eye: "PART-TIME CHECKER WANTED. NO EXPERIENCE NECESSARY. SEE MR. GLEASON, ASSISTANT MANAGER."

Mr. Lin spoke with Mr. Gleason and was hired immediately. "You'll be trained by an experienced checker," Mr. Gleason told him, "and within a week, you'll be ready to take over[6] your own register. You'll be paid the minimum wage,[7] but you can choose your hours. We're open twenty-four hours a day, seven days a week." Mr. Lin thanked Mr. Gleason and said, "That's fine with me. See you tomorrow." Mr. Lin then did his shopping, went home, and prepared a delicious meal. Both his neighbors enjoyed the meal and were amused by the events of the day.

QUESTIONS

1. When did Mr. Lin realize that he would have to get a part-time job?
2. Where did he look for a job first?
3. What did the placement officer give him?
4. What happened every time he called to find out about one of the jobs advertised around the campus or in the local newspaper?
5. What is the disadvantage of getting a job through an employment agency?
6. What did Mr. Lin decide to do on the way home?
7. What happened when Mr. Lin went to the supermarket?
8. Who will train Mr. Lin?
9. When will he be able to take over his own register?
10. How much will he be paid?
11. When can he start working?

II. DIALOGUE

Mr. Lin enters Waldgreen's Supermarket to apply for the job advertised in their window.

MR. LIN: Hello, I'd like to see the manager about the job you have posted in your window.

---

[5]a lift: an improvement in one's mood or spirit.
[6]take over: to take control, charge of, responsibility for.
[7]minimum wage: the lowest salary an employer can legally pay an employee.

CLERK: Oh, sure. Just a second and I'll get him for you.

MANAGER: I understand you're interested in a job as a checker.

MR. LIN: Yes, sir. I saw the notice in your window and came right in.

MANAGER: Have you ever done this kind of work before?

MR. LIN: No, I haven't, but I'm willing to learn, and I'm sure I can be trained quickly.

MANAGER: I'm sure you can, too. It's not that difficult a job. What hours can you work?

MR. LIN: Well, I'm a graduate student and my hours vary. Most of my classes are in the late afternoon, though.

MANAGER: That's okay. The hours are flexible, so I think we can arrange something. By the way, you're not here on a student visa, are you? If you are, I can't hire you because it's not legal for you to work.

MR. LIN: Oh no, I have a green card.[8]

MANAGER: OK. The job is yours if you want it.

MR. LIN: Sure, but can I ask how much the salary is?

MANAGER: You'll be paid the minimum wage.

MR. LIN: All right. When can I start?

MANAGER: Come in tomorrow, and we'll work out[9] a schedule. You'll also have to fill out some application forms. Can you make it at 11 A.M.?

MR. LIN: That's fine. See you then.

QUESTIONS

1.   What does Mr. Lin want to see the manager about?
2.   How did Mr. Lin find out about the job?
3.   How much experience does Mr. Lin have?
4.   Why does the manager feel that Mr. Lin can be trained quickly?
5.   Why does the manager want to know if Mr. Lin is in America on a student visa?
6.   How much will Mr. Lin be paid?
7.   What will Mr. Lin do when he comes in tomorrow?

III. GRAMMAR

A. Active vs. Passive Voice

In the Active Voice the subject is the *doer* of the action. In the Passive Voice the subject is the *receiver* of the action. We use the Passive Voice when we want to emphasize the receiver of the action rather than the doer.

---

[8]green card: permanent resident certificate for aliens.
[9]work out: to devise; arrange.

FORM: | be + Past Participle |

Present Tense
Active: Phil usually fixes the typewriter.

Passive: | be (Present Tense) + Past Participle |

The typewriter *is* usually *fixed* by Phil.

Present Continuous Tense
Active: Phil is fixing the typewriter now.

Passive: | be (Present Continuous Tense) + Past Participle |

The typewriter *is being fixed* (by Phil) right now.

Past Tense
Active: Phil fixed the typewriter yesterday.

Passive: | be (Past Tense) + Past Participle |

The typewriter *was fixed* (by Phil) yesterday.

Past Continuous Tense
Active: Phil was fixing the typewriter all morning.

Passive: | be (Past Continuous Tense) + Past Participle |

The typewriter *was being fixed* (by Phil) all morning.

Present Perfect Tense
Active: Phil has already fixed the typewriter.

Passive: | be (Present Perfect Tense) + Past Participle |

The typewriter *has* already *been fixed* (by Phil).

Past Perfect Tense
Active: Phil had already fixed the typewriter when we arrived.

Passive: | be (Past Perfect Tense) + Past Participle |

The typewriter *had* already *been fixed* (by Phil) when we arrived.

Future Tense (will)
Active: Phil will fix the typewriter.

Passive: | be (Future Tense (will)) + Past Participle |

The typewriter *will be fixed* (by Phil).

Future Tense (be going to)
Active: Phil is going to fix the typewriter tomorrow.

Passive:	be (Future Tense (be going to)) + Past Participle

The typewriter *is going to be fixed* (by Phil) tomorrow.

Modals (may, might, must, have to, should, ought to, can, would)
   Active: Phil should fix the typewriter.

Passive:	modal + be (base form) + Past Participle

The typewriter *should be fixed* (by Phil).

Complete the following exchanges using the appropriate tense in the *Passive Voice*.

Example: On the phone:
    A: Hello. I'm calling to find out about the job opening you advertised in the newspaper yesterday.
    B: Oh, I'm sorry. Someone <u>was hired</u> for that position this
                                     (hire)
   morning.

1. A: Doesn't Kurt work in this area anymore?

    B: Oh, no. He _____ . He works upstairs on the twenty-second
                   (promote)

   floor now.

    A: I didn't know that! When _____ he _____ ?
                                          (promote)

    B: Just last week. I'm sure he _____ a raise, too.
                             (give)

2. A: I'm not going to report this income.[10] It's off the books[11] anyway.

    B: Listen, it's a crime to cheat on your income tax returns. You could _____

   _____ or even _____ to prison!
        (fine)   (send)

3. A: You have to work overtime twice a month.

    B: Really?

    A: Sure. Didn't you know?

---

[10]report (one's) income: to tell the government how much money one earned (for tax purposes).
[11]off the books: not recorded in the official accounting books.

B: No, I _____ that when I _____ .
(tell; negative)   (hire)

A: Well, I'm sorry you _____ , but nevertheless it is company
(inform; negative)

policy and the rules have to _____ by everyone.
(follow)

4.   A: I'm so depressed.

B: What's the matter?

A: I _____ by six accounting firms last month, and I
(interview)

_____ by every one of them.
(turned down)[12]

B: Well, you went to a good school and got excellent grades, so I don't think it's a

matter of your ability. Maybe you just don't know how to present yourself well in an

interview.

A: You might be right.

B: Sure I am. You need to _____ on how to do well in an interview.
(train)

Lots of books _____ on it. Why don't you go to the library and
(write)

start doing some research?

A: You're right. That would be more useful than sitting around and being depressed!

5.   A: When do I have to file my income tax return?

B: What! Haven't you filed yet? All returns must _____ by April 15.
(file)

And today's the twentieth!

A: Well, now what'll happen?

B: You _____ probably _____ a percentage
(fine)

of what you owe. In other words, you'll have to pay a penalty for filing late.

---

[12]turn down: to refuse; not accept.

6. A: You're a new employee here, aren't you?

B: Yes, I am.

A: Do you know that today's payday? The checks are ready now. They _____

_____ in the accounting office on the eleventh floor.

(distribute)

B: Yes. I know. I just picked up my check. It was a lot less than I expected. I forgot that

Social Security[13] tax _____ every week in addition to federal and

(deduct)

state taxes.

7. A: Congratulations on your promotion!

B: Thank you. To tell you the truth, I have mixed feelings[14] about it.

A: Why is that?

B: Well, of course I'm happy that my salary _____ by quite a bit, but

(increase)

I'm a little nervous, too.

A: About what?

B: I _____ so many new responsibilities.

(give)

A: It's natural to be nervous when you start a new position, but I'm sure you will be

able to handle it.

8. A: Are you still looking for a job?

B: Yes, I am.

A: Three new openings _____ on the bulletin board just outside the

(post)

college placement office yesterday.

---

[13]Social Security: a government program requiring contributions from all working people. The government returns these contributions in monthly payments when the person retires.
[14]mixed feelings: to have positive and negative feelings about something or someone at the same time.

B: Oh, I saw them, too. But when I called this morning, I found out that they

_____ all _____ already.
                                       (fill)

9. A: Can you tell me how to fill out these time sheets?[15] And I don't know who to give

them to either.

B: Oh? _____ all that _____ to you yet?
                                              (explain; negative question)

A: No, not yet.

B: Well, you should have _____ how to handle those forms by the
                                  (tell)

personnel department, but since you weren't, I'll show you what to do with them.

10. A: I handed in a job application to you a few weeks ago, but I haven't heard anything

yet. _____ some kind of notification _____
                                                                    (send)

out soon?

B: Notifications _____ out last week. You should have received
                         (mail)

one already.

A: Well, it might have _____ by the post office. Several letters
                                (lose)

of mine _____ before.
                 (lose)

B: Well, if you come here in person and tell the personnel director what happened, I'm

sure you _____ another copy of the notification.
                    (give)

B. Sequence of Tenses

Recall this sentence from the narrative:
    Mr. Lin *knew* all along that sooner or later he *would have* to work part-time . . . .

When the following verbs are used in the *Past Tense* in the main clause, the verb in the dependent clause is also used in the *Past Tense* (showing that the action takes place *after* that of the main verb).

---

[15]time sheet: a form which shows how many hours an employee has worked during the week.

364
Help Wanted

Immediate opening on our Coronado Office for experienced secretary. Good typing, organizational skills, and phone manner a must. Please call Mr. Campagna after 9:00 a.m.

Fountain Waitress Wanted. Part time. Apply at fountain. 918 Orange Avenue.

Maintenance man - odd jobs, Navy. Also, in home work, prefer female by day or week. 555-6953.

Childcare my home. 3 days per week. 555-0573 after 5:00.

Single Female Employed Part-time with need for additional income on Part-time basis. Experience in General Clerical, Accounts Receiveable, Pegboard, Monthly Reports, Property Management, Billing & Collections. Work Part-time in exchange for rent or rental cost reduction. 555-4759.

LCDR and wife wish to housesit while own being remodeled Aug. to Dec. 1984 or portion thereof. No smoking/drinking. No children/pets. References. Please call 555-5511 after 6:00 p.m.

Companion / babysitter needed for 10 & 12 yr. old for summer. Flexible hours. Own transportation. Prefer college age or older. Office 555-3097. Evenings 555-8192.

Retired Navy chief or person mechanically inclined to work shipyard toolroom. Apply at First & A Ave.

Floor Covering Installation Trainee - apply at 845 Orange Ave.

Hairdresser - Part-time at the Beauty Salon. 555-8262.

Help wanted advertisement

hope	say	hear	realize	doubt
know	think	tell	ask	promise

Examples: I hope that he will be able to start soon.
I *hoped* that he *would* be able to start soon.

He says he is going to quit next week.
He *said* he *was* going to quit next week.

Complete the following exchanges using the correct tense in the dependent clause.

Example: A: Jim's quitting next week.
B: I didn't know that. What happened?
A: I'm not sure. He just said that he *wasn't satisfied* with his
(satisfied)
job anymore.

1. A: Guess what! I finally found a job.

    B: Congratulations!

    A: Thanks. To tell you the truth, I had been looking for a job for so long that I doubted

    whether I _____ ever _____ one.
    (find)
    B: Oh, I knew you _____ a good job sooner or later.
    (get)

2. A: The boss is furious. I think he's going to fire some people.

    B: Don't worry. He's always blowing his top.[16] Last week he said he _____

    _____ all of us. Of course, he didn't.
    (get rid of)
    A: I know. But this time he said he _____ .
    (be kidding; negative)

3. A: Aren't we getting a salary increase soon?

    B: Didn't you see the latest memo?[17]

    A: No. What did it say?

    B: It said that we _____ a raise at the end of the year.
    (get)

---

[16]blow one's top: to become very angry; to lose one's temper.
[17]memo (short for *memorandum*): a brief communication used within a company or office.

4. A: Are we going on strike?[18]

B: I thought we _____ , but now I don't think so.
(be)

A: Well, I never thought we _____ this year. None of us can afford
(strike)

to be out of work[19] now.

5. In an office:

A: Isn't there someone coming in for an interview today?

B: Yes, Ms. Jenson.

A: Well, I think she told me she _____ at three o'clock.
(come)

B: Oh, I'm sorry. I forgot to tell you that she called about an hour ago and said she

_____ .
(be late)

6. In the accounting department of a large company:

A: Here's my time sheet.

B: Did you know that you _____ hand this in yesterday?
(be supposed to)

A: No. My supervisor told me I _____ hand it in today.
(can)

B: Well, I'd better speak with him because that's not correct. All time sheets are due on

Wednesday.

7. A: You promised that you _____ me how to do this work today.
(show)

B: Well, I thought I _____ time today, but I'm really too busy now.
(have)

A: Oh, I knew you _____ that.
(say)

---

[18]go on strike: to stop working in order to obtain higher pay, better working conditions, or more
benefits.
[19]be out of work: to not be working; unemployed.

C. Sentence Patterns

Recall this sentence from the narrative:

No matter which company he called, however, the answer was always the same . . . .

PATTERNS

no matter + Question Word + Subject of + Verb of
                                          clause   clause

No matter where she moves to, she always finds work right away.

no matter + how + <u>Adjective</u> + Subject of + Verb of
                       Adverb   clause   clause

No matter how well he does his job, his supervisor never praises him.

no matter + how <u>many</u> + Noun + Subject of + Verb of
                     much   clause   clause

No matter how many times I tell him, he just won't listen.

Complete the following exchanges with an appropriate response using the above pattern.

Example: A: I think I'm going to start looking for another job.
                    B: What's the matter now?
                    A: *No matter what* I do, the manager criticizes me.
                    B: Oh, she's only correcting your work. Don't be so sensitive.

1.   A: Why didn't you take that part-time job you were offered?

     B: Well, I have an M.B.A. now. I didn't think that job was good enough for me.

     A: So you're still unemployed?

     B: Yes.

     A: Well, _____ you have, don't forget you still need to get some
                        (education)

          experience.

     B: You're right. I guess I should have taken that job just for the experience.

2. A: How come you didn't punch in on the time clock[20] yesterday?

    B: Oh, I got to work so late that I completely forgot.

    A: Well, in the future, don't forget to punch in, _____ .
        (arrive)

3. A boss and her secretary:

    A: I'm not taking any calls for the next hour. I need to get some paperwork done.

    B: No calls at all?

    A: None. _____ , I don't want to be interrupted.
        (call)

4. A: I just got a promotion and I'm still having trouble making ends meet. I can't believe it.

    B: I know how you feel. It seems like _____ , there's still
        (earn)

        not enough.

    A: Well, I guess that's because the more we make the more we spend.

5. A: I don't know if I can complete this by the deadline.[21]

    B: Oh, I'm sure you can. Every time you make up your mind[22] to do something you

        always do it, _____ .
        (difficult)

IV. EXPRESSIONS AND IDIOMS

*   *all along:* all the time; from the beginning.

Recall this sentence from the narrative:
> Mr. Lin knew *all along* that sooner or later he would have to work part-time . . . .

Complete the following exchanges with an appropriate response using *all along*. Be sure to follow the rules for sequence of tense.

---

[20]punch in (on the time clock): to record the time when one arrives at work.
[21]deadline: the date which a job, assignment, or paper is due.
[22]make up one's mind: to decide; to become determined to do something.

APPLICATION FOR EMPLOYMENT

PERSONAL INFORMATION

DATE _____ SOCIAL SECURITY NUMBER _____

NAME _____
LAST _____ FIRST _____ MIDDLE _____

PRESENT ADDRESS _____
STREET _____ CITY _____ STATE _____ ZIP CODE _____

PERMANENT ADDRESS _____
STREET _____ CITY _____ STATE _____ ZIP CODE _____

PHONE NO. _____

IF RELATED TO ANYONE IN OUR EMPLOY.
STATE NAME AND DEPARTMENT
(OMIT NAME OF SPOUSE) _____ REFERRED BY _____

EMPLOYMENT DESIRED

POSITION _____ DATE YOU CAN START _____ SALARY DESIRED _____

ARE YOU EMPLOYED NOW? _____ IF SO MAY WE INQUIRE OF YOUR PRESENT EMPLOYER _____

EVER APPLIED TO THIS COMPANY BEFORE? _____ WHERE _____ WHEN _____

*The Age Discrimination in Employment Act of 1967 prohibits discrimination on the basis of age with respect to individuals who are 40 years of age or older.

EDUCATION	NAME AND LOCATION OF SCHOOL		DID YOU GRADUATE? *	SUBJECTS STUDIED
GRAMMAR SCHOOL				
HIGH SCHOOL				
COLLEGE				
TRADE BUSINESS OR CORRESPONDENCE SCHOOL				

SUBJECTS OF SPECIAL STUDY OR RESEARCH WORK _____

WHAT FOREIGN LANGUAGES DO YOU SPEAK FLUENTLY? _____ READ _____ WRITE _____

ACTIVITIES: CIVIC. ATHLETIC. ETC. _____
(EXCLUDE ORGANIZATIONS. THE NAME OR CHARACTER OF WHICH INDICATES THE RACE. CREED. SEX. MARITAL STATUS. AGE. COLOR OR NATIONAL ORIGIN OF ITS MEMBERS.)

LAST

FIRST

MIDDLE

(CONTINUED ON OTHER SIDE)

APPLICATION FOR EMPLOYMENT

Job application

FORMER EMPLOYERS (LIST BELOW LAST FOUR EMPLOYERS, STARTING WITH LAST ONE FIRST.)

DATE MONTH AND YEAR	NAME AND ADDRESS OF EMPLOYER	SALARY	POSITION	REASON FOR LEAVING
FROM				
TO				
FROM				
TO				
FROM				
TO				
FROM				
TO				

REFERENCES: GIVE BELOW THE NAMES OF THREE PERSONS NOT RELATED TO YOU, WHOM YOU HAVE KNOWN AT LEAST ONE YEAR.

	NAME	ADDRESS	BUSINESS	YEARS ACQUAINTED
1				
2				
3				

IN CASE OF
EMERGENCY NOTIFY
_____ NAME _____

_____ ADDRESS _____ PHONE NO. _____

I AUTHORIZE INVESTIGATION OF ALL STATEMENTS CONTAINED IN THIS APPLICATION. I UNDERSTAND THAT MISREPRESENTATION OR OMISSION OF FACTS CALLED FOR IS CAUSE FOR DISMISSAL. FURTHER, I UNDERSTAND AND AGREE THAT MY EMPLOYMENT IS FOR NO DEFINITE PERIOD AND MAY, REGARDLESS OF THE DATE OF PAYMENT OF MY WAGES AND SALARY, BE TERMINATED AT ANY TIME WITHOUT ANY PREVIOUS NOTICE.

DATE _____ SIGNATURE _____

DO NOT WRITE BELOW THIS LINE

INTERVIEWED BY _____ DATE _____

REMARKS: _____

NEATNESS _____

ABILITY _____

HIRED	FOR DEPT.	POSITION	WILL REPORT	SALARY WAGES

APPROVED: 1. _____ 2. _____ 3. _____
EMPLOYMENT MANAGER   DEPT. HEAD   GENERAL MANAGER

Job application (continued)

Example: A: I heard that Scott was promoted to assistant manager
last week.

B: Well, I knew *all along he'd be promoted*. He's an excellent worker and he has a lot on the ball.[23]

1.   A: I got a call from Bache Company today.

B: Well? Did you get the job?

A: No, I didn't.

B: I guess you're disappointed.

A: A little. But to tell you the truth, I knew _____ the
                                                              (I-get; negative)
job. I didn't do very well on the interview.

2.   A: John has just been named vice-president. It was announced this morning. He's the
youngest vice-president the bank has ever had.

B: I'm not surprised. I said _____ .
                                        (he-go places[24])

3.   A: Did you hear the news? One hundred workers were just laid off.[25]

B: What are you so surprised about? We knew _____ .
                                                          (company-in financial trouble)
They even told us they would have to lay off some workers sooner or later.

4.   A: It's been a month and I still haven't found a job.

B: Well, I told you _____ .
                            (it-difficult to find a new job)

A: I know. I shouldn't have resigned until I had found a new position first.

5.   A: I can't believe we have to work overtime again today!

---

[23]have a lot on the ball: to be smart, clever.
        be
[24]go places: to become successful.
[25]lay off: to put out of work; to lose a job.

B: What are you complaining about? You knew _____ .
                                             (we–busy this week)

They told us a long time ago that we would have to put in[26] a lot of overtime this

week.

V. SITUATIONAL DIALOGUES

1.   On the telephone. Mr. Adams is responding to a help-wanted ad he saw in the newspaper.

OPERATOR: Good morning, I.T.C. Corporation.

MR. ADAMS: Hello, I'd like to speak with Ms. Evans in personnel.

OPERATOR: OK. I'll connect you.

MS. EVANS: Personnel. Good morning.

MR. ADAMS: Good morning. I'd like to speak with Ms. Evans.

MS. EVANS: Speaking.

MR. ADAMS: Oh, Ms. Evans, I'm Frank Adams and I'm responding to your ad in the
Sunday Times. I have a Bachelor's degree in Business Administration and I'm bilin-
gual, so I have the necessary qualifications.

MS. EVANS: Do you have any job experience?

MR. ADAMS: Well, yes, I've worked as a salesman for Muller's Beer for the past two
summers.

MS. EVANS: Oh, I see. Well, the job calls for[27] someone with a minimum of three years
experience in sales . . . .

MR. ADAMS: Oh, but I have worked for at least five years as a salesman for my uncle's
company. That's been part-time, of course, and excluding the past two summers.

MS. EVANS: OK. Please send me your résumé and make sure you state exactly what
your responsibilities were and the number of customers you dealt with.[28]

MR. ADAMS: I'll get it right in. When do you think I'll hear from you?

MS. EVANS: If you are selected for an interview, we'll contact you within two weeks.

MR. ADAMS: Thank you for your time.

MS. EVANS: Don't mention it. Have a good day now.

MR. ADAMS: You, too. Bye.

QUESTIONS

1.   How did Mr. Adams find out about the job opening at I.T.C. Corporation?
2.   What type of degree does Mr. Adams have?

---

[26]put in (an amount of time): to spend time (doing something).
[27]call for: to require.
[28]deal with: to have relations with: to manage; attend to.

3. What experience does Mr. Adams have?
4. How much experience is required?
5. What does Mr. Adams have to send to Ms. Evans?
6. What additional information should his resume include?

2. At a job interview:

MR. JONES: Please be seated, Ms. Brookes. I see that you have had experience as a computer programmer at two major international corporations. Since the position of senior programmer here requires supervision of other programmers, we'd like to know if you have had people working under you.

MS. BROOKES: Yes, at both corporations I was the supervisor of other programmers. At Metell I supervised five programmers and at Boman Systems I had nine people under my supervision.

MR. JONES: How about languages? I mean, we use DATA IV and VISION.[29] Are you familiar with those?

MS. BROOKES: No problem. I also have used COBOL, M.P.E., and IMAGE.[29]

MR. JONES: Well, your background and qualifications are impressive. Now do you have any questions you'd like to ask us?

MS. BROOKES: Well, I'd like to know about your health benefits and pay scale.

MR. JONES: Certainly. This folder outlines our health and medical benefits, and this chart has our pay scale. For new employees there is a two-week, paid vacation.

MS. BROOKES: Thank you, I'm sure all my questions will be answered by the information in this packet. I look forward to hearing from you soon.

MR. JONES: Oh, you will. We'll give you a call this afternoon as soon as we've finished our interviews. Goodbye now.

MS. BROOKES: Goodbye.

QUESTIONS

1. What kind of experience has Ms. Brookes had?
2. What does the position of senior programmer require?
3. What computer languages is Ms. Brookes familiar with?
4. What does Mr. Jones think of Ms. Brookes's qualifications?
5. What would Ms. Brookes like to know about?
6. When will Mr. Jones let her know whether she has the job or not?

VI. VOCABULARY BUILDER

job   full-time job/high-paying job/job benefits/job description/job interview/job market/part-time job/job placement office/jobless/temporary job

[29]DATA IV, VISION, COBOL, M.P.E., IMAGE: the names of different computer languages.

employment	employment agency/employment listing/unemployment insurance
labor	labor contract/labor leader/labor union
worker	blue-collar worker/co-worker/factory worker/part-time worker/white collar worker

VII. ROLE PLAY SUGGESTION

1. Go on a job interview. Discuss qualifications, experience, benefits, salary.

VIII. PREPOSITION PRACTICE

A. Prepositions

USE **THROUGH** TO SHOW:

motion from one side to another	He drove **THROUGH** town to get to the interview.
motion past	He drove **THROUGH** several red lights.
by means of; because of	He found out **THROUGH** Robert.
movement within a large space	The plane flew **THROUGH** the air.
from the beginning to the end	Computer programmers often work **THROUGH** the night.
to and including	The bank is open Monday **THROUGH** Saturday.

USE **THROUGHOUT** TO SHOW:

| in every part of | They have corporate offices **THROUGH-OUT** the United States. |
| during a whole course or period. | Those skills served him well **THROUGH-OUT** his career. |

USE **BEYOND** TO SHOW:

on the far side of	The entrance to the personnel office is **BE-YOND** the elevators.
not able to understand	I can't understand your paper. It is **BEYOND** me.
surpassing; exceeding	In everything I've done, I've gone **BEYOND** what was required.

Complete the following exchanges with the appropriate preposition.

1.   In an office:

   A: I'd like to apply for the typing position you have open.

   B: Fine. How did you find out about the opening?

   A: _____ the Apex Employment Agency.

   B: How many words a minute can you type?

   A: Approximately seventy.

   B: All right. Just go _____ the door on your left and see Mr. Fuller.

   He'll give you some forms to fill out.

2.   On the phone:

   A: Good morning, Engineering Department.

   B: Yes, I've read your ad in the career section of the *News*, and I'd like to come down

   for an interview.

   A: Fine. We are located on Sixteenth and Holbrook in the Westville section.

   B: I'm not too familiar with the Westville section. How do I get there from East Hook?

   A: OK. Drive _____ the Glen Oaks area until you reach Sixteenth.

   Turn right and go straight. Be careful not to go _____ any stop

   signs. They are often hard to see because of the trees. After two miles you'll come

   to Holbrook. The personnel office is just _____ the front gate.

3.   On the phone:

   A: Hello, college placement office, Jan speaking.

B: Hi. I need a good paying part-time job. I don't care what I do but I have to make more than the minimum wage.

A: Are you willing to work _____ the night?

B: No problem. _____ my college career I've worked crazy hours.

A: OK. Well, there's a job as a night watchman at A. B. Systems Corporation.

B: They're a large firm with offices _____ the state. Where's the job located?

A: Right here in Eastport.

B: I'll be right over to fill out the forms.

4.   A: Have you read Dr. Leonard's new paper yet?

B: Well, I looked through it, but to be honest with you, it's really _____ me.

A: I'm glad you said that, because I couldn't understand it either.

5.   A: I heard Nancy was promoted again.

B: I'm not surprised. She's an excellent worker.

A: That's true. She always goes _____ the minimum required in anything she does.

B. Additional Preposition Combinations

work on (IS):
to do work   I'll *work on* that problem until I solve it.
to try to influence or convince   He won't agree, so you'll have to *work on* him.

work up (S):
   to develop, create   You'd better *work up* a new résumé.

work up (IS):
   to get excited, enthusiastic   I can't get *worked up* about that job.

work out (S):
   to solve; find an answer to   I'm sure we can *work* this problem *out*.
   to arrange; devise   Let's sit down and *work out* a schedule.

work out (IS):
   to result   I'm sure your new job will *work out* well.

Complete the following exchanges with the appropriate preposition combination.

1.   A: Haven't they finished repairing the copy machine yet?

       B: No. They've been _____ it all morning, but they haven't

           fixed it yet.

2.   A: I don't think the manager will let me take tomorrow off.

       B: Well, just _____ him a little. I'm sure he can be persuaded.

3.   A: What time are you going home tonight?

       B: I don't know. My supervisor doesn't want me to leave until I _____

           this problem _____ .

4.   A: What are you _____ ?

       B: Well, the boss didn't like the plan I proposed, so I'm trying to _____

           a new one. I don't know what I'll do if she doesn't like this one.

       A: Oh, don't worry. It will all _____ .

5.   A manager and an employee:

       A: Just look at this schedule! I can't believe you want me to work three Saturdays in a

           row.[30] How could you do this to me?

---

[30]in a row: consecutively: one after the other.

B: There's no need to get so _____ . I didn't realize I had scheduled

you to work so many Saturdays. Have a seat and I'll _____ a

new schedule for you right now.

A: OK. I'm sorry I flew off the handle.[31]

---

[31]fly off the handle: to become very angry.

12 THE BARBECUE

I. NARRATIVE

One day in early June, Mr. Lin received an invitation from his boss, Mr. Grove, to attend a Fourth of July barbecue.[1] As he looked at the invitation, he noticed that the letters R.S.V.P. were written at the bottom. Since he had no idea what these letters stood for,[2] he decided to ask his neighbor, Mr. Sharon, what they meant. Mr. Sharon explained that R.S.V.P. stands for the French phrase, "Répondez s'il vous plaît," which means please let the host know if you plan to attend. Before Mr. Lin could thank him, Mr. Sharon said, "By the way, I suggest that you bring your host a small gift. When I am invited to a party, I bring a bottle of wine or some pastry." Suddenly, Mr. Lin began to worry about what he should wear and what other customs he needed to be aware of.[3] Mr Sharon was again helpful. He told Mr. Lin, "Barbecues are held in the backyard, so dress is casual. And really, there's nothing else you need to know, except, maybe, that Americans tend to be open and friendly people. Relax! When you get there, they'll make you feel right at home."

Mr. Lin got to Mr. Grove's front door at the same time as a middle-aged couple. The couple and Mr. Lin were politely greeting each other on the doorstep when Mrs. Grove opened the front door. With a broad smile, she bent over so that her two friends could kiss her on the cheek. She then greeted Mr. Lin. He didn't know if he was supposed to shake her hand or kiss her cheek. He stood frozen[4] until Mrs. Grove firmly shook his hand and with her left hand motioned for him to enter. Mr. Lin then met the rest of the family. First he was introduced to Alyssa, the teenage daughter. Makeup and a stylish dress made Alyssa look much older than fifteen. A few seconds after saying "Hi" to Mr. Lin, she ran off to answer the telephone. The phone must have rung twenty times during the course of the barbecue; each time it was for Alyssa. Mr. Grove jokingly said, "Whenever I want to talk to Alyssa, I call her on the phone."

---

[1]barbecue: cooking outdoors on a charcoal fire.
[2]stand for: to represent; signify.
[3]be aware of: to realize; to know.
[4]frozen: not moving; unable to move.

There were tables set up in the backyard. The Groves had prepared a huge spread.[5] "Please help yourself to whatever you'd like," said Mrs. Grove. "As you can see, there's enough food here to feed an army! There's also beer, wine, punch,[6] and soda to drink." Mr. Lin helped himself to some barbecued chicken, baked clams, salad, and French bread, and took a can of soda. "If that soda isn't cold enough yet, there's plenty of ice in the cooler[7] over there," said Mrs. Grove.

As Mr. Lin began eating, the Groves' second daughter, Margaret, came over and introduced herself. Margaret was in her thirties and recently divorced. She was a successful lawyer with a large firm in the city. Both she and her ten-year-old son were very knowledgeable about China and spent a lot of time talking to Mr. Lin. He felt very comfortable with her. This was not the case with Brad, the only son. Brad was quite conceited and loud. He and his date constantly tried to be the center of attention, but this was difficult because Florence, Mr. Grove's mother, stole the show[8] with her witty and interesting stories.

Florence was a seventy-two-year-old widow; she was very active in programs which tried to gain benefits for senior citizens.[9] Mr. Lin had just read an article about homes for the aged, and he was surprised to find out that elderly people usually ended up at these homes. Since he was curious to know why old people did not spend their last years living with their families, he asked Florence. She said, "Well, I think that at one time many older people would stay with their children, but times have changed. In many American families both the husband and wife work, so if a parent is sick or disabled, there's no one around to take care of him or her. Besides, many senior citizens don't want to be dependent on their children. To tell you the truth, I wouldn't live here with my children. I like my independence. Also, some elderly people just can't adapt to the lifestyles of their children, so they **would just as soon** live alone. Of course, there are still many Americans who are eager to have their parents live with them."

After the barbecue was over, and Mr. Lin was on his way home, he thought to himself, "When I first came to this country, I knew almost nothing about American lifestyles. I've certainly learned a lot since then!"

QUESTIONS

1. What does R.S.V.P. stand for?
2. How did Mr. Lin find out what R.S.V.P. meant?
3. What did Mr. Sharon suggest?
4. What kind of gift does Mr. Sharon usually bring when he is invited to a party?

---

[5]spread: a large amount of food.
[6]punch: a mixed drink usually made from fruit juices; sometimes liquor is added.
[7]cooler: a large container filled with ice which is used to keep food and drinks cold.
[8]steal the show: to capture everyone's attention.
[9]senior citizen: an older person (usually someone over sixty-five years old).

5. What was Mr. Lin worried about?
6. What kind of dress is appropriate for a barbecue?
7. How did the middle-aged couple greet Mrs. Grove?
8. Why did Alyssa look older than she actually was?
9. What was Brad Grove like?
10. What was Florence Grove like?
11. According to Florence Grove, why don't many older people spend their last years living with their children?
12. What did Mr. Lin realize as he was on his way home?

II. DIALOGUE

1. Mr. Lin arrives at the Groves' house and rings the doorbell.

MRS. GROVE: Oh, Le-Tian, how nice to see you! I'm so glad you could make it.

MR. LIN: Thank you. Mr. Grove's been talking about this barbecue for so long that I wouldn't have missed it.

MRS. GROVE: Well, come into the backyard and make yourself at home! There's plenty to eat and drink. Now help yourself to whatever you'd like. Don't be polite!

MR. LIN: Thank you. You've really prepared quite a spread here. Everything looks delicious.

(Mr. Lin helps himself to some food. After a few moments, Mrs. Grove returns with her daughter Alyssa.)

MRS. GROVE: Oh, Mr. Lin. Here's someone I'd like you to meet. This is my daughter, Alyssa.

ALYSSA: How do you do?

MR. LIN: How do you do? I'm glad to meet you finally, Alyssa. I've heard a lot about you.

ALYSSA: Only good things, I hope!

MR. LIN: Of course.

(Margaret, Mrs. Grove's other daughter, comes over.)

MARGARET: Oh, you must be Mr. Lin. My father has told us a lot about you. I'm Margaret. Nice to meet you.

MR. LIN: Nice to meet you, too.

MARGARET: My father tells me you're always busy working and studying. I'm glad you were able to take time out to[10] join us today.

---

[10]take time (out) to (do something): to stop doing one thing in order to have time to do something else.

MR. LIN: Well, it seems that between going to school and working part-time, I never have a minute to myself.[11] So I decided that I deserved a day off.

ALYSSA: C'mon. I see some more people I want to introduce you to.

MR. LIN: OK. See you later, Margaret.

MARGARET: OK. Have fun!

QUESTIONS

1.   Who greeted Mr. Lin at the door?
2.   How did Mr. Lin know about the barbecue?
3.   Who did Mrs. Grove introduce Mr. Lin to?
4.   What did Margaret say when she introduced herself?
5.   Why did Mr. Lin decide to take time off and come to the party?

III. GRAMMAR

A. Time Clauses

PRESENT TENSE

Recall this sentence from the narrative:
   When I *am invited* to a party, I *bring* a bottle of wine or some pastry.

When talking about the present, use the Present Tense in both the time clause and the main clause.

Time Clause	*Main Clause*
Time Expression + Subject + Verb (Present Tense)	Subject + Verb (Present Tense)

After he *comes* home from a party, he *goes* straight to bed!

PAST TENSE

Recall this sentence from the narrative:
   When I first *came* to this country, I *knew* almost nothing about American lifestyles.

When talking about the past, use the Past Tense in both the time clause and the main clause.

Time Clause	*Main Clause*
Time Expression + Subject + Verb (Past Tense)	Subject + Verb (Past Tense)

As soon as she *got* the invitation, she *accepted*.

---

[11]have (an amount of time) to oneself: to have free time, leisure time.

FUTURE TENSE

Recall this sentence from the narrative:

When you *get* there, they *will make* you feel right at home.

When talking about the future, use the Present Tense in the time clause and the Future Tense in the main clause.

Time Clause	Main Clause
Time Expression + Subject + Verb (Present Tense)	Subject + Verb (Future Tense)

Before I *leave*, I'll *have* another piece of cake.

Complete the following exchanges with an appropriate response using the correct tense.

Example: A: Do you go to parties often?

B: Not now, but *when I lived in Manhattan I went to parties*

<u>(live)</u>   <u>(go)</u> .

all the time.

1. A: When you and Laurel go out to dinner, who usually _____ ?

(pay)

B: We always _____ when we _____ together.

(go dutch¹²)   (eat)

2. A: When did you realize you loved Carolyn?

B: Oh, as soon as I _____ her I _____ in love

(see)   (fall)

with her.

A: Oh, it was love at first sight!¹³

3. A: Aren't you going to have a housewarming¹⁴ party?

B: Sure. After we _____ , we _____ a big bash.¹⁵

(get settled)   (throw)

A: Well, don't forget to invite me!

B: C'mon. When we _____ a party, _____

(have)

we always _____ you?

(invite; negative question)

A: Yes, of course. I'm only kidding.

---

¹²go dutch treat: to share expenses.

¹³love at first sight: to fall in love the first time you meet.

¹⁴housewarming party: a party given to celebrate getting a new house or apartment.

¹⁵throw a bash: to have a party.

4. A: I heard you're going to Denver this week. Do you plan to see Joann?

    B: Of course. I always _____ her a visit[16] when
                             (pay)

        I _____ in Denver.
            (be)

    A: Please say hello to her for me, okay?

    B: Sure. When I _____ her I _____ sure to give
                      (see)   (be)

        her your regards.

    A: Thanks. In fact, would you mind delivering a note to her?

    B: Of course not. But I'm leaving tomorrow.

    A: All right. I _____ the note today and _____
                     (finish)   (give)

        it to you before you _____ .
                               (leave)

5. A: You must have had a wild party here last night!

    B: What makes you say that?

    A: Well, the place is a mess. How about cleaning up a little before you go out again?

    B: Listen, I have to meet someone right now, but don't worry. I _____
                                                                      (straighten)

        everything up[17] when I _____ . I promise!
                                  (return)

B. Would

We use *would* many ways. We use it in certain phrases (e.g., would like) and in the Conditional (see chapter 8). It is also used to show (1) past habit and (2) that something is likely to happen.

FORM: | would + Verb (base form)

(1) *Past Habit*: We use *would* to show what we did as a habit in the past.

---

[16]pay someone a visit: to visit someone.
[17]straighten up: to make neat; to clean.

Recall this sentence from the narrative:
> . . . at one time many older people *would stay* with their children . . . .

(2) *Likely*: We use *would* to show that we are likely to do something. *Would not* shows that we are not likely to do something.

Recall this sentence from the narrative:
> . . . I *wouldn't live* here with my children.

Complete the following exchanges with an appropriate response using *would* to show (1) past habit or (2) that something is likely.

> ***Example:***   A: Did you forget to ask Jenny to come to the family reunion?[18]
>   B: Of course not! *I wouldn't forget to ask Jenny!*

1.   A: Would you like to go skiing with us?

      B: I'd love to!

      A: Great! Do you know how to ski?

      B: Sure. When I was in college, I _____ every other week.

2.   A: Have you decided who you're going to invite to the dinner party?

      B: Yes. In fact, I'm going to sit down and write out the invitations right now.

      A: Well, please don't leave out[19] my cousin Eunice.

      B: _____ I _____ her _____ ?
>   (leave out)

      A: You might! The last time she was here you told me you thought she was boring and

            tacky![20]

      B: Well, she is. But, after all, she's still your cousin, so I have to invite her.

3.   A: Do you like to dance?

      B: Well, when I was a teenager, I _____ every Friday night, but
>   (go dancing)

            I seldom go any more.

---

[18]family reunion: when all the members of a family get together.
[19]leave out: to forget; to not include.
[20]tacky: not elegant or sophisticated; lacking good taste.

A: How come?

B: I don't like all these new dances, not to mention[21] disco music!

4. A: I'm really upset with you. I never thought you _____
   (do)

   such a thing!

   B: What? What are you talking about? Do what?

   A: Lie to me!

   B: I _____ that! We'd better sit down right now and get to the

   bottom of this.[22] I'm sure there's been a misunderstanding.

5. A: Some of us are going out to the bar after work. Want to come along?

   B: No, thanks.

   A: Don't you drink?

   B: To tell you the truth, I don't. When I was a college student, I _____
      (go drinking)

   almost every weekend, but I can't take alcohol any more.

6. A: Did my remark offend you?

   B: Yes, it did.

   A: Then I apologize. I _____ you on purpose.[23] I didn't
      (hurt; negative)

   realize that what I said _____ you.
      (offend)

   B: That's okay. Forget it.

   A: Do you really accept my apology?

   B: Yes, I do.

---

[21]not to mention: besides; in addition to [emphasizes the importance of what follows it].
[22]get to the bottom of (something): to find the real cause.
[23]on purpose: not by accident; to mean to do something.

7.   A: How about going to a movie tonight?

   B: No, I don't feel like²⁴ it.

   A: Don't you like movies? You never want to go with us.

   B: Well, when I lived in Kansas I _____ all the time, but now that

   I'm in San Francisco I prefer to spend my money on the theater and concerts.

C. Whatever/wherever/whenever/whichever/who(m)ever

Recall this sentence from the narrative:
Please help yourself to *whatever* you'd like.

PATTERN

(1)   In this pattern, the Question Word-ever means *any* (anything, any time, anyone, etc.)

[Question Word-ever] + Subject of clause + Verb of clause

You can take *whatever* you want.
Leave *whenever* you need to.
Please feel free²⁵ to invite *who(m)ever* you'd like.
Whatever you decide is okay with me.
Tell him to choose *whichever* one he likes.

(2)   We also use Question Word-ever to mean *no matter* (see Chapter 11).

   Example: __*Whatever*__ he does, I always forgive him.
                     No matter what

                     __*Wherever*__ you want to go, I'll take you there.
                     No matter where

Complete the following exchanges with an appropriate response using *whatever, wherever, whenever, whichever* one, or *whoever*.

   Example: A: It's a beautiful day. Let's go for a drive!
                     B: Okay. Where do you want to go?
                     A: It doesn't matter. *Wherever you want to go is fine with me.*

1.   A: What time should I arrive for the party?

   B: Well, it's an open house so come _____ .

---

²⁴feel like: to want to; to desire.
²⁵feel free (to do something): don't hesitate (to do something).

2.   A: Oh, I really blew it.[26] I don't know how I can face[27] Gail again.

B: Oh, listen, _____ , I'm sure Gail will forgive you.

(do)

3.   A: I'd like to borrow John's car, but I'm afraid to ask him for it.

B: What are you afraid of?

A: Well, what if he refuses?

B: Are you kidding? He's crazy about[28] you. He'll give you _____ .

(want)

A: Do you think so?

B: Of course. _____ something, don't hesitate to ask him.

(need)

4.   A: Who should I invite to our wedding reception?

B: You can ask _____ , but keep in mind[29] that we can only

(would like)

have a hundred guests.

5.   A: I understand you're leaving for Europe tomorrow. What places do you plan to visit?

B: I don't have an itinerary.[30] I am just going to take a month and go _____

_____ .

(want)

A: Well, _____ , have a good time.

(go)

6.   A: I really don't want to go over to Cindy's house on Saturday, but I don't know what

to tell her. Help me think of a good excuse.

B: Well, _____ , she's still going to be angry, so you might

(tell her)

as well tell her the truth.

---

[26]blow it: to make a serious mistake; to fail.
[27]face (someone): to meet confidently.
[28]be crazy about (someone/something): to like very much; to love.
[29]keep in mind: to remember; stay aware of.
[30]itinerary: a plan of places to visit on a trip.

7. In a restaurant:

A: It's really nice of you to treat me to dinner.

B: Well, after all the favors you've done for me, this is the least I can do.

A: But this is such an expensive restaurant!

B: Listen, order _____ and don't worry about the prices.

Everything's on me.[31]

8. In a department store:

A: There are so many skirts here, I don't know which one to choose.

B: This is your birthday present, so pick _____ .

A: Some of them are quite expensive though!

B: Please! Money is no object.[32]

D. Subjunctive

Recall this sentence from the narrative:

   . . . I *suggest that* you *bring* your host a small gift.

We use the subjunctive to show that one person wants another person to do something.

PATTERNS

Subject + Verb + that + Subject + (not) + Verb (base form)

I *requested* that he *tell* you first.
He *insisted* that we *stay* home.

Common verbs used in this pattern include:

advise	demand	prefer	require
ask	insist	recommend	suggest
command	order	request	urge

[31] be on one: to treat; pay for someone else.
[32] money is no object: the price or cost doesn't matter.

We can use another pattern when we want to talk about one person wanting another person to do something:

```
Subject + Verb + Indirect Object + (not) + to + Verb (base form)
```

Common verbs used in this pattern include:

advise	command	remind	request	teach	want
ask	order	prefer	tell	urge	warn

He *told* me *not to leave early*.

Complete the following exchanges with an appropriate response using one of the preceding patterns.

Example: A: What are you bringing to the party tonight?
B: Well, Mr. Ryan requested *that I bring some dessert*.

1. A: What time should we leave tomorrow?

    B: Well, what time does the picnic begin?

    A: It starts at noon.

    B: Then I suggest _____ because it's a good[33] two-hour
        (no later than 10 A.M.)

        drive from here to the state park.

    A: That's fine with me.

2. A: Phil says he doesn't know what to bring to the party tonight.

    B: I prefer _____ . We have more than enough food now.
        (not bring anything)

3. A: Albert is very angry with me. I stood him up[34] last night. Now I don't know what

        to do.

    B: Well, I recommend _____ .
                          (apologize)

    A: Do you think he'll accept my apology?

---

[33]a good (amount of time): no less than that amount of time; at least that amount of time.
[34]stand (someone) up: to fail to meet an appointment.

B: I don't see why not.

4.   A:.   Sylvia said that she had a terrible time at the dance last night.

B: Well, I thought she wasn't going to go to that dance. Why did she change her mind?

A: Monica insisted _____ .
                          (go)

5.   A: I heard that you went to the luncheon yesterday. I thought that you didn't want to

go.

B: I didn't, but Lee requested _____ there.
                                      (be)

6.   A: Why did you split up with[35] Tom?

B: Well, to tell you the truth, all my friends kept urging _____ .
                                                              (stop seeing him)

7.   A: Why is Barry so angry at you? He's been bad mouthing[36] you all over the place

lately.

B: Well, I demanded _____ the money he owes me. He promised
                          (pay back)

to pay me back two months ago.

8.   A: Didn't you ask _____ on the camping trip with us?
                            (Susan-go)

B: No, I didn't.

A: Why not?

B: What do you mean "why not?" You told _____ her!
                                              (me-invite; negative)

E. Sentence Patterns

Recall these sentences from the narrative:
      . . . there's *enough food* here to feed an army!
      If that soda isn't *cold enough* yet, there's plenty of ice in the cooler . . . .

---

[35]split up: to separate; to end a relationship with someone.
[36]bad mouthing: to say bad things about someone.

PATTERNS

> enough + Noun + (for + Object) + to + Verb (base form)

Is there *enough food* for everyone to eat?

> Adjective + enough + (for + Object) + to + Verb (base form)

This room isn't *large enough* to hold a party.

Complete the following exchanges with an appropriate response using an *enough + Noun* or *Adjective + enough* pattern.

> *Example:* A: Hey, there's not *enough volume*. Turn up[37] the stereo.
> B: You must be kidding! The music is *loud enough* to wake the dead.

1. A: Josh goes out partying[38] almost every night of the week.

   B: I'd be exhausted if I did that.

   A: I would be too, but he's _____ to take it.
   (young)

2. A: Does our student club have _____ to throw a New
   (money)

   Year's Eve party?

   B: We have _____ , but the members don't have
   (money)

   _____ to set it up.[39]
   (time)

3. A: Hey Brenda, do you want another drink?

   B: Oh, no thanks. I've had _____ tonight. I'm getting drunk.[40]
   (liquor)

   A: Not you. You really know how to hold your liquor.

   B: Sorry Ben. I'll pass[41] on this one.

---

[37]turn up: to make louder.
[38]party: to have a good time; to go from party to party.
[39]set up: to organize; to establish.
[40]get drunk: to lose control due to too much liquor.
[41]pass on: to not accept.

Party invitation

Thank you note

4.   A: Thanks a million for your help. You've been great.

  B: It was my pleasure, and I really didn't do that much.

  A: Well, you did more than _____ to get our class reunion off the
                                        (work)

  ground[42] and now all we have to do is send out the invitations.

5.   A: Jack, I'm worried about tonight's reception.

  B: What are you worrying about? We have _____
                                                  (hors d'oeuvres[43] and drinks)

  for an army.

  A: I know. But there are over fifty people coming. I hope that this place is _____

  _____ .
                                (roomy)

6.   On the phone:

  A: Oh, did I wake you?

  B: Yes, but never mind. I had _____ anyway.
                                        (sleep)

IV. EXPRESSIONS AND IDIOMS

● *would just as soon:* to prefer to do one thing
rather than another; rather.

> would just as soon + (not) + Verb (base form)

Recall this sentence from the narrative:
   Some elderly people just can't adapt to the lifestyles of their children, so they'*d just as
   soon* live alone.

Complete the following exchanges with an appropriate response using *would just as soon.*

   Example: A: Do you want to go to the movies with me tonight?
               B: What's playing?

---

[42]get (something) off the ground: to get (a project) started.
[43]hors d'oeuvres: a French phrase meaning a small portion of food served before meals. Often
   served for parties in the evening as well.

A: A war picture.

B: No thanks. *I'd just as soon stay home and read.*
                (stay home and read)

1.   A: I'm going away for the weekend.

   B: Are you going by yourself again?

   A: Yes.

   B: Why not ask your cousin Harold to go with you? Wouldn't it be nice to have some

        company?

   A: Harold? He'd drive me crazy.[44] I'd _____ .
                                              (go alone)

2.   A: Listen, you really should apologize to Stanley.

   B: Me apologize? It was all his fault. I _____ again
                                              (see; negative)

        than _____ .

3.   A: We're going for a ride this afternoon. How about coming along?

   B: No, thanks.

   A: How come you're never willing to join us?

   B: To be frank, I don't like the crowd[45] you hang around[46] with. I _____

        _____ .

4.   A: Do you mind if I go out for awhile?

   B: Well, I _____ . I'm not in the mood[47] to be alone tonight.
              (you-stay home)

5.   At a party:

   A: Do you want to stay awhile longer?

   B: No, this party is boring. I _____ now.
                                      (leave)

[44]drive (one) crazy: to annoy; to bother one.
[45]the crowd: a group or type of people.
[46]hang around with: to spend time with; associate with.
[47]in the mood: to feel like; desire. *Also,* in a good/bad mood: in a good or bad state of mind.

V. SITUATIONAL DIALOGUES

1.   On the telephone. Ted is calling to ask Julie out.[48]

TED: Hello, is Julie there?

JULIE: Yes, speaking.

TED: Hi, Julie. This is Ted Rodgers. I'm Jim Mitchell's roommate. Jim said he thought you and I would hit it off[49] right away, so I should give you a call.

JULIE: Oh, yes, he's mentioned you quite a few times. I'm glad you called.

TED: So am I. Well, I'd like to ask you out this Saturday night. I've got tickets for the film festival, so I thought we might go to dinner first and then to the movies.

JULIE: Great. I love old movies.

TED: I'll be by[50] at six o'clock, if that's OK.

JULIE: Sure.

TED: See you then.

JULIE: Wait. You don't have my address. I live at 1478 West Holly Drive. It's the rear apartment.

TED: OK. See you later.

JULIE: Bye now.

QUESTIONS

1.   Who suggested that Ted call Julie?
2.   Why did Ted call Julie?
3.   What time are they going to meet?
4.   Where are they going?

2.   On campus.

SAM: Tarik, I'm glad I bumped into you. I'd like to invite you to my parents' house for a Thanksgiving[51] turkey dinner.

TARIK: Oh, gee, I'd love to; but I just told Paul Sullivan I'd be happy to go to his home on Thanksgiving.

SAM: Well, I see I should have invited you earlier. How about coming over for Christmas dinner?

TARIK: Yes, I'd love to.

SAM: Okay. I'll send you a little note with the details.

---

[48]ask out: to ask someone to go on a date.
[49]hit it off: to get along well; to like each other.
[50]be by: to come over (to visit someone; pick someone up, etc.).
[51]Thanksgiving: The fourth Thursday in November. A day when Americans give thanks for what they have. Originally celebrated with Native Americans in honor of the fall harvest. Turkey, yams, corn, and pumpkin pie are usually part of the meal.

TARIK: Thanks. I look forward to seeing you then.

SAM: Right. Take care.

QUESTIONS

1.   Why is Sam glad he ran into Tarik?
2.   Why can't Tarik make it to Sam's house for Thanksgiving?

3.   Jerry was invited to a dinner party at Colleen and Denny Gold's house. The dinner party is now over and Jerry is leaving.

JERRY: Well, it's getting late. I must be going.

COLLEEN: Oh, so soon? It's not that late.

JERRY: Oh, I don't want to overstay my welcome. Besides, it's almost midnight, and I do have to go to work tomorrow morning. I want to thank both of you for a lovely evening.

DENNY: Well, we're glad you enjoyed it.

JERRY: I really did. The dinner was delicious. You're a marvelous cook, Colleen.

COLLEEN: Thank you. Actually, Denny's a pretty good cook, too. Next time I'll have him cook for you.

JERRY: Great. But first I'd like to have you two over[52] to my place for dinner.

DENNY: We'd love to do that.

JERRY: Good. I'll call you this week, and we'll arrange a date. Good night, and thanks again.

QUESTIONS

1.   What did Jerry think of the dinner?
2.   Who cooked the dinner?
3.   What would Jerry like to do?
4.   Why is Jerry going to call Colleen and Denny this week?

VI. VOCABULARY BUILDER

party   anniversary party/birthday party/Christmas party/cocktail party/costume party/engagement party/fraternity party/fund raising party/going away party/graduation party/Halloween party/housewarming/New Year's Eve party/office party/retirement party/sorority party/sweet sixteen party

---

[52]have (someone) over: to invite someone to your house.

HOLIDAYS

January 1	New Year's Day
January 15	Martin Luther King, Jr.'s Birthday
February 12	Lincoln's Birthday
February 22	Washington's Birthday
May (second Sunday)	Mother's Day
May 30	Memorial Day
June (third Sunday)	Father's Day
July 4	Independence Day
September (first Monday)	Labor Day
October (second Monday)	Columbus Day
November (first Tuesday)	Election Day
November 11	Veterans Day
November (fourth Thursday)	Thanksgiving
December 25	Christmas Day

VII. ROLE PLAY SUGGESTIONS

1. Turn down an invitation to a party.
2. Accept an invitation to dinner.
3. Invite someone on a date.
4. Invite someone to your home for dinner.

VIII. PREPOSITION PRACTICE

A. Prepositions

USE **ONTO** TO SHOW:

    motion to the top of   The cat jumped **ONTO** the table.

USE **OFF** TO SHOW:

    separation from, removal   I took the cat **OFF** the table.

    a lack of engagement   They are **OFF** duty.

    a distance from   The picnic grounds are **OFF** the main road.

Complete the following exchanges with the appropriate preposition.

1. A: Listen, can you give me a lift[53] to the bus stop?

    B: Sure, at 3 o'clock. I'm _____ work then.

2. A: Barbara, do me a favor?

    B: Sure.

    A: Take those books _____ the chair, and put them in the bookcase.

    B: You're still weak from the flu, huh?

    A: Yeah.

3. On the phone:

    A: Jackie, this is Irv. I'm having a hard time finding your house. Can you give me the

       directions again?

    B: OK. Take River Road until you get to Bella Vista Avenue. Go three blocks and we

       are just _____ to the right. It's a yellow frame house.

4. A: Boy, that's quite a bruise on your leg. How'd it happen?

    B: I got it when I tried to jump _____ John's boat. The deck was

       wet and I slipped.

B. Additional Preposition Combinations

break up with (IS):
  to end a relationship   Cynthia *broke up* with Mark yesterday.

get along (IS):
  to manage; to progress   Despite their lack of money, they *get along*
                                          fine.

---

[53]give a lift: to give someone a ride.

to be friendly; to be compatible

Please don't invite Jim. We never *got along* when we were kids, and now it's worse.

get over (IS):
recover from (emotional pain, illness, or fright)

Henry doesn't want to date anyone. He still hasn't *gotten over* Helen.

get to (IS):
to bother; to annoy

That Jeff is so nosy; he really *gets to me*.

go with (IS):
to date regularly
to be suitable for; to harmonize with

Jill has been *going with* Raul for over a year.
He's a terrible dresser. His pants never *go with* his jacket.

go through (IS):
to experience

Breaking up was very painful. I don't want *to go through* that again.

go through with (IS):
to complete

She *went through with* her plans to buy a house.

Complete the following exchanges with the appropriate preposition combination.

1. A: I've been working on our office Christmas party for the past week and I'm sick and tired of it.[54]

    B: Don't let it _____ you. Besides, you'll have a good time at the party.

    A: Maybe, but I think it's going to take me a week to _____ all of this.

2. A: Is Debby still _____ Ralph?

    B: No. She _____ him last week.

    A: It's no wonder. They never _____ . I don't know how their relationship lasted this long.

---

[54]sick and tired: to really not want to do something any longer.

3.   A: How's Duffy?

      B: He's getting better, but boy did he _____ a lot! First he got the

           flu; then when he _____ that, he fell and broke his leg, and then

           Brenda _____ with him.

      A: Wow! I think I'll give him a call. I'm sure he could use a little moral support.[55]

4.   A: Did you hear about Larry and Kathy?

      B: No, what happened?

      A: Well, they never got married! The invitations were sent; the reception hall was

           rented; everything was set. Then Larry took off for Seattle, and no one has heard

           from him since.

      B: I'm not surprised. I knew he would never _____ it. He's

           too young.

---

[55]moral support: encouragement.

III REVIEW CHAPTER AND POPULAR EXPRESSIONS

I. CREATE A DIALOGUE

Create a dialogue using the words and expressions listed.

1. In a police station:
    A: be mugged
    B: how
       happen?
    A: be about to
       cross the street
       two men
       jump on
    B: try
       fight off?
    A: no
       take wallet
       run away
    B: lucky
       could have
       be killed
    A: if only
       not go out
       so late
       not happen
    B: from now on
       more careful

_____

_____

_____

_____
_____

2. A husband and wife are talking. The husband feels ill:
    A: get sick
    B: call
        doctor
    A: there is no need to
    B: what if
        serious
        had better
        just in case

_____
_____
_____
_____

3. A patient is being examined by a doctor:

    PATIENT: sore throat
              chest pains

    DOCTOR: probably
             come down with
             flu
             chest x ray
             just in case

_____
_____
_____
_____

4. Two co-workers are talking:
    A: what time
        get off
        last night
    B: ten o'clock
    A: how
        can stand
        work late
        all the time
    B: be used to
        work overtime
        besides
        make ends meet

    _____

    _____

    _____

    _____

5. Two roommates. One of them is going downtown:
    A: be off to
        bank
    B: as long as
        go downtown
        would mind
        pick up
        stamps
        for me
    A: might as well
        buy
        for myself
        too

    _____

    _____

    _____

    _____

6. Two friends are talking:
   A: how
       date
       last night
   B: be stood up
       can't help
       upset
   A: too bad
   B: get over it
       soon

_____

_____

_____

_____

_____

7. Two friends are talking about a couple they know:
   A: Julie
       split up
       Henry
       she said
       can't go through
       another argument
   B: to tell you the truth
       know
       all along
       break up
       sooner or later
       never get along very well
       in the first place

_____

_____

_____

_____

_____

8. Two colleagues are talking:
   A: sick and tired of
       put up with
       job
       get to me
   B: quit
       whenever
       want
       have a lot on the ball
       sure
       find another job

   _____

   _____

   _____

   _____

   _____

9. Two friends:
   A: ask Joan out last night?
   B: yes, but
       turn down
       she
       go with
       someone else

   _____

   _____

   _____

   _____

   _____

10. Two friends on the telephone:
    A: eat lunch out together
        sometime
    B: can't afford
        out of work

```
          lay off
          last week
   A:     why don't
          try my company
          come to think of it
          opening in my department
          ought to
          work up
          new résumé
   B:     work on
          for the past three days
   A:     as soon as
          ready
          give it to me
          show it
          my boss
```

II. POPULAR EXPRESSIONS RELATED TO FOODS

Expression	Definition	Example
(be) in hot water	to be in trouble	Margaret's younger brother had another car accident. That boy is always *in hot water*.
(be) chicken	to be afraid	Don't *be chicken*! Ask her for a date.
butter up	to flatter	Mel thinks that if he *butters up* the vice president of the bank, he'll get the loan he wants.
(be) nuts	to be crazy to be enthusiastic about/ like very much	He's really *nuts*. She's *nuts about* gymnastics. He's *nuts about* her.
(be) fishy (sound)	to be suspect/strange	When I saw a young kid driving your car, I knew something *was fishy*, so I called the police.

1. On the phone:

   A: Hello, Sparkle, this is Sue. Listen, I'm really _____ . I've just

   been arrested for drunk driving. I need a lawyer.

   B: Don't worry. Tell me where you are and I'll be right there.

2. A: Alex, you looked so handsome last night and you danced so well!

   B: Okay, what do you want? Why are you _____ me

   _____ ?

   A: I'm not trying to flatter you! What I'm saying is true.

   B: All right. Well, thanks for the compliment then.

3. Two friends are talking at a dance party:

   A: Let's dance.

   B: Oh, no. I don't know how to disco.

   A: C'mon. Don't be _____ .

   B: No. I don't want everyone to see me.

   A: No one cares if you can dance well or not. Just relax and enjoy yourself.

4. Two managers are discussing an applicant for a job:

   A: Well, Edwin, what did you think?

   B: His educational background was quite good, but he's had four jobs in the last year

   and a half.

   A: Yes, that seemed a little _____ to me, too.

5. A: Warren is really _____ about you.

   Why don't you go out with him?

B: He's never asked me.

A: Oh, he's just _____ . Why don't you ask him?

6. On the telephone:

A: Carl? This is Peter. Listen, I borrowed Dad's car and had an accident. I'm fine, but the car is wrecked.

B: You borrowed Dad's car? Are you _____ ?

You're really _____ now.

III. GRAMMAR REVIEW

A. Past Modals

Complete the following exchanges using the appropriate past tense modal: *could have, should have, might have,* or *must have.*

1. A: How many bottles of wine did you get for tonight's dinner party?

B: Two. One white and one red.

A: You _____ more. Two bottles won't be nearly[1] enough.
   (buy)

2. At the dinner table:

A: Have another piece of meat. There's plenty.

B: Oh, no thank you. I _____ four or five pieces already.
   (have)

I'm stuffed.[2] It was really delicious.

3. A: Where are the beer and soft drinks for tonight's cocktail party? Don was supposed to pick everything up. Do you think he _____ ?
   (forget)

B: Impossible. When Don says he's going to do something you can count on it.

---

[1]not nearly: not at all; not close.
[2]stuffed: full.

A: You're right . . . Oh, I know. He _____ the drinks in the
                (put)

refrigerator in the basement. Let me go downstairs and check right now.

4. A: Thank you for preparing all the food tonight. It was a big job. You _____

_____ all day.
                (work)

B: Oh, it was nothing. I'm glad I was able to help out.

A: Well, I really appreciate it. Thank you again.

B: You're welcome.

5. A: Did you just get back from the grocery store?

B: Yes.

A: You _____ me you were going food shopping. You
           (tell)

_____ up a few things for me.
      (pick)

B: Oh, I'm sorry. I didn't think to[3] ask you.

A: That's all right.

6. A: Who stole my cake? I left a piece of cake in the fridge and now it's gone. Who ate it?

B: How do I know? It _____ Jack, or Irene _____ it.
             (be)   (eat)

A: Jack is on a diet, so it _____ Irene.
                        (be)

B: All I know is that I didn't eat it.

B. Gerunds and Infinitives

Complete the following exchanges with either a gerund (Verb + ing) or an infinitive (to + Verb).

---

[3]think to: to remember (to do something).

1. A: What smells so awful?

   B: I burnt the vegetables. I have to admit _____ is not one of
      (cook)

      my strong points.

   A: I guess not. It's not easy _____ vegetables.
      (burn)

2. A: You shouldn't skip lunch again. It's important _____ properly.
      (eat)

   B: Well, I always have a big dinner and I usually eat a good breakfast, so I don't think

      that _____ lunch everyday is that important.
           (eat)

3. A: Can I help you set the table?

   B: Oh, that's okay. I'll ask one of the kids _____ it.
      (do)

   A: Do your children always help you around the home?

   B: Sure. _____ the table is one of their jobs and so is
           (set)

      _____ the dishes.
           (do)

4. A: How was your tennis match?

   B: Great, but now I'm starving. _____ tennis always gives me a
      (play)

      good appetite.

   A: There are plenty of cold cuts in the fridge. Help yourself to whatever you'd like.

5. A: I wish I could cook as well as you do!

   B: It's not that hard _____ how to cook.
      (learn)

      Would you like me _____ you?
      (teach)

   A: Listen, I can't even boil water! _____ me would be
      (teach)

      very difficult!

C. Passive

Complete the following exchanges with the passive voice.

1. A: What time are the caterers going to bring the food?

    B: Don't worry! Everything _____ before six o'clock.

(deliver)

2. A guest and the host at a dinner party:

    GUEST: Can I help you with anything?

    HOST: Oh, no. Everything _____ already _____

(prepare)

    Just relax and enjoy yourself.

3. A: Didn't you order the liquor?

    B: No. You told me the liquor _____ already _____ .

(order)

    A: No. I said that it _____ yet.

(order; negative)

    B: I'm sorry. I must have misunderstood you. I'll call the liquor store right now then.

4. Preparing for a dinner party:

    A: _____ the salad _____ yet?

(make)

    B: No, the tomatoes and celery _____ even _____

(cut; negative)

    up yet.

    A: Would you do that for me, please?

    B: Okay, but I'm not finished with these hors d'oeuvres yet.

    A: Never mind, then. Finish what you're doing. I'll do the salad.

    B: All right. Oh, the lettuce _____ already _____ .

(wash)

    It's in the bottom drawer of the fridge.

5. At a buffet:[4]

A: This is quite a spread. When did you have time to prepare all of this?

B: Well, my sister and I have been working on it for three days. The turkey _____

_____ last night. The pies _____ the day
        (bake)   (make)

before yesterday. The ham and the roast beef _____ this
                                                       (cook)

morning.

A: Wow! You two have been at it nonstop.[5] You certainly did a great job. Everything is

delicious.

B: Oh, thank you. Now help yourself to some more!

6. The host and hostess of a party are talking after the last guest has gone home:

A: Well, the party's over.

B: Do you think everyone had a good time?

A: Well, all the food _____ up!
                                              (eat)

B: What do you say[6] we call it a night?[7]

A: Fine with me. We can straighten up tomorrow.

B: And begin planning our next party!

---

[4]buffet: a meal set out on a table for people to help themselves.
[5]nonstop: without stopping; continuously.
[6]what do you say: let's; how about.
[7]call it a night: to end the evening; i.e., go to bed, go home, stop what one is doing.

GLOSSARY of COLLOQUIAL TERMS

INDEX